T0334195

Management

Management

Inventing and Delivering
Its Future

Edited by
Thomas A. Kochan and
Richard L. Schmalensee

The MIT Press
Cambridge, Massachusetts
London, England

This book was set in Palatino by SNP Best-set Typesetter Ltd., Hong Kong.

Library of Congress Cataloging-in-Publication Data

Management : inventing and delivering its future / edited by Thomas A. Kochan and
  Richard L. Schmalensee.
    p. com.
  "MIT Sloan School of Management: 50th anniversary."
  Includes bibliographical references and index.
  ISBN 978-0-262-11282-6 (hc. : alk. paper)— 978-0-262-52767-5 (pb)
    1. Management.   2. Organizational change.   3. Corporate governance.
  4. Personnel management.   5. Human capital.   6. Technological innovations—
  Management.   I. Kochan, Thomas A.   II. Schmalensee, Richard.   III. Sloan
  School of Management.
  HD31.M2928   2003
    658—dc21   2003044503

The MIT Press is pleased to keep this title available in print by manufacturing single
copies, on demand, via digital printing technology.

Contents

Foreword

The 50th anniversary of the MIT Sloan School of Management offers an auspicious moment to look to the past with pride and to the future with boldness and confidence. It also is a moment to celebrate the deep and important synergies of the Sloan School and the other elements that comprise MIT.

The beginning of management education at MIT predates 1952, when the Sloan School opened its doors as the School of Industrial Management. Its roots reach much further back in time. MIT's first curriculum in 1865 included subjects that today's MBAs would find familiar—economics and statistics, principles of industrial development, business law, taxation, and banking.

As the industrial world developed in the early 1900s, the concept of providing business training in the academic environment gained popularity. So did the demand for these courses, prompting MIT to create Course XV—Engineering Administration—in 1914. For the next three decades, the relevance and demand for programs in management only continued to grow. And in 1952, the MIT Sloan School was born.

The concept of the school was the idea of MIT alumnus and innovator Alfred P. Sloan, Jr., Class of 1895—the man credited with the invention of the modern corporation. Mr. Sloan sought to solve the complex problems of modern industry through the sort of rigorous research that MIT has always been about, and his generosity made it possible for MIT to create the new school.

For MIT, with its long history of working on practical problems affecting society and the economy, this progression was natural.

The MIT Sloan School was shaped by bringing MIT's quantitative approach to the management of organizations, and through the strong traditions of innovation that have been the hallmark of MIT.

Today, innovation—both technological and organizational—creates new pathways to serve society and drives the strength of businesses and, indeed, entire economies. Contemporary industry is fast-paced, knowledge-based, global, electronically interconnected, and often created by entrepreneurs. It thrives on innovation. So does the Sloan School.

MIT is blessed with an intellectual environment of remarkable creativity, generated by the synergy among world-class programs in science, engineering, and management, together with extraordinary programs in the arts, humanities, architecture, and the social sciences. The Sloan School leverages these strong collaborative links across the Institute to prepare the next generation of engineers, scientists, and innovative, technology-savvy managers to shape the world around us.

This has created an ideal educational setting, not just for the last half century, but for the next 50 years and beyond.

I cannot imagine MIT without its Sloan School, and I cannot imagine the Sloan School without MIT. It is a comparative advantage, and competitive advantage for all of us.

Charles M. Vest, President
Massachusetts Institute of Technology

Preface

Alan Greenspan recently gave a talk here in Boston on corporate governance. He began by stating the undeniable fact that free market capitalism is based on trust. I would take this a step further: Trust in free market capitalism is based on trust in the collective integrity of the companies that make up the market. A company's integrity depends on trust—the trust it shows its employees, its customers, its suppliers, its stockholders, and all the other constituencies that surround it. This trust is not just a matter of virtue for virtue's sake; it is an indispensable element for any business that wants to survive over the long haul.

Having run a successful electronics company for almost 40 years, a company that became a world leader and a billion-dollar enterprise in a very demanding business, I am often asked what it was that made this company so successful. Competence, especially in technology, is critical. But it is not enough. A strong sense of ethics must guide the company in all its dealings with people inside and outside the company. Not just a strong sense, but an *uncompromisingly* strong sense of ethics. Bend the rules, and you might as well break them. You just cannot get away with being a little bit unethical, or being unethical once in a while. As soon as you're found out—and you will be found out—that vital sense of trust is shattered forever. The current newspaper headlines show this to be sadly true.

The importance of ethics comes through loud and clear in the dialogue and speeches from the MIT Sloan School's 50th Anniversary Convocation which is the subject of this book. As chair of The MIT Corporation, I am gratified by the attention given to the subject, first because it is so important for business leaders to reflect on what they must do to build trust; and second, because our schools must ask whether they are instilling a sense of ethical behavior in the next generations of business executives and leaders.

We are all proud of the Sloan School's rich heritage, but we will be even prouder if, years from now, we can see in this anniversary celebration an event that signaled a turning point in the journey to a world of business practice and education that recognizes the role of trust as the cornerstone of our whole economic system. Our collective responsibility is to take Alan Greenspan's macro-vision and apply it to every company and every situation we touch. The ideas expressed at the convocation and presented in this volume are an excellent starting point.

Alex d'Arbeloff
Chair, The MIT Corporation

Acknowledgments

Preparation of this volume and the splendid anniversary convocation on which it is based required support and leadership of a large number of loyal and dedicated people and organizations. General Motors Corporation has supported management at MIT since before the Sloan School was founded. So it is fitting that they served as our primary partner in hosting the 50th Anniversary Convocation. The Boeing Company, the Sloan Foundation, Deutsche Bank, Empirix, and Fleishman Hillard International Communications also provided valuable support to the event. We thank these organizations for their continued commitment to the Sloan School.

A large number of Sloan staff and faculty helped to plan and manage the convocation. We owe special thanks to Lori Correale, Eliza Dame, Paul Denning, Bernie Lord, and Robert St. Cyr for the countless hours they put into making sure the event came off flawlessly. Their best reward lies in the universal view of those who attended that it was a landmark event. Never before had such a large gathering of Sloan School alumni, students, faculty, and distinguished guests come together to both renew acquaintances and to engage in a thoughtful discussion about the current state and future directions for management practice and education. These hard working and creative people exemplify the important roles Sloan staff members play in the school day in and day out. We thank them, and all the Sloan School staff, for their ongoing dedication and professionalism.

We asked a small committee of faculty and staff to help us design the program for a 50th anniversary event that would be both a celebration and an intellectually engaging and challenging look into the future. For getting this combination just right we thank Eliza Dame, Thomas Kochan, John Little, Stewart Myers, Stephen Sacca, and David Weber.

Transforming the richness of the dialogue and the presentations into what we hope is a readable and coherent text was a daunting challenge. Andrea Meyer organized the materials and edited the papers and panel discussions into the chapters that follow. Jackie Curreri kept track of the various pieces of the book, brought them together to create a single text, and throughout managed to keep her sanity and humor intact. Paul Denning coordinated efforts with our colleagues at The MIT Press, and John Covell managed the process of turning a loose manuscript into the final product. Their individual and collective good work illustrates how a modern team works effectively and cooperatively across boundaries and distances.

Finally, our thanks go to the alumni, students, faculty, and other guests who joined us and helped shape the rich dialogue that took place at the convocation. This book is the product of their ideas and the articulate fashion in which they expressed them. We hope it does justice to both the substance and the spirit of their remarks.

1   Introduction

Richard L. Schmalensee and
Thomas A. Kochan

At MIT, Alfred Sloan had a vision of a different kind of business school, one that promoted a closer association between science, engineering, and industry. Sloan imagined a school that did more than just teach best practices—he foresaw a school that helped define them.

Richard Wagoner, Chief Executive Officer, General Motors

In the early 1950s, the Carnegie Corporation and the Ford Foundation commissioned reports that called on universities to build a new management profession based on rigorous academic research, particularly in economics and behavioral science. About the same time, Alfred P. Sloan, the architect of both the modern day General Motors and the dominant corporate form of the twentieth century, proposed that MIT create a School of Management that would leverage the Institute's rich scientific and technical strengths and build on the strong tradition of management education at MIT extending back to the previous century. So began an experiment in inventing the modern management profession and professional education programs at MIT and in other universities in America and, later, in other parts of the world.

As the above quote from GM's current CEO Richard Wagoner suggests, Alfred Sloan, the Ford Foundation, and the Carnegie Corporation would be proud of what has been accomplished. In the ensuing years:

• The tools of modern corporate finance and capital market analysis were developed, drawn heavily on theoretical advances in economics. The widespread use of these tools has enabled capital to flow more efficiently to its best uses, in particular to the new entrepreneurial ventures that would usher in the information age. At Sloan in the early

1970s, Robert Merton, Fisher Black, and Myron Scholes developed the mathematical theory of option pricing, which both reshaped financial markets and was recognized by a Nobel Prize.

• Theories and practices guiding management-employee relations moved from methods developed largely for military organizations to principles based on economics and behavioral science for motivating and empowering employees, building high performance work systems based on teamwork, and better negotiating organizational change and resolving conflicts. In 1957, MIT's Douglas McGregor introduced his famous Theory Y and challenged managers to reexamine their assumptions about employees. Following in this tradition, over the next three decades Sloan faculty would call for a transformation of labor management policy and practice, be among the first to study and propose how to better integrate work and family life, and develop an entirely new field for managing the process of technological innovation.

• The advances in computing power led to creation of another new field, the study of Management Information Systems. Sloan School faculty pioneered in the development of "decision support systems," which demonstrated the power of information technology to inform management decisions, not just to automate payroll and billing. Sloan research demonstrated the importance of organizational factors in determining the value of information technology, a lesson being learned anew in the Internet age.

• Management science was born out of the fields of operations research and statistics, computer modeling became the dominant tool guiding research and teaching in this area, and the field of operations management (or production) was transformed. At MIT and Sloan, the field of system dynamics was born, and generations of students were trained to use this and other modeling tools to understand complex situations and solve complex problems.

The list could go on. A few other management schools could cite comparably important breakthroughs and contributions by their faculty. But no profession can afford to sit still, especially when the world around it continues to change. So flash forward fifty years to the present. Is it once again time to ask basic questions about what principles should guide the second fifty years of management practice and education?

On the weekend of October 10–12, 2002, alumni, faculty, and students of the MIT Sloan School of Management took up these basic questions as we celebrated the School's 50th Anniversary. Our goal was to engage a broad range of leaders from all corners of the world in an exploration of the present challenges, future opportunities, and expectations facing managers, the organizations they build, and the constituencies they should serve in the next 50 years.

This book summarizes the discussions that took place at the convocation and presents the research papers, prepared by student-faculty teams, that served to stimulate them. We present this not simply to report on the convocation, though it was an unforgettable event, but to begin similar discussions with others who share a commitment to using the knowledge, tools, and experience of management scholars, educators, and professionals to address the critical issues and problems we encounter in our world today and to prepare for tomorrow's management challenges. We invite you to engage in this discussion with us by exploring the vision for the future that emerged from the convocation.

Challenges and Opportunities

It is often said that we live in a time of crisis or of rapid change. It is even more trite to say that we are at a critical turning point in the world of business and that the changes to come in the future will be far greater than anything experienced in the first 50 years of the development of the management profession. But just now, there is a fair chance that all these familiar statements are true.

The intensity of the challenges management faces today reflects the confluence of several developments. The past decade witnessed a full and powerful swing of the economic pendulum from years of steady and strong economic growth that peaked with the rise of the dot.coms only to be followed by the steep decline when the bubble burst. The same swings occurred globally with the rise and fall of the Japanese, other Asian, and Latin American economies. Though the dot.com bubble burst spectacularly, the breathtaking pace of technological advance has not perceptibly slowed, and businesses of all sorts struggle to keep up. Throughout both the rise and decline of the global economy, the gaps between the richest and poorest, both in the United States and internationally, grew to what many now believe are intolerable and unsustainable levels. Then came September 11, 2001, and its aftermath of international tensions, uncertainty, and war. Add to this the crisis in corporate confidence brought on by corporate scandals in the United States and it is easy to see why many believe that this is a critical moment for the business community and the management profession—and perhaps for the global economy.

There is obviously much to be concerned about today. But if the energy and creativity expressed at the Sloan convocation and reflected in the pages that follow are any indication, there are good reasons to be optimistic about our ability to meet these challenges and to prepare for the future. To do so, however, we will once again need to return to first principles and use the power of our advancing knowledge creatively and responsibly to improve the practice of management.

Broad Themes

What are these first principles? Three linked, overlapping themes dominated the analysis and dialogue of the convocation. Many of the contributions to this volume reflect more than one of these themes.

Managers must build and maintain the trust of a broad set of stakeholders through openness, transparency, and accountability

As Alex d'Arbeloff makes clear in the foreword to this book, business runs on trust. No system of laws and contracts, no system of corporate governance can cover all contingencies or detect all wrongdoing. For any firm to function effectively, its management must be trusted by shareholders, customers, employees, communities, regulators, and other stakeholders to behave in an ethical fashion—to live up to the spirit of regulations and agreements, not just the letter, to conform to social norms, and to do all this even when it costs money and nobody is watching. U.N. Secretary General Kofi Annan's opening remarks remind us forcefully of the breadth of business responsibilities and stakeholder relations in our global economy. And Carly Fiorina's talk demonstrates that building trust on the many relevant dimensions is not just another top management task; trust depends on how management at all levels performs all its tasks—on the DNA of the organization, as she puts it. We believe these two important statements, which we present together in chapter 2, deserve careful consideration by all in the business community.

In most of the convocation sessions, trust emerged as an issue of great, often over-riding, bottom-line importance. We saw, in many contexts, how trust depends on openness, transparency, and accountability. The examination of the Nike case in chapter 3 illustrates the value of being trusted by customers and others not to exploit workers and the difficulty of rebuilding that trust once it is lost. Both the importance of trust along this dimension and the difficulty of rebuilding it have increased markedly in recent years. And the discussion of the organization of the future in chapter 4 shows that, particularly in knowledge-based firms, employee loyalty and creative engagement are essential. Both these, of course, must rest on trust.

The theme of building trust beyond the organization is central to the discussion of the changing role and power of consumers in chapter 5. It has always been recognized that in a free market economy the needs and preferences of consumers should drive the goods and services supplied. But for the past 50 years, marketing science and practice have led a sort of schizophrenic life. On the one hand, the tools of marketing have helped companies to increase profits by better understanding and in some case better shaping consumer behavior to fit the products and services offered. This is what Glen Urban and his students describe as "push marketing." Thanks to an important extent to the power of the Internet, however, these same tools can now be used to empower consumers to increase their satisfaction by shaping the products and services offered by businesses. For this to happen, consumers need to trust information supplied by firms and react honestly to it, and this will require marketing practice to focus on supporting as well as influencing consumers and to build longer lasting and more trusting relationships between consumers and producers. Urban labels this "trust-based marketing," an exciting new paradigm for the next 50 years of marketing science.

Trust-based marketing is another example of the shift in management perspective called for by conference speakers and participants. In his speech to the convocation, GM CEO Richard Wagoner reinforced the importance of listening to and meeting the needs expressed by customers by recounting the story of Buck Weaver, GM's director of consumer research back in the 1930s. Weaver was a voice for the customer inside the corporation then, and he serves as a model for the shift in marketing called for today. In recognition of the importance of this shift, Wagoner announced that GM is creating a Buck Weaver Prize to be awarded by MIT Sloan to individuals who advance theory and research in marketing science over the course of their careers.

In chapter 6 we turn to the issue of corporate governance and its role in rebuilding investors' trust. Citizenship, accountability, and performance must rest on sound and effective principles and practices of corporate governance. Recent corporate scandals in the United States have both given visibility to debates over corporate governance and opened these debates to a broader array of voices than those that dominated this topic in the past decade or so. This is a healthy development that, if taken seriously, could usher in an era of experimentation and change in who participates in corporate governance and how organizations are held accountable to their different stakeholders.

Are there some fundamental theoretical principles that should underlie all governance models, regardless of the specific institutional forms they take? Is there value in institutional variation, both for the sake of learning and experimentation, and to reflect differences in cultural norms, economic conditions, and societal expectations? Chapter 6 reports our discussion and analysis of these important questions. In his introduction to this topic, Stewart Myers outlines what he sees as the fundamental tasks of an efficient governance system. It must allocate capital and human resources to their optimal uses. There is little debate about these fundamental requirements. The debate comes in how to structure governance arrangements to meet them.

This debate is not limited to the United States. The same debates are alive and well in Asia and Europe, fueled by their own financial crises, the emergence of new market economies, and historical differences in institutional development. We therefore bring an explicit international lens to these issues. This is done in part out of a new sense of modesty and recognition that in the past some have too aggressively promoted the American model of corporate governance as the ideal the rest of the world should emulate. It is clear now that, in order to improve the American model, we must both examine that model and work to better understand and learn from the experiences of governance models found in Asia and Europe. The two papers prepared by Myers and his student teams do just this. The front-line views from Europe presented by Dr. Rolf Breuer, and from Asia presented by Dr. Victor Fung, then show how these issues look from vantage points outside the United States. These views give a sense of some of the relevant institutional issues and complexities.

Managers must be prepared to deal with increasingly complex problems involving broadening sets of stakeholders

It is much easier to talk about trust-based marketing than to solve the complex problem of being both credible and effective. And it is much easier to talk about improving corporate governance than to figure out exactly how to do it—much less how to ensure by laws and regulations that it is done. More generally, as the global economy becomes more tightly linked, as business performance depends more on creativity and less on easily measured effort, as new technologies present an increasing flow of challenges and opportunities, and as customers and shareholders become better informed and more demanding, the problems faced by management involve new stakeholders and levels of complexity undreamt of a few decades ago. There was no suggestion at the convocation that any of these drivers of complexity will slow in the foreseeable future.

U.N. Secretary General Kofi Annan's opening remarks both described an important dimension of this complexity and set the tone for a broader vision in his call for corporations to join together in a Global Compact to "embrace nine universal principles in the areas of human rights, labor standards, and the environment, and to enact these principles within their spheres of influence." Hewlett Packard CEO Carly Fiorina agreed and announced that her company is joining the Global Compact. She went on to state even more clearly the responsibilities of CEOs and other executives: "Management serves at the pleasure and for the benefit of our shareowners, our customers, and our employees—and not the other way around."

These are not calls for business leaders to sacrifice enduring shareholder returns in pursuit of social objectives. Rather, they call on business leaders to recognize that the long-term health of their organizations requires them to be broadly accountable and to address issues heretofore generally viewed as not business concerns.

The complex challenges that businesses face as they attempt to be good corporate citizens in our global economy are brought to life in chapter 3 through examination of a concrete case study prepared by Richard Locke. The case asks: What, if any, labor standards should the Nike Corporation require of its global contractors, and to whom should the corporation be held accountable? As the comments that follow the case illustrate, the case stirred considerable debate among participating alumni. The answers to these questions offered by different alumni turned on how broadly they defined the term "corporate citizenship." The minimalist answer that dominated much of public discourse and business school teaching in recent years is that corporations should be accountable for enhancing today's shareholder value. And, of course, managers are responsible to the individuals and institutions that put at risk the financial capital needed to build and sustain a firm. Yet most of the alumni who discussed this case view an exclusive focus on shareholder value as leading to decisions that are both myopic and socially unacceptable. They too want to hold corporations to a higher standard of corporate citizenship. But, as the Nike case makes clear, it is far from simple to translate these aspirations into effective policies.

In chapter 4, the legacy of Douglas McGregor serves as a launching pad for a rich discussion of the features of the complex and evolving organization of the future and its implications for management practice and education. The paper prepared with Sloan students and alumni by Thomas Kochan, Wanda Orlikowski, and Joel Cutcher-Gershenfeld suggests that realizing McGregor's vision will require questioning and challenging some of the very basic assumptions regarding the role of people, work, technology, leadership, and organizational goals that dominated twentieth century organizations. The sustainable organization of the twenty-first century, according to this view, will be one that leverages the full potential of its human capital to add value to the firm *and* returns fair value to its workforce and their families. Because modern organizations depend so much on intangible assets—like intellectual property, loyalty, trust, and firm-specific knowledge—traditional financial measures may provide misleading indicators of performance and viability.

The panel discussion that accompanies this paper reinforced the points that Carly Fiorina made about the need for openness and transparency, not just to investors but to employees as well. Panelist Meg O'Leary, a senior manager at PriceWaterhouseCoopers, noted that the culture of openness, trust, and flexibility present in her organization made it possible for her to work at home and to integrate her work and family life. James Goodnight, CEO of SAS Institute, stated succinctly the importance of the workforce in the twenty-first-century organization and the personal responsibility of the modern CEO to gain and maintain its trust and commitment: "95 percent of a company's assets drive out the front gate every night; the CEO must see to it that they return the following day."

Peter Senge, a founder and president of the Society of Organizational Learning, reinforced a point made in the earlier discussions of globalization, namely, that transparency, openness, and engagement no longer stop at an organization's boundary. He argued that a truly sustainable networked organization of the future will need to engage and address the interests and needs of a broader set of groups and organizations in civil society, whether this be NGOs, unions, or governmental entities. He put it bluntly: "15 percent of the people having 85 percent of the 'goodies' is not sustainable." Fifty years ago, only a few would have thought of this complex issue as a concern of business.

Managers must be prepared to harness advances in science and technology that will transform organizations and markets

Perhaps the most visible reason why managers' roles have become more complex in recent decades is that the pace of technological change has accelerated across a broad front. Organizations that do not harness the potential of new technologies and solve the problems they pose do not survive long in most markets. Successful companies with able CEOs are regularly pushed aside by technologies that were unknown when those CEOs were in school.

The paper presented in chapter 7 by Rebecca Henderson and her students, and the panel discussion that follows it with leading MIT scientists and engineers, provide a glimpse of some of the powerful new technologies that will shape the business world of the near future. As our colleagues from the Schools of Science and Engineering pointed out, these technologies have the potential to do enormous good as well as harm; every innovation is both an opportunity and a challenge. Professor Susan Linquist, for example, described work underway on how adding vitamin A to rice production could reduce the number of malnourished children who go blind by the time they enter school. She also described an innovative but simple technology developed at MIT for purifying drinking water that if made widely available to families in developing countries would have major payoffs to world health. On the other hand, convocation participants were amused and at the same time appalled at the demonstration of a prototype "person finder" that might join us in our homes, keep track of our whereabouts so presumably others (like our bosses?) can locate us and reach us anytime, anywhere, and under any circumstance. And while we delighted in the sight of a personal robot that we might have doing household chores, preparing our meals, and helping us to monitor our children from work or other remote locations, we were less enamored with the idea that others might likewise tune in and observe all aspects of our family and personal lives.

In his remarks summarized in chapter 7, MIT provost Robert Brown notes that most of the really big scientific innovations come not from established disciplines or departments at MIT but out of the laboratories and research centers that bring together scholars from two or more disciplines. This is equally true in management organizations and processes today. Translating scientific discoveries and technical breakthroughs into actual products and services requires building, leading, and coordinating multi-disciplinary and multi-functional teams. This is the heart of the innovation process in organizations.

In remarks summarized in chapter 4, Boeing's CEO Phillip Condit captured the changes in management and organizational designs that are needed to manage the innovation process efficiently and seamlessly. He, like others, sees the organization of the future as a network more than a hierarchy. To be successful, the networked organization needs to draw on and return fair value to its workforce, suppliers, customers, and communities. Condit's remarks provide a good introduction to the discussion of the broader range of features needed in twenty-first-century organizations presented in chapter 4.

It is important to note that many of the organizational changes discussed in chapter 4 are driven by changes in information technology, just as the emergence of trust-based marketing rests importantly on the power of the Internet. Technology, particularly information technology, has had—and will continue to have—profound implications for how businesses are managed, as well as changing the goods and services they produce.

Implications for the Future of Management Education

What are the implications of this discourse for the future of management education? What should the Sloan School do to lead the way in realizing this vision? The key lesson we take away from the convocation is that management education should endeavor to develop principled leaders who earn trust, who are able to address a broader set of problems and stakeholders, and who are able to identify and exploit opportunities to innovate, many of which will be provided by advances in science and technology.

In practical terms, what does this imply? First, it clearly requires us to pay more attention to the ethical dimensions of being a professional manager, to the sort of leadership that is required to earn stakeholders' trust. Management schools cannot change their students' characters by preaching at them, but students can learn what sort of behavior is expected of them as professionals, and they can learn to be more effective leaders and more sensitive to ethical issues. We believe that this is most effectively done in context, not in isolated lectures or courses focused on ethics. Ethics cannot be taught to aspiring managers as abstract philosophy. It must be grounded in the real work managers do, the issues they encounter, and the decisions they are called upon to make independently and in concert with other groups and institutions. As we at Sloan are redesigning our curricula, we are placing great emphasis on the effective teaching of ethical principles—on developing leaders who are principled as well as effective and are able to enhance long-run viability and performance.

Second, as managers are expected to address broader responsibilities and deal with new, complex issues, so too must the management schools that educate them. To ensure that we are addressing the most important problems of the day, the management school of the future will need to be an open forum where a diverse set of people and stakeholders come together to learn and explore how to address these problems and meet these challenges. This means doing more than periodically bringing business leaders to campus to share their vision and problems with faculty and students. It means engaging leaders from all parts of society—business, government, and civil society.

Since the ideas, tools, and evidence that will be used to build this new management education system will only be as good as the research that generates them, management research will likewise need to broaden its focus to provide the theories and tools needed to meet these broader expectations and to examine how well organizations are performing on these broader dimensions. Breakthroughs such as those listed at the beginning of this introduction came from research that was then translated into our educational programs. Accordingly, we believe that it is essential in this era of rapid, complex change that MIT Sloan and other management schools continue to be research-driven. Greater complexity in the executive suite has increased, not reduced, the need for sound and rigorous analysis, and it has broadened the set of problems that need to be analyzed. Business schools must develop leaders who can deploy new management methods in response to new management challenges.

Third, future managers will need an understanding of the potential benefits, risks, and ethical challenges posed by emerging technologies, including nanotechnologies, personal robotics, bioengineering, and others not yet in view. Businesses must innovate, and innovation depends increasingly on exploiting the potentials of new technologies. Moreover, ethical and technical analysis will need to be closely coupled in management decision-making if we are to guide science and technology in appropriate directions.

This does not mean all managers need to have Ph.D. degrees in specific technical disciplines that underlie their products or services. While this would not necessarily be a bad thing, it would not guarantee that managers understand the details of technologies that emerge decades after their graduation. Managers, whether they have technical degrees or not, need to learn to speak the language of science and technology and to be able to challenge and engage experts in an informed discussion of the scientific data needed to make sound and prudent decisions. In short, managers need to know how to learn about new technologies and to think creatively about their implications and likely evolution.

In order to equip our students to lead successful innovation, we at MIT Sloan believe it is vital that we engage our colleagues in science and engineering even more directly and creatively in the future than we have in the past. If Provost Brown is correct that most of the fundamental breakthroughs in science and engineering at MIT have come out of its multi-disciplinary laboratories and centers, the management school of the future must be an open and inviting setting where scholars from multiple disciplines interact and bring the best of their disciplinary knowledge to bear in teams working on the most critical problems of the day. The results of this work and these interactions must be translated into innovative curricula that prepare management students to drive successful innovation in new products and processes. The era in which business schools can wall themselves off from the rest of their universities and still be successful is very likely over!

Ultimately, realizing the vision and meeting challenges outlined here will require transforming our traditional curricula and mode of operations. Like our sister universities, we have structured the lives of our students and faculty around a set of independently taught, sequential courses fitted into full or half-semester time blocks, punctuated by times set aside for students and faculty to visit and study companies around the world. The fixed semester, sequential-course model was designed for faculty to teach their discipline-based knowledge in a relatively pure fashion, unencumbered by the multi-faceted complexities of many important problems.

To be sure, there is both efficiency and merit to the conceptual clarity which this structure allows in teaching basic disciplinary principles. Some of this knowledge will undoubtedly need to continue to be delivered in this fashion. But increasingly, we need to find ways to apply the same insight to our teaching as we do in our multi-disciplinary research laboratories and centers. We need to link research to teaching by engaging students in the application of knowledge from multiple disciplines to real-world problems. This means more cross-disciplinary, cross-functional, problem-oriented teaching. It means building more direct links between classrooms and real organizations, their problems, and the people involved in them. Some of this can be done remotely by taking advantage of the wonders of modern communication technology. But much of it requires personal interaction and engagement in order to see the problems and challenges first hand in their actual cultural and organizational settings. Doing this will reek havoc on traditional semester and course designs. But it will create new opportunities for better linking research, ensure more rapid testing and application of new theoretical breakthroughs and research findings, and in doing so will help harness the advances of science, technology, and human capacity called for by participants in the convocation.

The two-year MBA degree program was a natural byproduct of a model that saw education and training as a one-time ticket needed to enter a profession. Management education in the future will need to break out of this one-time, sequential model of education and practice by translating the rhetoric of "lifelong learning" into reality. Alumni and managers of corporate partners will need to be viewed as extended family members who come together on a regular basis and as new developments arise. New, shorter degree-granting programs may emerge, and new technologies and new teaching methods are likely to transform executive education as we know it. So stay tuned—these are interesting times in management education, as well as in the broader management profession.

We believe the analysis and dialogue that occurred at the Sloan Convocation and is recorded on the pages to follow can serve as a starting point for rethinking and reforming the profession of management. We invite you to explore the ideas presented here and then add your own voice to the debates and dialogue about the future of management that we hope our convocation and this volume will launch.

2 Challenges and Responsibilities

2.1 Corporate Citizenship in a Global Society

Kofi Annan

Over the course of half a century, the Sloan School of Management has built itself into one of the world's academic powerhouses. I say "world," and not just "country," because right from the start, Sloan looked well beyond the confines of this campus, encouraged people from many nations to study here, and was eager to advance the cause of international cooperation, scholarly and otherwise.

Three decades ago, I was fortunate enough to become part of the Sloan community. I recall in particular that Sloan exposed me to some very interesting work in organizational culture and planned change. That may sound like jargon to some, but I can assure you it has come in very handy at the United Nations.

Back in 1982, when I was working with the High Commissioner for Refugees, I invited my good friend Professor Ed Schein[1] to Geneva to help us improve our internal communications and coordination.

We gathered for what we thought would be a straightforward, hour-long briefing. Three hours later, we were all physically and emotionally drained from what had quickly turned into a frank, soul-searching exercise on our mission: what it means to work for the United Nations and how different people can best work together.

Some frustrations had been bottled up for years. But once the floodgates were open, we found new ways forward and, truly, a new sense of unity and purpose. The session was so successful that in 1990, when I was head of human resources, I asked Ed to come in again—this time with Professor Lester Thurow. About 30 senior officials from throughout the U.N. system, and from 26 different countries, came together and achieved a similar breakthrough.

---

1. Edgar H. Schein, Sloan Fellows Professor of Management Emeritus.

I like to think we are replicating that exercise on a global level, among peoples and nations, as we strive to build the trust, confidence, and sense of shared responsibility needed to address the urgent issues and threats of our times.

We are all aware that more and more challenges—from environmental degradation to drug trafficking and the spread of diseases such as AIDS—have a global dimension. Through work and travel and trips to the store, we can see that trade and communications are stitching the human family ever more closely together.

These phenomena have also helped to make the early twenty-first century a very troubling time for our global village. Distrust between cultures and religions often leads to violence and has been aggravated by the terrorist attacks of 11 September. Concern is mounting because of global economic uncertainty, and because the benefits of globalization have been shared so unevenly. Confidence in markets has been dealt a further blow with a series of corporate scandals in the United States and the gathering feeling that markets, by themselves, cannot respond to the real needs of society or provide the public goods that humankind needs to survive.

In an age of interdependence, global citizenship is a crucial pillar of progress. In a series of global meetings and conferences over the last two years in particular, world leaders have tried to define just what that citizenship means. They have been trying to build an inclusive, responsive, effective international system, from which all people can benefit—and in which all feel they have a stake.

Shared responsibility was at the heart of the declaration adopted at the Millennium Summit in September 2000. All countries came together—not just to express their general hopes for peace and development in the twenty-first century, but also to give their backing to a set of very specific, time-bound objectives which have since become known as the Millennium Development Goals.

The goals include reducing hunger, providing access to safe drinking water, and ensuring universal primary education. They will be closely monitored and measured—how many kids are in school, how quickly hunger and extreme poverty are being reduced. And we will advertise the results in a way that, we hope, will galvanize politics and policy-making so that the goals can be met by the target date of 2015.

Governments faced a first test of their commitment to these goals last November at the World Trade Organization meeting in Doha. There, trust was the main issue on the table. Developing countries have heard a lot of talk about free and fair trade, but seen far too little of it. They want to know that their products will have an equal chance to compete in the global market. That chance is currently denied them because of tariffs on their goods, and because of subsidies given to their competitors in rich countries—subsidies that also perpetuate unsustainable practices in farming, transport, and energy use.

The new round of negotiations agreed to at Doha offers the prospect that markets will be opened—but it is too soon to say that trust in the trading system has been achieved or will be achieved.

The Monterrey Conference on Financing for Development last March was also an exercise in recognizing shared responsibilities. The Conference generated substantial new pledges of official development assistance, reversing a decade-long decline, and made good progress on issues such as debt relief, investment, and corruption. Just as important, developed and developing countries reached a common understanding on their respective responsibilities in the pursuit of balanced, equitable development.

Finally, in September 2002, at the World Summit on Sustainable Development in Johannesburg, global citizenship took center stage. All leaders committed themselves to a path of development and economic growth that safeguards resources and ecosystems for succeeding generations. Rich-country leaders in particular agreed to reduce their nations' ecological footprint on the planet.

Taken together, these summits and conferences give us a blueprint that puts people—not states, and not GDP statistics—at the center of policy-making. The over-riding challenge now is implementation. And for that we shall need people from different sectors—public, private, and civil society—to forge more and better partnerships.

One of the most welcome developments at the United Nations in recent years has been the steadily growing engagement of the business community—both in policy forums and in projects on the ground.

Although the relationship is not without its difficulties, there is growing recognition that we must move beyond the politics of confrontation, and that solutions to poverty, environmental degradation, and other challenges can only be found if the private sector is involved. More and more businesses are themselves recognizing how much they depend on international norms and standards for the conduct of business on a global scale, and on the U.N.'s wide-ranging work for peace and development.

The Global Compact initiative I launched in 1999 at the World Economic Forum in Davos was based on my belief that open markets and human well-being can go hand in hand. Over the long run, human well-being can be dramatically advanced by well-functioning markets. But markets themselves can be sustained only if they ensure human well-being.

I asked business to embrace nine universal principles in the areas of human rights, labor standards, and the environment, and to enact these principles within their spheres of influence. I picked these areas because I was worried by a severe imbalance in global rule-making: while there are extensive and enforceable rules for economic priorities such as intellectual property rights, there are few strong measures for equally vital concerns such as human rights and the environment.

The compact has since become more than a call to action. Today it involves not only business but also labor federations and nongovernmental organizations. It has promoted the importance of universal values and encouraged investors to look harder at opportunities in the least developed countries, particularly in Africa. The compact has also created a learning forum—a worldwide academic network that examines case studies, trying to determine what works and what doesn't. I am pleased that the Sloan School plays an important role in this forum.

None of this is meant as a substitute for action by governments, or as a regulatory framework or code of conduct. Rather, the compact is a voluntary initiative, a platform for showing how markets can be made to serve the needs of society as a whole.

Businesses may ask why they should go down this path, especially if it involves taking steps that competitors might not, or steps they feel are rightly the province of governments. Sometimes, doing what is right—for example, eco-efficiency or creating decent workplace conditions—is in the immediate interest of business.

Sometimes, we must do what is right simply because *not* to do so would be wrong. And sometimes, we do what is right to help usher in a new day, of new norms and new behaviors. We do not want business to do anything different from their normal business; we want them to do their normal business differently.

Openness is the emerging hallmark of our time. But we need to make it work. Otherwise, countries and peoples might retreat behind protectionism or, worst of all, reject global citizenship in favor of narrow concepts of national interest not at all appropriate for an interdependent world.

Business is well placed not only to generate employment, investment, and growth, but also to advance global citizenship.

Sloan is well placed to teach more than accounting and finance, and to help define the parameters of corporate citizenship. I am delighted that its program is already evolving in this direction.

And the United Nations is well placed to promote dialogue that will build trust, and to create the multilateral norms and frameworks needed to fulfill our shared responsibilities.

All of us—the private sector, civil society, labor unions, NGOs, universities, foundations, and individuals—must come together in an alliance for progress. Together, we can and must move from value to values, from shareholders to stakeholders, and from balance sheets to balanced development. Together, we can and must face the dangers ahead and bring solutions within reach.

Discussion

Q. Do you see a link between corporate responsibility and corporate citizenship on one hand and the gulf between haves and have-nots on the other? Do companies have a positive role to play in creating a sustainable future?

A. I see a very important role for the corporate world. Corporations that respond to norms of sustainability do make a difference in the communities and societies in which they operate. Corporations and their leaders can influence policies of governments and steer decision-making in the right direction.

But they also make a difference in the daily lives of individuals. Corporations don't have to wait for countries to pass laws to know that they should not pollute the water that produces the fish for the village. They do not have to wait for government to tell them to pay a decent wage or to train their people.

Take the case of HIV-AIDS. Corporations have done some fantastic things around the world to address this problem. Look at what Volkswagen has done in Brazil. For years it watched its good managers contract this disease. So the company developed a program of education and treatment and then they saw these creative men and women live on and pass on this knowledge on how to protect themselves to their families and communities. So the roles of corporations in development and the health of society are extremely important and some corporations are doing quite a lot.

Q. What special responsibilities do American corporations have in the global community?

A. I am extremely happy that U.S. corporations are beginning to join the Global Compact. We have had tremendous response from Europe, Asia, Africa, and Latin America and recently Hewlett Packard and Pfizer have joined, and I expect others to follow in the future.

Today, corporations have become the main motor for the creation of wealth. They have technology, they have money, they have management, and they have global operations. In some ways, corporations understood faster and better than government that we live in a global world. Corporations that operate around the world should see their role not only as headquartered in New York or in Silicon Valley. They should also see it as their responsibility to pass on some of the knowledge, technology, and training to the people and communities where they operate. When they fail to do this, they inadvertently become part of the problem or the conflict.

Let me give you an example of what happened in Nigeria with Shell. Some of the villages around Shell's production sites felt they had seen nothing of the benefits accruing to them from the exploitation of the oil. The money was going to the central government and the profits were going to the shareholders while the people continued to live in squalor. Two or three months ago, women demonstrated and took over one of the sites. Now, Shell has announced that it will put some of the money back into the villages. Even if it is not just the responsibility of individual companies like Shell, they should be pressuring the government and saying, "don't you think we should be doing something for the villages around here?" and pull together and do something for these people. These gestures go a long way. I know some companies are doing this and I would urge others to do so.

Q. What can we at MIT, Sloan, and our alumni do in particular to advance the Global Compact initiatives?

A. I think you are already on the right track by training your students and discussing the Global Compact with them and with the many companies you advise. I have had a chance to discuss this issue with the Sloan Fellows and I am struck by how enthusiastic they are about this. And quite a few of your professors are already working on it. These are important ways of spreading the word.

Another thing we can do is to promote the learning forums that we have introduced. These forums are places where companies can come together to discuss what their responsibilities are, what their posture should be if they find themselves in areas of conflict. What is expected of corporations and to whom should they turn for advice and how can they work together? All this will be extremely helpful.

2.2

Restoring Trust: Corporate Responsibility and the CEO

Carly Fiorina

All of us share an enormous pride as Sloan School graduates because the Sloan School has managed to stay on the cutting edge through 50 years of enormous change in our free enterprise system while never losing sight of the fundamental values that make that system work in the first place, namely: trust, honesty, integrity, accountability, and responsibility.

There are a number of things I'd love to discuss with you today. I'd love to talk about the transformation we see in technology today, which is that physical processes are becoming digital processes. I'd love to tell you how that transformation is driving a fundamental shift in the value proposition in the technology industry, away from those companies that can provide simple point products—like isolated servers or personal computers—toward those companies that can put information technology ingredients together to provide end-to-end solutions. And I would love to tell you why the new HP, which we fought so hard to create, is uniquely positioned at the center of this industry to lead this revolution.

But the truth is, I think all corporate leaders today have a responsibility that goes beyond simply expounding on the particular trends in their particular industries. In light of the corporate abuses we have seen in the past year, I think all of us have a unique responsibility to help restore faith in the American economy.

Whether we've been touched by scandal or not, I believe it's incumbent on all corporate leaders to take ownership of this problem, and to lead by example at our own companies. As a group, we as corporate leaders have an opportunity to make clear, in our words as well as our actions, what we have always known to be true: that management serves at the pleasure and for the benefit of our shareowners, our customers, and our employees—and not the other way around.

Restoring that faith—and rebuilding that trust—is what I'd like to spend a few minutes talking about here today.

I do so knowing that to be a CEO giving a speech on corporate governance is to immediately invite inspection. But if CEOs don't speak out because they don't want to draw scrutiny, then corporate leaders will lose their voices in this discussion, which will give the initiative to people who know a lot about regulating businesses but not quite as much about running them.

It was in October 2001 that Enron took a $1 billion write-down of investments. Within three weeks, it would report that it had overstated its earnings since 1997 by $586 million. Within six weeks, the company—which was valued at more than $60 billion just a year before—filed for bankruptcy.

The stunning collapse of Enron not only cast a long shadow over our capital markets; it quickly gave way to headlines that more Enrons were to come. And sure enough, they *have* come—more than ten in all—leading one newspaper this week to refer to the parade of fallen business leaders as the "corporate perp walk" of the week.

Let's call this what it really is: it is greed, pure and simple. In every company accused of abuse, the traits are all the same: abuses of power, breach of ethics, undermining of honest accounting, deception of both public and private watchdog groups, and sometimes, the willing cooperation of such groups. In each case, checks and balances failed, and people tried to get away with gains made at somebody else's expense.

It is also true that these abuses occurred in an era when many quarters—some media, some analysts, some management teams—seemed to forget the fundamentals. Fundamentals like: management should manage the company not manage the share price. Between 1992 and 1999, the number of companies who beat estimates by exactly one penny quadrupled. Nearly 1,000 companies have restated their earnings in the last year.

Fundamentals like: management means balancing short-term returns with long-term investment; and that a CEO must think of a decade, not simply a quarter. Fundamentals like real profit, real cash flow, and real balance sheets matter. Fundamentals like trust, integrity, and responsibility matter.

There is no question who has paid the biggest price: it's been average investors, and ordinary people, who have either lost their jobs, lost their life savings, lost their pension funds—or lost all three.

Unlike the half-century between 1930 and 1980—when 5 to 15 percent of Americans invested in the market—the explosion of defined contribution plans in the 1990s means that today, more than 60 percent of Americans own stock. Which means that to a degree unprecedented in American history, corporate wrongdoing is being felt not just at the boardroom table, but at the kitchen table as well. In the last 10 years, average Americans bought into the idea of a market-driven society.

And now their anger is pointed in many directions. As the *New York Times* recently pointed out, "many issues have been blended together in the public mind-set, from cooking the books and stealing corporate cash to excessive pay and perks," making no distinction between crime and common practices. That's because, to many, there *are* no distinctions.

Similarly, many investors put all companies in the same boat. The Secretary-General of the United Nations, Kofi Annan, has said that the most frustrating thing about Africa today is that investors don't yet differentiate between countries in Africa. They hear about something bad happening in Zimbabwe, and they take it as proof that they shouldn't invest in Uganda—because hey, Africa is Africa, they think—so they keep their investments away.

In this atmosphere, the same is true of corporate America. The misdeeds of some have cast aspersions on every corporate office in America. After all, if a dozen companies either issued make-believe accounts or made-up earnings numbers, why should anyone believe that dozens of other companies aren't practicing the same deceptions? So they keep *their* investments away—and the Dow falls below 7,500 for the first time in five years.

According to one poll, public confidence in big business is at its lowest point since 1981.

As is their role, into this breach, regulators and government officials have stepped in with ideas for new regulation and legislation. As one report put it, while the federal government has taken a hammer to conflicts of interest among auditors and executives, the New York Stock Exchange has done the same thing for boards of directors. From the integrity of certified financial audits to appropriate accounting principles and auditing standards, what used to be the legal ceiling is increasingly becoming the legal floor. And if that will help restore investor confidence, it's an important step.

But if we are truly embarking on a new Age of Reform—such as the one America went through a century ago following a similar decline in public trust—leadership is not going to come from the government or other oversight organizations. True leadership—as it did 100 years ago—must come from corporate America itself.

So how do we do it? Managing a company, not a share price, means balancing the requirements of shareowners, customers, employees, and communities. And managing a company for the long term, not just the short term, requires building sustainable value for shareowners and customers and employees and communities. And these relationships of sustainable value require real trust and real candor.

Coming as I do from a company of scientists and engineers, it probably comes as no surprise that I believe trust begins first and foremost as a DNA question: If you don't have ethics strongly coded in your own business, it's going to be difficult to project those values in the larger market.

After all, what is trust? It's no accident that the word "trust" derives from the Scandinavian word *truste*, which means firm, solid, steadfast. In a phrase, I think trust means being counted on to do the right thing when nobody is watching. It means doing what you say you are going to do. It means that your word is your bond.

In the end, business practices aren't driven by corporate culture—they reflect corporate culture.

When I was a student here, it was called values-based management, the famous Theory Y. It was based on the profound idea that the most valuable resource a company has doesn't lie in its products or plants or plans: it lies in its people. And it was driven by the equally profound idea that if you treat people right, you'll get the best they have to give. In the real world, I think we've all learned that this has a lot more to do with common sense than it does with any theory.

We all know: people want to do a good job. They want to be treated with consideration and respect. They want to feel a real sense of accomplishment in their work, to have their ideas considered and their achievements recognized. They want to feel like they're part of something larger than themselves—to be a part of the larger vision, direction, and goals that a company is working toward. There is now a mountain of evidence to support the idea that a company's objectives can best be achieved by people who understand and support a company's vision, and who are allowed flexibility in working toward common goals.

The difficulty comes in communicating not just what a company is trying to do, but how it is trying to do it. Any corporation can sit down and write a high-minded statement of values. But we all know: It is in living those values that is the hard part.

At HP, we understand that values need to be constantly reinforced in an organization to be real. We know that how we do things is as important as what we do.

Forty-five years ago, HP pioneered the idea of a corporate values statement. Realizing that the rapid growth of HP made it impossible to have the daily one-to-one contact with employees that the founders had long enjoyed, in 1957, Bill Hewlett and Dave Packard convened a group of HP employees together at the aptly named Mission Inn in Sonoma, California, to put those values in writing—so new employees and future employees would understand not just *what* we did but *how* we did it. That's how the famous "HP Way" was born.

What's sometimes forgotten about the HP Way is that it didn't happen overnight. It grew out of 20 years of experience in the company itself, and it was an attempt to *capture* the values of the company, not to *create* them. In turn, those values were reinforced everywhere. Our values are fundamentals, not rocket science. Trust, respect, integrity, contribution, teamwork and collaboration, passion for customers.

Of course, one of the challenges we've had in the past year in our merger with Compaq is how to combine two large organizations—145,000 employees—into one team without sacrificing the values that made us successful. So, before the merger was even announced, we undertook a cultural due diligence study in both companies to learn what employees value—what motivates them, what gives them pride and commitment.

The study involved in-depth interviews with 127 executives and 138 focus groups involving more than 1,500 managers and employees from both companies in 22 countries around the world. We also conducted team-building meetings to examine our cultural perceptions, share ideas, and develop common goals. In the end, we were able to identify the key attributes of HP and Compaq, a set of values we all aspired to.

The interesting thing is, the values that came out of that work were the same ones that made up the original HP Way, with one notable addition that says more about the times than anything else—speed and urgency. The point is people everywhere aspire to the same things.

Values are reflected in how we do things. At HP, we have something called the "open door" practice: anyone can raise any issue with anyone else, anytime. We reinforce this in interesting ways. Our board members are free to interact with any employee they choose—and they do.

Our employees are free to contact anyone—any board member included, and they do. I think the thing that's impressed me the most in my three years at HP is that every communication I've ever received has been signed. Even during the emotion and turmoil of the proxy contest, every communication I've received has been signed.

It is also true that one can never take these fundamentals of how we do things for granted. And particularly I think in times of turmoil, people need reinforcement on the most fundamental things. In times of turmoil like a merger, in times of turmoil like the threat of war, in times of turmoil like a down economy, in times of turmoil like corporate scandal, it is more important than ever to reinforce these fundamentals because people think if they don't hear it, it must no longer be true.

As I and the rest of the management team travel around our new company, we talk always, always about how we do things. That our character as a company is as important as our capability and our results. We have reinforced the open-door policy with all of our employees, not just our new employees. We make it clear that it is not simply a right, it is an obligation. It is our expectation that employees raise their hand and raise issues about which they have concern or an important point of view.

And because we are pulling together a new company for the first time, we are reinforcing these open-door policies with other means. We are using a belt and suspenders, if you will, not simply setting a tone at the top, not simply reinforcing existing policies, but also creating some new ones like 800 numbers, like ombudsman roles to make sure that people understand *how* we do things is as important as *what* we do.

I began by talking about the basic DNA of a company, the way values are acted upon every day by employees, the way trust and integrity are displayed every day all up and down the management chain, from the boardroom to the shop floor, because this is where it all starts. Without this foundation of integrity and candor, no amount of regulation will fix what ails corporate America.

It is, of course, integrity and candor in the boardroom that has riveted everyone's attention and concern.

Finally, the values that govern the boardroom should be no different than the values that govern the shop floor. Which means truly open debate, truly open dialogue, truly open access.

Of course, asking the tough questions, and engaging in truly open and honest debate and dialogue, is a board member's job. And providing truly open access to employees, and information—insight to the good, the bad, and the ugly—is management's job.

But what I've found serving as chairman and CEO of HP—particularly during our proxy contest—is that practicing these fundamentals is more than compliance with a board's or management team's responsibilities. They make a board and a company more effective.

People have asked me—"How did you keep the board together during the proxy battle?" The answer is, they kept themselves together. They kept themselves together because they exercised the highest standards of governance. They asked the hard questions—over, and over, and then asked them again. They debated the merits of the merger, and all its risks—and compared it to every other alternative. They routinely met without me. They routinely talked with the management team, with the auditors.

Open debates, open doors, and open access make all teams more effective, and these fundamentals should be as much a part of the boardroom as anywhere else. Of course, processes and controls and regulations can, and should, play an important role. But it is how we conduct ourselves in our companies and our boardrooms that will have more lasting impact than the certification we sign.

And if the fundamental DNA of the shop floor and the boardroom are the same, then policies and practices must be aligned and consistent and equitable from top to bottom, and bottom to top.

Nowhere is this more true than pay. At HP, this has been a longstanding practice. When employees forgo a bonus in the tough times of the last few years, everyone forgoes one. No one is eligible for a raise until everyone is eligible.

If open doors and open access and open dialogue are part of the fundamental DNA of effective groups, so are the principles of equity, consistency, and alignment. And once again, these fundamentals must apply in the boardroom as surely as on the shop floor.

I want to close on a final point. I mentioned balancing the needs of employees, customers, shareowners, and communities. And I believe communities belong as equal members in the balanced equation that management teams are responsible for.

In this day and age, we are not just corporate citizens—we are global citizens. With global reach must come global responsibility. We live in a world today where there is more prosperity than ever before—but it's also a world where two billion people are living on less than two dollars a day; where 130 million children will never go to school; where one in five people has never had a clean glass of water. If we learned anything on September 11th, we learned that a global economy that is creating prosperity for millions will not be sustainable if billions of people feel they have no stake in it.

There has never been a time when corporations have had the reach, the resources, the knowledge, and the expertise to make a difference that we do today. Now, more than ever, corporate leaders have an opportunity to redefine the role of the corporation on a world stage— to leverage our ability to improve the lives of people, communities, and nations.

On one hand, it means being good global citizens, maintaining high standards and setting a good example in areas like the environment, ethics, labor, and human rights. On the other, it means being part of the communities in which we do business.

Too often, corporations look at disparities in the developing world and ask two fundamental questions: first, how do we use our money to provide people with the resources they need to make a difference? or second, how do we use our talents to make sure citizens in the developing world have the training to use the technology or equipment we provide once they've got it?

That's what traditional philanthropy has been about—but if we have learned anything in this new global economy, we have learned that traditional philanthropy is no longer enough. In asking those two questions, we rarely take a leap to a fundamental third question, which is: How do we engage their talents? How do we engage local citizens in local communities in the developing world to learn what's important to them, and what goals they hope to achieve?

I think we in the multinational community rarely ask local citizens what they think and what they need—either because the market share hasn't been there, or the profit motive hasn't been there. But if we never make the leap to that third question, corporations leave off the table those very assets—our ability to invent locally relevant products, our project management skills, and our ability to set goals and meet them— that make us most relevant. The truth is, financial capital alone is not the greatest wealth multinationals can bring to the developing world—

it is human capital. It is experience and knowledge, and the ability to transmit that into capacity building. Especially at a time when the challenges are so great, we need to apply all of our best talents to solving those problems.

But that can't happen if multinationals remain faceless entities from far-away places. It can only happen if corporations engage local citizens in the developing world in the places where they live and work. HP, and other companies, are working to create a new model of involvement, one that taps more deeply into the things we do best.

Instead of simply committing resources—like computers or printers—and wishing them well, we are committing some of our best talent to underdeveloped communities from East Palo Alto to Kuppam, India to South Africa; putting our people in place for up to three years and charging them with working with local citizens to set goals and create solutions for the challenges the community prioritizes. In the process, we're working hand in hand with local governments, NGOs, and humanitarian organizations. This isn't about imposing solutions—it's about listening to the needs of the community and helping them acquire the tools they need to make their own goals and dreams come true.

Why do it? This is not an argument for compassion; it's an argument for enlightened self-interest. First, because of the security dimension—poverty anywhere undermines stability everywhere. Second, because if we look beyond the next quarter or two, particularly for an industry where only ten percent of the world is in a position to buy our products, we have to acknowledge that many of the ideas and markets of the future will come from the developing world.

But our ability to make a difference abroad starts with integrity here at home. The good news is that for all the trouble our economy and our country have been through the past year, our economy—and our system of free enterprise—remains the strongest in the world. American capitalism has shown a remarkable ability to react, recover, adapt, evolve, and triumph over change. And let's remember: American capitalism is not some unseen force. It is us—all of us. As Senator Joe Lieberman has said, the force that's kept America strong for two centuries is not the hidden hand, but the credible handshake.

No one of us alone can restore faith in the market. This is a challenge that all corporations share—which is why I believe it's up to all of us, as corporate leaders, to solve. To me, the important thing is to understand that good corporate governance is not something that is being done *to* us. It is not something being foisted *upon* us. The values we are being asked to live by today are the same values we used to build the greatest economy on earth.

The values we are being asked to live by are the same fundamental values we know we must act upon every day to build effective teams and companies.

As the regulations and investigations mount, as our lawyers and auditors focus on our compliance, let's focus on these fundamentals. Because there simply is no substitute.

Discussion

Q. The general public doesn't see a difference between corporate fraud and excessive executive compensation. Where do you draw the line between these two issues?

A. I understand why the public doesn't see a distinction. If it is difficult to justify CEO compensation based on the value that they provide, then they are taking money out of the shareholders' pockets. That is why consistency, equity, and alignment are so important. Employees must be able to understand why they get paid what they do compared to what the CEO gets paid. That is why at HP we have the concept of *total rewards*. This includes base pay, benefits, bonuses, and long-term equity. We have the same structure from the CEO right down to the first-level employee. Everyone has to be able to see this and understand it so they can draw this line for themselves.

Q. Contemporary CEOs are expected to forecast quarterly earnings without sacrificing long-term profitability and growth. In the current environment, a CEO who manages quarterly earnings risks the accusation of being deceptive and one who fails to manage long-term growth is labeled incompetent. How does the CEO set and meet targets without managing earnings?

A. There is some conflict and it is also true that Wall Street is talking out of both sides of its mouth. It is virtually impossible in turbulent times like these to always land a plane on a dime. So companies will sometimes miss a target. That's a fact. And it is also a fact that there are temptations, there are choices that can be made every quarter to manage the numbers and those choices simply have to be walked away from. No amount of regulation can substitute for integrity.

Let me give you a personal example. I can remember missing the target in the fourth quarter of 2000. The truth is, we could have made that quarter but it was the wrong thing to do. The pressures that arose when we missed that quarter were intense, including calls for my resignation. But the truth is, we are responsible for managing the company, not the media, not the analysts, not even the shareholders. That is why it is important to remember that the CEO's job is not to safeguard a quarter but to safeguard the company to provide sustainable value for decades to come, not just for quarters.

Q. How do you measure the long-term success of the company?

A. You have to measure it in a variety of ways. Just as financial indicators are a lagging measure of success, there are some leading indicators. One of the leading indicators we use is total customer experience. We believe this is a leading indicator of whether customers will continue to purchase things from us in the future. And that is a predictor of future success.

In a technology company, it also means deciding how much R&D spending to invest in projects that will only pay off a few years down the road. Shareholders who are interested in the underlying value of the assets they own, not those who just are interested in the change in the value of the currency, expect managers to do their job. I'm not talking about those shareholders only interested in the value of the currency. Those who value the assets know that it is management's job to balance the short and long term. When I go and talk to those shareholders, I find that they ask as many questions about the long term as the short term.

Q. Are analysts a positive or negative factor?

A. Some help and others do not. One of the curious things about all the current debate is frankly a lack of accountability among the media and financial community for failing to also take responsibility for creating the dot.com bubble. I think it would be a good idea if some in the financial community and in the financial media also raised their hand and said, "yes, we were also pushing the stock prices up by saying to the people 'ignore the fact that there won't be any profits for the next five years.'"

Q. What is your view of the division of the respective responsibilities of the board and management?

A. I have talked about the need for boards to operate on the principle of open access and dialogue. Some people ask, won't this lead to the board taking over the job of management? I honestly don't think so. It is clearly the board's job to oversee management and to reinforce management for doing their jobs in the right way. But I also think that that oversight responsibility is impossible unless board members have the information needed to know what is really going on. And what is really going on is not completely reflected in the beautiful power point slides presented in boardrooms. What is really going on is what managers really think, what customers really think, and what managers say when they talk in the hall outside the board meetings and have a chance to tell a board member how things are really going.

Q. A related question is about the composition of the board, particularly in light of the new responsibilities and potential liabilities. Is this an issue that affects whom you can attract?

A. I think it is an issue. While there is an upside to all the scrutiny and controls, and there are upsides, there will be a downside if in the end they create an overly risk-averse climate. After all, the business of business is taking prudent risks. Board members are worried about the amount of time, the administrative trivia, and the liability involved. This makes it all the more essential for potential board members to ask how the board will operate and whether they will have access to the information they need.

3 Globalization

3.1

The Promise and Perils of Globalization: The Case of Nike

Richard M. Locke

How should global corporations behave in the new international world order? What constitutes good corporate citizenship when the stakeholders are diverse and dispersed around the globe and where no clear or consensual rules and standards exist? These questions shape the behavior of most multinational corporations (MNCs) today. Although multinationals are eager to pursue the opportunities of increased global integration, they are more and more aware of the reactions which their strategies induce—both at home and abroad. Thus, they tread warily, lacking clear and agreed-upon definitions of good corporate citizenship.

Through a case study of Nike, Inc.—a company that has come to symbolize both the benefits and the risks inherent in globalization—this paper examines the various difficulties and complexities companies face as they seek to balance both company performance and good corporate citizenship in today's global world.

This paper is divided into three parts. First, it examines current debates over the basic conception of corporate citizenship. Second, it analyzes the evolution of Nike's global strategies, illustrating how this particular company has redefined its understanding of corporate citizenship in the light of the challenges and opportunities it has faced. The paper concludes by pondering the more general lessons this case study may have for management education and business strategy in the future.

Corporate Citizenship in a Global Economy

The issue of corporate citizenship and the role of corporations in society have been debated for centuries. The debates move through various waves of intensity, often provoked by revelations of corporate scandals and/or problems arising from various business practices (e.g., product safety and labor relations during the Industrial Revolution, defense-related corruption scandals in the 1970s, and accounting abuses and the impact of globalization today). Notwithstanding this long history, and the fact that each year dozens of articles on this topic are published and numerous prizes for corporate social responsibility are awarded, there exists no agreed-upon definition of corporate citizenship. In fact, both in the literature and in the more general corporate social responsibility movement, there coexist alternative—sometimes even competing—conceptions of what constitutes good corporate citizenship, why it is important, and how it should be implemented.

Alternative Models of Corporate Citizenship

Although the literature on corporate citizenship (sometimes referred to as corporate social responsibility—CSR) is extensive and contains many subtle distinctions, it can be divided among four highly stylized models: (1) minimalist, (2) philanthropic, (3) encompassing, and (4) social activist conceptions of corporate citizenship. These four models differ both in terms of the supposed beneficiaries of corporate action (shareholders vs. broader societal stakeholders) and in the motivation behind these actions (instrumental vs. moral/ethical). (See table 3.1.1.)

The more traditional or *minimalist* conception of corporate citizenship was perhaps best articulated by the economist Milton Friedman. According to Friedman, "the social responsibility of business is to increase the wealth of its shareholders" (1970). In other words, the sole responsibility of business is to those who have invested capital in the company. By maintaining a singular focus on wealth creation, businesses will promote efficiency and achieve optimal economic performance, which in this view is the ultimate good that a business can do for society. Of course, corporations should not violate laws or engage

Table 3.1.1
Alternative models of corporate citizenship

		Motivation	
		Instrumental	Moral/ethical
Beneficiaries	Shareholders	Minimalist	Philanthropic
	Stakeholders	Encompassing	Social activist

in any irregular activities that could harm the wealth of shareholders, but any attempt to incorporate social goals into core business activities will, according to this conception, lead to inefficiencies. Moreover, given that most managers do not have expertise in the area of social responsibility, engaging in these activities will simply distract them from their primary fiduciary responsibility, which is to protect and promote shareholder wealth.

The *philanthropic* model is an extension of this traditional view. Although it, too, is concerned primarily with the optimization of efficiency and shareholder wealth, it does recognize that individual managers, shareholders, and sometimes even companies can, at times, engage in various philanthropic activities. However, these activities are seen *not* as important or even related to core business activities, but rather as motivated by various moral or ethical concerns.

A more inclusive stakeholder view of the corporation underlies the third, more *encompassing* model of corporate citizenship. According to this view, management is responsible not solely to shareholders but also to other groups (e.g., employees, consumers, creditors, suppliers, and local communities) that may be affected by the company's practices. Therefore, managers must consider the interests of these other groups when making decisions. Some proponents of this approach contend that corporate responsiveness to a wide constellation of stakeholders enhances the resiliency of the firm in the face of external threats (Freeman 1984 in Brummer 1991). This, in turn, promotes the long-term survival of the firm. Others argue that company engagement in broader societal issues directly increases company profitability and hence shareholder wealth.[1] Thus, according to this third model of corporate citizenship, corporate behavior may be directed toward a wider constellation of actors, but it is nonetheless instrumental, geared toward maximizing benefits to this broader (albeit still limited) group.

The *social activist* view of corporate citizenship, the fourth model, extends the boundaries of supposed beneficiaries beyond those groups directly affected by company decision-making and toward society at large. According to this view, corporations should act to enhance broader societal goals and not merely to benefit a more restricted number of shareholders and/or stakeholders. Corporations should act not merely out of instrumental concerns but rather out of moral or even

---

1. See Elizabeth Murphy, "Best corporate citizens have better financial performance," *Strategic Finance*, January 2002.

ethical considerations. In fact, because corporations are usually powerful and wealthy actors in society, they have a moral obligation to act in a way that aids their less fortunate fellow citizens.

Of course, there are many other, more subtle views of corporate citizenship. (See the references for a sampling of other views.) The point here is *not* to provide a comprehensive review of the literature on corporate citizenship but rather to highlight the existence of significant divergent opinions about several key dimensions of this issue, including:

1. *The role of management:* Should managers behave solely to enhance shareholder wealth? Or should they act to benefit other groups (both within and outside the firm) as well? Do managerial responsibilities extend beyond what is required either by law or contractual obligation?

2. *The relation to profit:* Should corporate decision-making be driven solely by economic considerations? Or are other (social) factors equally important? How does one measure and account for these other considerations? Is there an economic benefit to being a good corporate citizen?

3. *The realm of responsibility:* Are corporations responsible for only the direct effects of their decisions and strategies or also the indirect effects? What are the boundaries or limits of these responsibilities?

Globalization

The debates surrounding competing conceptions of corporate citizenship have become more complex and heated as a result of globalization. During the last two decades of the twentieth century, global trade and global capital mobility increased dramatically. For example, trade among the industrial democracies grew at almost twice the rate of total economic output during the 1970s and 1980s.[2] Whereas global trade amounted to about one-third of total world output in the early 1970s, it approached 45 percent in 1995. Intra-industry trade, an indication of competition within similar product markets, far outstripped interindustry trade, thus heightening competition among producers for similar markets. At the same time, world trade became progressively

---

2. Geoffrey Garrett, *Partisan Politics in the Global Economy* (Cambridge University Press, 1998), p. 51.

less dominated by exchanges within the OECD nations, since various newly industrialized countries (e.g., South Korea, Singapore, Brazil, Mexico, India, and China) increased their exports after the oil crisis of the 1970s. A recent study by the World Bank shows that 24 developing countries, home to about 3 billion people, increased their integration into the world economy since 1980. Manufactures rose from less than 25 percent of developing country exports in 1980 to more than 80 percent in 1998.[3] As a result, these countries achieved higher growth in per capita incomes (on average 5 percent growth), longer life expectancies, and better schooling.[4]

Financial integration and movement of capital across borders also increased dramatically in these years. For example, international bank lending grew from around $200 billion in 1973 to almost $4 trillion in 1992.[5] Although the raw numbers on international capital flow are staggering, some economists, including those working at the International Monetary Fund, believe that the best indicator of capital mobility is the existence of government restrictions on international capital movements. In the early 1970s, less than 15 percent of countries had no capital controls. By the mid-1990s, about 30 percent of countries had removed controls on capital mobility.[6] This trend continued throughout the decade.

This increased flow of trade and capital, as well as the dramatic improvements in information, communication, and transportation technologies, has opened up all sorts of opportunities for MNCs to invest in or source from lower-cost developing countries. Yet these opportunities are not without risk. As corporations increasingly disperse parts of their value chain throughout the developing world, they encounter a number of issues that challenge their original conceptions of corporate citizenship. How should these corporations behave when they are operating in several different countries, each with its own wages, regulations, customs, and standards (or lack thereof)? What standards should they abide by and who—national governments, international organizations like the ILO, or the corporations

---

3. World Bank, *Globalization, Growth, and Poverty* (The World Bank, 2002), p. 5.
4. However, this same study shows that not all developing countries have benefited from increased globalization. In fact, much of the developing world trades less today than it did 20 years ago. This explains, in part, the growing poverty and income inequality manifest in much of the developing world.
5. Garrett, *Partisan Politics in the Global Economy*, p. 54.
6. Richard Herring and Robert Litan, *Financial Regulation in the Global Economy* (The Brookings Institution, 1995), pp. 26–27.

themselves—should set these standards? To whom are these corporations responsible? To their shareholders and direct employees? To their
vendors, suppliers, and customers? Or even to the employees of their
third-party vendors and the local communities in which those factories
are located? What are the boundaries or limits of a corporation's
responsibilities? In short, globalization has exacerbated the tensions
and debates already present within the corporate social responsibility
movement.

In order to better illustrate the complexity of these issues, we now
turn to an examination of Nike, Inc.—a company that has come to symbolize both the promise and the perils of globalization.

The Athletic Footwear Industry

The athletic footwear industry experienced an explosive growth in the
last two decades. In 1985, consumers in the United States alone spent
$5 billion and purchased 250 million pair of shoes.[7] In 2001, they spent
over $13 billion and bought over 335 million pair of shoes.[8] Although
the industry is highly segmented—by different sports, models, and
price—the branded shoe segment is dominated by a few large companies (e.g., Nike, Reebok, and Adidas). In fact, the top 10 footwear companies control over 70 percent of the global athletic footwear market
(see table 3.1.2). Since displacing Adidas in the early 1980s and Reebok
in the early 1990s, Nike has become the largest and most important
athletic shoe company in the world. (See figure 3.1.1.)

The Promise of Globalization: Nike, Inc.

Founded in 1964 through an investment of $500 each by Phil Knight
and Bill Bowerman, the company (then called Blue Ribbon Sports—
BLS) has evolved from being an importer and distributor of Japanese
specialty running shoes to becoming the world leader in the design,
distribution, and marketing of athletic footwear. Nike has stated: "Our
business model in 1964 is essentially the same as our model today: We
grow by investing our money in design, development, marketing and

---

7. Miguel Korzeniewicz, "Commodity Chains and Marketing Strategies: Nike and the
Global Athletic Footwear Industry," in *Commodity Chains and Global Capitalism*, ed. Gary
Gereffi and Miguel Korzeniewicz (Greenwood Press, 1994), p. 248.
8. National Sporting Goods Association, 2002; www.sbrnet.com

Table 3.1.2
Market share

Athletic footwear market share	1991	1992	1993	1994	1995	1996	1997	1998	1999
Nike	22.5	25.4	24.4	22.7	27.1	32.1	35.3	N/A	30.4
Reebok	18.8	20.0	18.9	18.3	17.4	14.7	14.5	N/A	11.2
Adidas	13.6	10.0	9.3	10.3	9.9	10.2	10.3	N/A	15.5
Fila	0.9	2.1	2.7	3.0	4.1	6.0	5.7	N/A	3.9
Converse	3.4	3.5	4.0	4.2	3.3	2.7	3.2	N/A	2.2
New Balance	1.8	1.8	2.1	2.2	2.5	2.9	3.1	N/A	3.8
ASICS	4.7	5.4	5.2	4.7	4.2	3.5	3.0	N/A	2.5
Puma	4.6	3.8	4.3	3.1	2.4	2.4	2.1	N/A	2.1
Keds/Prokeds	3.0	3.9	3.9	3.0	2.4	1.9	1.5	N/A	0.0
Airwalk	0.0	0.0	0.4	1.1	1.2	1.4	1.1	N/A	0.0
Top 10	73.3	75.9	75.2	72.6	74.5	77.8	79.8	0.0	71.6
Others	26.7	24.1	24.8	27.4	25.5	22.2	20.2		28.4
Totals	100.0	100.0	100.0	100.0	100.0	100.0	100.0	0.0	100.0

Sources: HBS Case #9-299-084 "Nike, Inc.: Entering the Millennium," March 31, 1999, and *Footwear News*, December 27, 1999

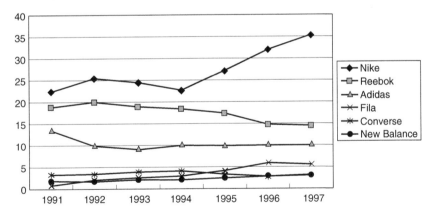

Figure 3.1.1
Global athletic footwear market share—top 6.

sales and then contract with other companies to manufacture our products."[9]

According to company legend, Nike's business model was developed by Knight while he attended Stanford Business School in the early 1960s. Knight realized that while lower-cost, high-quality Japanese producers were beginning to take over the U.S. consumer appliance and electronic markets, most leading footwear companies (e.g., Adidas) were still manufacturing their own shoes in higher-cost countries like the United States and Germany. By outsourcing shoe production to lower-cost Japanese producers, Knight believed that BLS could undersell its competitors and break into this market. As a result, BLS began to import high-tech sports shoes from Onitsuka Tiger of Japan. As sales increased to almost $2 million in the early 1970s, BLS parted ways with Onitsuka and began to design and subcontract its own line of shoes. The Nike brand was launched in 1972, and the company officially changed its name to Nike, Inc. in 1978.

Nike first developed a strong working relationship with two Japanese shoe manufacturers, Nippon Rubber and Nihon-Koyo. But as costs and prices increased in Japan over the course of the 1970s (owing to a combination of a tighter labor market, the impact of the first oil crisis on Japan's economy, and a shift in the dollar/yen exchange rate as a result of the so-called "Nixon shock"),[10] Nike began to search for alternative, lower-cost producers. During these same years, Nike opened up its own shoe factories in Maine and New Hampshire, hoping to develop a reliable and high-quality source to supply its growing domestic market. At the same time, the company also began to cultivate potential suppliers in South Korea, Thailand, China, and Taiwan. By the early 1980s, as costs continued to increase in both Japan and the United States, and as the Korean government created a number of incentives to develop South Korea's footwear industry,[11] Nike closed its U.S. factories and sourced almost all of its production from Asia. In 1982, 86 percent of Nike's athletic footwear came from Korea and Taiwan.[12]

---

9. As reported on Nike's web site, nikebiz.com
10. For more on this period, see Yasusuke Murukami, "The Japanese Model of Political Economy," in *The Political Economy of Japan: Volume 1, The Domestic Transformation*, ed. Kozo Yamamura and Yasukichi Yasuba (Stanford University Press, 1987).
11. These and other government incentive programs are nicely described in Alice H. Amsden, *Asia's Next Giant* (Oxford University Press, 1989).
12. "International Sourcing in Athletic Footwear: Nike and Reebok," HBS Case #9-394-189, pp. 2–5.

Over time, as South Korea and Taiwan also began to develop, costs began to rise in these sources as well. As a result, Nike began to urge its suppliers to relocate their operations to other, lower-cost countries. The company worked with its lead suppliers to open up manufacturing plants in Indonesia, China, and Vietnam. By guaranteeing a significant number of orders and by placing Nike employees at these new factories to help monitor product quality and production processes, Nike was able to help its lead vendors establish an extensive network of footwear factories throughout Southeast Asia.[13]

Today, Nike's products are manufactured in more than 700 factories, employing over 500,000 workers in 51 countries (see table 3.1.3). Nike has only 22,658 direct employees, the vast majority of them working in the United States.[14] Over the years, Nike has broadened its product range. Whereas in 1980, Nike sold 175 different styles of shoes,[15] it offered 772 different styles in its spring 1990 collection and almost 1,200 different styles in its spring 2000 collection.[16] Nike has also moved into other sectors (apparel and sports equipment) and expanded its sales beyond the United States into Europe, Latin America, and Asia. (See appendix A.) In 2001, the company made about $9.5 billion in revenues, of which 59 percent came from footwear sales and 29 percent from apparel.

Important differences exist among the sectors in which Nike competes. Although still primarily known as a footwear company, only 68[17] out of its 736 suppliers are producing shoes. Most of these suppliers are located in Asia. (See appendix B.) In contrast, Nike apparel products are manufactured in 579 factories distributed throughout the world. These differences are due both to the rules governing international trade in the two industries and to the underlying nature of these industries (footwear factories are usually large, capital-intensive facilities, whereas garment factories are usually smaller, easy to set up, and extremely labor-intensive operations). Whereas footwear quotas were

---

13. For more on the evolution of Nike's strategy, see "Nike (A)," HBS Case #9-385-025; "International Sourcing in Athletic Footwear: Nike and Reebok," HBS Case #9-394-189; and J. B. Strasser and Laurie Becklund, *Swoosh: The Unauthorized Story of Nike and the Men Who Played There* (Harper Business 1991).

14. Nike, Corporate Responsibility Report, FY 2001, p. 1.

15. This includes different color combinations of shoes.

16. These figures come from various Nike catalogs. We thank Jody McFarland for helping us obtain these data.

17. Twenty of these footwear suppliers manufacture shoes for Cole Hann, a Nike subsidiary. Thus, only about 50 suppliers are manufacturing Nike brand shoes.

Table 3.1.3
Regional and product distribution of suppliers

Country	# of factories	Apparel	Equipment	Footwear	# workers
Albania	1	1	0	0	200
Belarus	1	1	0	0	70
Argentina	4	3	0	1	436
Australia	11	9	2	0	400
Bangladesh	4	3	1	0	14,120
Brazil	9	3	1	5	5,488
Bulgaria	4	4	0	0	881
Cambodia	2	2	0	0	2,021
Canada	21	20	1	0	2,300
Chile	1	1	0	0	100
China	74	35	22	17	175,960
Dominican Rep	5	4	1	0	3,995
Ecuador	1	1	0	0	353
Egypt	3	3	0	0	600
El Salvador	8	8	0	0	4,044
Germany	2	2	0	0	30
Greece	19	19	0	0	5,300
Guatemala	2	2	0	0	816
Holland	3	3	0	0	81
Honduras	5	5	0	0	2,438
Hungary	1	1	0	0	1,650
India	23	19	1	3	16,071
Indonesia	30	16	3	11	104,514
Israel	3	1	2	0	2,157
Italy	12	8	2	2	5,000
Japan	6	2	4	0	1,500
Korea	49	31	10	8	4,000
Laos	2	2	0	0	2,452
Lithuania	1	1	0	0	45
Macau	3	3	0	0	500
Macedonia	1	1	0	0	215
Malaysia	42	41	1	0	8,044
Micronesia	2	2	0	0	672
Mexico	41	39	0	2	12,258
Morocco	2	2	0	0	1,274
New Zealand	1	1	0	0	50
Pakistan	3	2	1	0	9,880
Peru	4	4	0	0	5,286
Phillippines	22	18	4	0	9,400
Portugal	23	23	0	0	1,872
Romania	3	3	0	0	2,900
Singapore	2	2	0	0	300
South Africa	2	2	0	0	660
Sri Lanka	16	16	0	0	10,286
Taiwan	35	24	7	4	15,600
Thailand	62	42	11	9	47,962
Turkey	16	15	1	0	7,944
UK	5	5	0	0	814
USA	131	117	14	0	13,369
Vietnam	12	7	0	5	43,414
Zimbabwe	1	0	0	1	7,000
Total	736	579	89	68	556,722

Source: Nike, Corporate Responsibility Report, FY 2001

eliminated by the mid- to late 1980s (leading to a consolidation of the industry), trade in garments is still very much shaped by the existence of quotas (e.g., the Multi-fiber Agreement).[18] In 2005, according to the World Trade Organization (WTO) Agreement in Textile and Clothing, quotas in garments produced in WTO member states should also end. At present, neither Vietnam nor Cambodia are WTO members, and thus quotas will remain in place after 2005.

These industry differences have a significant impact on the kinds of relationships that Nike can develop with its various suppliers. For example, in footwear, Nike has been able to develop long-term relations with several large South Korean and Taiwanese firms. With some of these firms, Nike designers create new footwear designs and styles for upcoming seasons and then relay them via satellite to suppliers, who in turn develop the prototypes. Once these prototypes are approved, these lead suppliers fax the product specifications to their various plants throughout Southeast Asia, where production can take place almost immediately. This level of trust and coordination facilitates both production and (usually) compliance activities for Nike. In apparel, given short product cycles and volatile trends, the situation is completely different. Nike works with numerous suppliers, most of whom are also working for other (often competitor) companies. Given that different apparel suppliers specialize in particular products or market segments, shifts in consumer preferences or fashion trends could translate into very short-term contracts with and/or limited orders from Nike. This alters both the level of influence which Nike has with these suppliers as well as Nike's ability to monitor regularly the production processes and working conditions of these factories.

The Perils of Globalization: Wages, Working Conditions, and the Rise of the Anti-Nike Movement

The same factors that permitted Nike to grow at an impressive rate over the last several decades—taking advantage of global sourcing opportunities to produce lower-cost products and investing these savings into innovative designs and marketing campaigns—have also created serious problems for the company in recent years. Already in the 1980s, Nike had been criticized for sourcing its products in

---

18. For a fascinating discussion of the impact of quotas on the international apparel industry, see David Birnbaum, *Birnbaum's Global Guide to Winning the Great Garment War* (Hong Kong: Third Horizon Press, 2000).

factories/countries where low wages, poor working conditions, and human rights problems were rampant. However, over the course of the 1990s, a series of public relations nightmares—involving underpaid workers in Indonesia, child labor in Cambodia and Pakistan, and poor working conditions in China and Vietnam—combined to tarnish Nike's image. As Phil Knight lamented in a May 1998 speech to the National Press Club, "the Nike product has become synonymous with slave wages, forced overtime, and arbitrary abuse."[19]

How Nike, a company associated with both athleticism, health and fitness, and innovative marketing and design, became the poster child for the antiglobalization movement provides an interesting window into the potential risks and problems which globalization creates for all multinational corporations. In what follows, we will not provide a comprehensive review of the various abuses of which Nike and its suppliers have been accused in recent years. Instead, we will examine three anecdotal illustrations of the kinds of problems the company has confronted.

Low Wages in Indonesia[20]

In the early 1990s, Nike products were being manufactured in six Indonesian factories, employing more than 25,000 workers. Four of these factories were owned by Nike's Korean suppliers. As Nike's presence in Indonesia increased, the factories supplying its products (about 6 million pairs of shoes per year) came under greater scrutiny. Reports by a variety of NGOs and labor activists claimed that these plants were rife with exploitation, poor working conditions, and a range of human rights and labor abuses. Many Indonesian shoe factories did not even pay the minimum daily wage (at the time, 2,100 rupiah/day or about $1). They petitioned the Indonesian government for exemptions to the legal minimum wage, claiming it would cause them "hardship" to pay. According to official Indonesian government calculations, this minimum daily wage only covered 70 percent of the basic needs of one

---

19. Quoted in "Hitting the Wall: Nike and International Labor Practices," HBS Case #9-700-047.

20. This section relies heavily on "International Sourcing in Athletic Footwear: Nike and Reebok," HBS Case #9-394-189, "Hitting the Wall: Nike and International Labor Practices," HBS Case #9-700-047, and "Nike: What's It All About?" electronic memo, Global Exchange, 1999.

individual—let alone a family. Nike's South Korean suppliers were seen as especially stingy with wages and abusive to local workers. One worker at Nagasakti Para Shoes, a Nike contractor, said that she and other Indonesians were "terrified" of their South Korean managers: "They yell at us when we don't make the production quotas, and if we talk back they cut our wages."[21]

The plight of workers in these factories became publicized through the skillful use of media by several NGOs. Jeff Ballinger, founder of Press for Change (but at the time employed by the Asian-American Free Labor Association, a branch of the AFL-CIO), spent nearly four years in Indonesia, exposing low wages and poor working conditions in factories producing Nike goods. In 1993, CBS aired a report featuring Ballinger, about workers' struggles at Nike's Indonesian suppliers. In 1994, harsh criticism of the company's practices appeared in an array of different publications: the *New Republic*, *Rolling Stone*, the *New York Times*, *Foreign Affairs*, and the *Economist.*

At first, Nike managers sought to ignore or deflect these criticisms. They argued that the Indonesian factories were owned and operated by independent contractors, not by Nike. Nike's vice president for Asia at the time claimed that Nike did not "know the first thing about manufacturing. We are marketers and designers." The company's general manager in Jakarta also argued, "They are our subcontractors. It's not within our scope to investigate [allegations of labor violations]."[22] But by the mid-1990s, Nike instructed its Indonesian contractors to stop applying for exemptions to the legal minimum wage. In April 1999, after the Indonesian government raised minimum wages to 231,000 rupiah/month (then about $26), Nike announced that it would raise wages for workers employed by its suppliers above the legal minimum wage, to between $30 and $37.50 per month.

Child Labor in Pakistan[23]

The city of Sialkot, Pakistan, is home to a cluster of small- and medium-sized firms specializing in an array of labor-intensive, export-oriented

---

21. "International Sourcing in Athletic Footwear," p. 5.
22. "International Sourcing in Athletic Footwear," p. 6.
23. This section draws heavily on Khalid Nadvi and Sajid Kazmi, "Global Standards and Local Responses," unpublished manuscript, Institute for Development Studies, Sussex, United Kingdom, February 2001.

goods, including hand-stitched soccer balls. About 70 percent of the world's high-quality soccer balls are produced in Sialkot—many of them for leading brands like Reebok, Nike, Mitre, and Adidas. About a dozen local firms dominate employment and production in the local sports goods cluster. In addition, a wide range of subcontractors and specialist input suppliers also work in the area. Home work is also common in this region.

In June 1996, *Life* magazine published an article on child labor in Pakistan that included a photo of a 12-year-old boy stitching a Nike soccer ball. This article and its accompanying photo unleashed another wave of criticism against Nike and a call by various consumer groups, trade unions, and NGOs to boycott Sialkot-produced soccer balls. According to Maria Eitel, vice president and senior advisor for corporate responsibility at Nike, this represented a "critical event" for the company in terms of its understanding of globalization, international labor standards, and corporate responsibility.

According to Dusty Kidd, vice president for compliance at Nike, Nike was already working with Saga, its supplier, to eliminate home work and produce soccer balls in more centralized stitching centers. But the impact of the *Life* magazine article was nonetheless devastating for Nike's brand image. Today, Nike sources soccer balls only from Saga's 12 stitching centers. In response to the wave of criticism generated by this episode, the Sialkot Chamber of Commerce and Industry signed the so-called "Atlanta Agreement" with the ILO, UNICEF, and several leading sports goods associations to implement a program to eliminate child labor from the soccer ball sector. As a result of the Atlanta Agreement, the ILO's International Program for the Elimination of Child Labor (IPEC) arrived in Sialkot to monitor local soccer ball producers and to provide various social protections, training, and other income-generating activities for families whose children used to work in stitching plants. Nike insists that any of its contractors caught employing child workers must remove the child from the factory, continue to pay the child's wages, and pay for the child's school fees until he/she reaches legal working age. Yet, notwithstanding the arrival of IPEC and Nike's new child labor policies, the ILO reports that many local employers continue to use children in their stitching centers and that in response to increased monitoring of standards in Sialkut, some soccer ball production has moved to other nearby but less regulated areas of Pakistan.

Health and Safety Problems in Vietnam[24]

In November 1997, an Ernst and Young audit of one of Nike's South Korean subcontractors, the Tae Kwang Vina Company operating in Vietnam, was leaked to an NGO called Transnational Resource and Action Center (TRAC, later renamed CorpWatch). At that time, Tae Kwang Vina employed over 9,000 workers and produced more than 400,000 pairs of Nike shoes per month. The Ernst and Young audit, commissioned by Nike, reported serious health and safety problems at the Tae Kwang Vina plant. Toluene concentrations were said to exceed between 6 and 177 times acceptable standards in certain sections of the plant. (*Toluene* is a chemical solvent that is known to cause central nervous system depression, damage to the liver and kidney, and various skin and eye irritations.) The report also claimed that chemical releases in the plant had caused numerous cases of skin and heart disease, and that respiratory ailments, owing to excess dust, were rampant in other areas of the factory. According to the report, personal protective equipment was not provided at the factory, and working conditions and work hours at the plant were in violation of Nike's code of conduct.

News of this report, which appeared in the *New York Times* and other leading newspapers, ignited another wave of indignation over Nike's relations with its suppliers. This incident was particularly damaging for Nike since the report came from Ernst and Young, a leading accounting and consulting firm that Nike had hired to audit its suppliers' factories. In addition, the Tae Kwang Vina factory had been one of the factories former Ambassador to the U.N. Andrew Young had visited previously, as part of a study tour of Nike suppliers sponsored by the company. In his report on Nike's suppliers, Young did not mention the serious health and safety issues at the plant.[25] In short, this episode was more than simply another example of poor working conditions at one of Nike's supplier's plants; it called into question the company's honesty about and commitment to labor and environmental/health standards.

24. This section draws heavily on Dara O'Rourke, "Smoke from a Hired Gun: A Critique of Nike's Labor and Environmental Auditing in Vietnam as performed by Ernst and Young," CorpWatch, November 10, 1997.

25. The Young Report on Nike's suppliers has been severely criticized as "limited" and "biased" by an array of different NGOs.

These three events, combined with the numerous others that were reported in the press, created a major public relations problem for Nike. (Appendix C traces the number of negative articles about Nike that appeared in major publications.) Increasingly, labor and environmental problems at Nike's suppliers' factories were becoming a major problem for Nike itself. These events made Nike a target for the antiglobalization and antisweatshop movements. Several NGOs decided to focus most of their attention on Nike and the various problems found among its suppliers. Web sites focusing solely on Nike and its alleged abuses appeared on the world wide web and were used by NGOs and various activist groups to share information, coordinate protests, and further embarrass the company.[26]

Consumer and labor groups organized boycotts of Nike goods and pickets at Nike shops. Under pressure from several student groups, some universities cancelled their orders with Nike to produce collegiate athletic products. As a result of these various activities, the company's hard-earned image began to tarnish.

Nike's Response: Learning to Become a Global Corporate Citizen[27]

At first Nike managers refused to accept any responsibility for the various labor and environmental/health problems found at their suppliers' plants. Workers at these factories were not Nike employees, and thus Nike had no responsibility towards them. By 1992, this hands-off approach changed as Nike formulated a Code of Conduct for its suppliers that required them to observe some basic labor and environmental/health standards. Potential suppliers for Nike were obligated to sign this Code of Conduct and post it in their factories. Critics have charged that Nike's Code of Conduct is a minimal response and not fully enforced. Posting the code in factories where most employees are functionally illiterate and/or do not possess the power to insist on its implementation is simply window dressing, critics claim. Nonetheless,

---

26. See, for example, Oxfam's NikeWatch Campaign, the Clean Clothes Campaign's "Nike Case," Press for Change's nikewages.org, and the Global Exchange's "Nike: What's It All About?" All can be found on the various web sites of these organizations. B. J. Bullert, an anti-Nike activist, has written a fascinating paper on the anti-Nike campaign by various NGOs. See B. J. Bullert, "Strategic Public Relations, Sweatshops and the Making of a Global Movement," Working paper #2000-14, Shorenstein, Center on the Press, Politics and Public Policy.

27. This section is based on interviews with several Nike managers in July 2002. See appendix D for a list of interviewees.

the evolution of this document indicates that Nike is seeking to address several of the most serious problems found in its suppliers' plants. (See appendix E for the latest version of this code.) Since 1998, Nike has increased the minimum age of footwear factory workers to 18 and all other workers (in apparel, equipment) to 16. It has also insisted that all footwear suppliers adopt U.S. Occupational Safety and Health Administration (OSHA) standards for indoor air quality. In fact, a quick review of some of Nike's recent efforts in the area of labor and environmental/health standards shows that the company is serious about doing the right thing.

New Staff and Training

In response to the growing criticisms, Nike created several new departments (e.g., Labor Practices [1996], Nike Environmental Action Team [NEAT] [1993]), which, by June 2000, were organized under its Corporate Responsibility and Compliance Department. In 2001, in an effort to strengthen the links between production and compliance decisions, the compliance department was moved into the apparel division. Today, Nike has 85 people specifically dedicated to labor and environmental compliance and all located in countries where Nike products are manufactured. These employees visit suppliers' footwear factories on a daily basis. In apparel, given the much larger numbers of suppliers, Nike managers conduct on-site inspections on a weekly or monthly basis, depending upon the size of the firm. In addition to its corporate responsibility and compliance managers, Nike has about 1,000 production specialists working at or with its various global suppliers. All Nike personnel responsible for either production or compliance receive training in Nike's Code of Conduct, labor practices, cross-cultural awareness, and in the company's Safety, Health, Attitudes of Management, People Investment and Environment (SHAPE) program. The company is also developing a new incentive system to evaluate and reward its managers for improvements in labor and environmental standards among its supplier base.

Increased Monitoring of Its Suppliers

In recent years, Nike has pushed its suppliers to obey standards through increased monitoring and inspection efforts. For example, all potential Nike suppliers must undergo a SHAPE inspection, conducted

by Nike's own production staff. The SHAPE inspection is a pre-
liminary, preproduction inspection of factories to see if they meet
Nike's standards for a clean and healthy workplace, respectful labor-
management relations, fair wages and working conditions, and
minimum working age. After this initial assessment, labor practices are
more carefully audited by Nike's own labor specialists as well as by
outside consultants like PriceWaterhouseCoopers (PWC). This second
audit looks more carefully at the company's wages, use of overtime,
availability of benefits, and age of its employees. In addition to the
SHAPE and labor practices audits, all factories are evaluated by Nike's
production personnel on a range of issues such as quality, flexibility,
price, delivery, technical proficiency, managerial talent, and working
conditions. The goal of these various inspections and audits is to sift
through Nike's vendor base and retain only those who meet not only
price, quality, and delivery expectations but also labor and environmental health standards.

Nike is currently developing a grading system for all of its suppliers. It will use the system to determine future orders and thus create a
strong incentive among its suppliers to improve working conditions.
Nike is also exploring new incentive schemes that will reward good
corporate citizenship among both its suppliers (again through increased and more value-added orders) and its own managers. Nike
managers responsible for supplier factories that show improvement
in labor practices and health and environmental standards will be
rewarded in still-to-be-defined ways. In addition to its own internal
inspections, Nike suppliers are regularly audited by external firms like
Ernst and Young, PWC, and various accredited nonprofits (e.g., Verite)
that specialize in this work.

Relations with International and Nonprofit Organizations

In addition to developing internal expertise and capacity in the area of
standards and corporate responsibility and working with its own suppliers to improve their performance in these areas, Nike has been active
in founding and/or supporting an array of different international and
nonprofit organizations, all aimed at improving standards for workers
in various developing countries. For example, Nike is actively involved
in the United Nations Global Compact. As Secretary General Kofi
Annan noted in chapter 2, the Global Compact seeks to promote
corporate citizenship among multinational companies. Companies

seeking to join the Global Compact adhere to a set of core standards in human rights, labor rights, and environmental sustainability. They engage in a variety of activities aimed at improving these standards in the countries where the MNCs operate. Nike is also a founding member of the Global Alliance for Workers and Communities, an alliance of private, public, and nonprofit organizations that seeks to improve workplace conditions and improve training opportunities for young workers in developing countries. Other members of the Global Alliance include The Gap, Inc., the MacArthur Foundation, and the World Bank. Finally, Nike is active in the Fair Labor Association (FLA, formerly the Apparel Industry Partnership). Initiated in 1996 by President Clinton, the FLA is an American nonprofit organization that seeks to bring together various industry stakeholders to develop a common set of standards and to monitor these standards around the world. Although the FLA has experienced controversy, including the defection of its union affiliates, it has recently begun to sponsor independent audits of the factories supplying its members.

These various activities have begun to produce some significant changes among Nike suppliers. For example, as a result of its various inspections, audits, and internal research, Nike has been able to virtually eliminate the use of petroleum-based chemicals in its footwear production. This is something even the company's critics acknowledge.[28] Nike has taken the initiative in organizing an industry-wide organic cotton consortium and is making major strides in improving working conditions among its various suppliers.[29] Of course, not all of Nike's critics are convinced. Many continue to complain about poor wages and working conditions at Nike's suppliers in Vietnam, China, and Indonesia. Others argue that Nike's initiatives are simply not enough and that the company could do much more in the areas of wages, working conditions, human rights, and local socio-economic development. Yet the continuing controversy over Nike and its various activities is not in any way particular to Nike. Rather, they reflect much broader debates about the definition of corporate citizenship and the process of globalization.

---

28. Interview with Dara O'Rourke, formerly of CorpWatch and now an assistant professor of Planning at MIT.

29. On the Organic Cotton Initiative, see Nike's Corporate Responsibility Report, FY 2001. For an example of improved working conditions and relations with unions among Nike suppliers, see Verite's *Comprehensive Factory Evaluation Report of the Kukdong International Mexico plant in Puebla, Mexico*, March 2001. This report can be found on Nike's web site, www.nikebiz.com

Implications for Management Education and Business Strategy

As this paper has illustrated, there is significant debate over the responsibilities of corporations. Should companies behave solely to enhance
shareholder wealth, or should they act to benefit other groups (both
within and outside the firm) as well? Should corporate decision-
making be driven solely by economic considerations, or are other
(social) factors equally important? How does one measure and account
for these other considerations? Are corporations responsible only to
their own employees and shareholders, or are they also responsible for
the employees of their suppliers and subcontractors? What are the
boundaries or limits of any individual company's responsibilities?
Given that there are no universal standards and that not all companies
are promoting labor and environmental standards as rigorously as
Nike is, how does one promote greater coordination and collective
action among major producers? If some companies promote and
monitor for higher standards and others do not, does this erode the
competitive edge of the "good" corporate citizens? These questions
will shape the future of business in the years to come, and they need
to be integrated into the core curriculum of business schools today.
Rather than treat discussions of corporate responsibility as a side (and
often "soft") issue, to be discussed in a special seminar (often not part
of the core curriculum) or as an afterthought (special session) in already
established courses, this topic needs to be moved to the fore of most
management courses and used as a lens through which other business
issues are discussed. In this way, our students, the world's future managers, will instinctively benchmark their other decisions and actions
against whatever standards for corporate citizenship they embrace.
The point is not to impose a particular view of corporate citizenship on
our students, but rather to encourage them to engage this issue and
make it part of their everyday decision-making process.

   Globalization and the controversial issues it raises will also absorb
management in the foreseeable future. Should multinational companies abide by so-called international labor and environmental
standards, or is this simply regulatory imperialism and de facto
protectionism in another guise? Will the imposition of these standards
on developing countries diminish their competitive advantage and
thus damage their economic development? Or will improved labor and
environmental standards lead these local producers to upgrade their

production processes and up-skill their workforces and thus enhance their long-term competitiveness? Who (which actors) should be responsible for developing these standards? National governments, international organizations, transnational NGOs, local trade unions and civil society groups, or even individual corporations (through their own Codes of Conduct)?

The standards (if any) which are implemented and the actors who set the standards will have dramatic effects on the future trajectory—and the relative winners and losers—of globalization Again, these issues need to be integrated into our basic international management and global strategy courses. As recent world events have dramatically illustrated, the uneven distribution of the benefits of globalization has provoked a major backlash against multinational corporations and the entire process of globalization. Only by redressing this inequality can we ensure the future success of this process and perhaps some semblance of stability in the world. This is as much a managerial challenge as anything else. Provoking our students to wrestle with these dilemmas and to think through possible strategic solutions to these problems will better equip them for their future careers in today's turbulent global economy. These questions—and how they are answered—will shape the future of business for many years to come. Thus, it is imperative that they move to the center of management education today.

Acknowledgments

This case was prepared with the active involvement and research assistance of the following Sloan MBA students: Vanessa Chammah, Brian Curtis, Elizabeth Fosnight, Archana Kalegaonkar, and Adnan Qadir. I would also like to thank Miguel Alexander, Maria Eitel, Dusty Kidd, Joseph Tomasselli, and Dara O'Rourke for their helpful comments and assistance during this project. In addition, many of the thoughts on the context of global citizenship were developed collectively with Professor Zairo Cheibub, of the Federal University Fluminense, Niteroi, Brazil, in a joint paper we wrote on the topic.

Appendix A: Nike Sales and Revenue

Table 3.1.4
Sales and net income

Sales (million US$)	1978	1979	1980	1981	1982	1983	1984	1985	1986	1987	1988	1989	1990	1991	1992	1993	1994	1995	1996	1997	1998	1999	2000	2001
US footwear	69	144	245	399	581	666	640	567	650	510	758	1,058	1,369	1,680	1,744	1,969	1,869	2,309	2,772	3,754	3,499	3,245	3,351	3,209
US apparel	1	2	8	33	70	107	122	160	165	131	143	208	266	327	369	361	339	424	831	1,407	1,556	1,293	1,154	1,260
US athletic equipment								2	3	1														
Non-US footwear														652	868	1,049	998	1,244	1,682	2,391	2,460	1,973.8	2,210	2,414.8
Non US footwear and Non-US apparel	1	4	17	26	43	94	158	217	252	235	303	348	479											
Non-US apparel														210	268	353	359	473	651	1,087	1,436	1,383.7	1,392.6	1,503.3
Other												96	121	135	157	199	223	312	534	548	602	881	886.6	1,101.5
Total revenue	71	150	270	458	694	867	920	946	1,070	877	1,204	1,710	2,235	3,004	3,406	3,931	3,788	4,762	6,470	9,187	9,553	8,777	8,995	9,489
Net income (Million US$)	4	10	13	26	49	57	41	10	59	36	102	167	243	287	329	365	299	400	555	796	400	451	579	590

Sources: a) 1978–97: HBS Case #9-299-084 "Nike, Inc.: Entering the Millennium," March 31, 1999; b) 1998–2001: Company financial information.

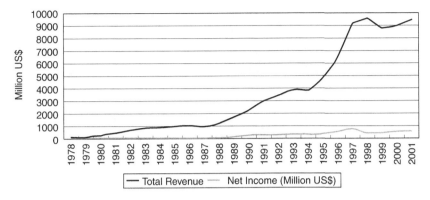

Figure 3.1.2
Total revenue—net income, 1978–2001. Sources: a) 1978–97: HBS Case #9-299-084 "Nike, Inc.: Entering the Millennium," March 31, 1999; b) 1998–2001: company financial information.

Appendix B: Regional Product Distribution of Nike Suppliers

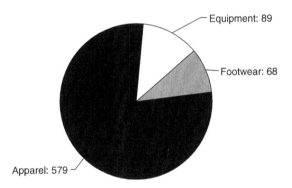

Figure 3.1.3
Factories per product. Total = 736. Source: Nike, Corporate Responsibility Report, FY 2001.

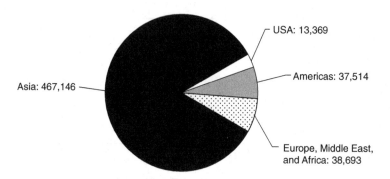

Figure 3.1.4
Number of contract workers by region (2001). Total = 556,722. Source: Nike, Corporate
Responsibility Report, FY 2001.

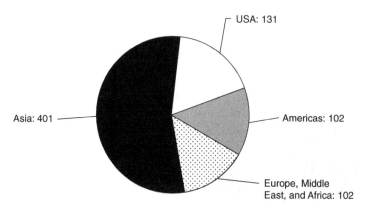

Figure 3.1.5
Factories per region. Total = 736. Source: Nike, Corporate Responsibility Report, FY 2001.

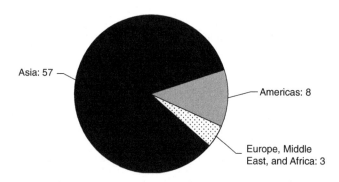

Figure 3.1.6
Footwear factories by region. Total = 68. Source: Nike, Corporate Responsibility Report,
FY 2001.

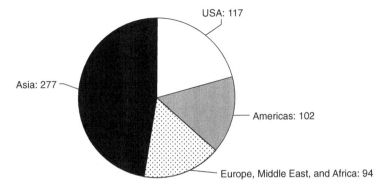

Figure 3.1.7
Apparel factories per region. Total = 579. Source: Nike, Corporate Responsibility Report,
FY 2001.

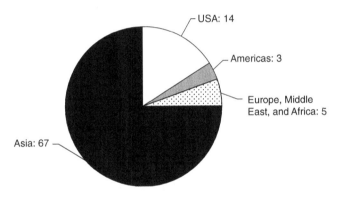

Figure 3.1.8
Equipment factories per region. Total = 89. Source: Nike, Corporate Responsibility
Report, FY 2001.

Appendix C: Nike Labor Relations Media Mentions

Source: Major World Newspapers through Lexis-Nexis database

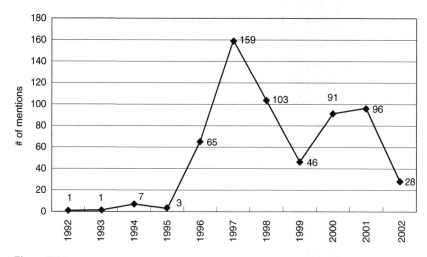

Figure 3.1.9
Media mentions with "sweatshop." Search words: Nike and Sweatshop. Time frame:
previous ten years. Number of documents containing both words: 600.

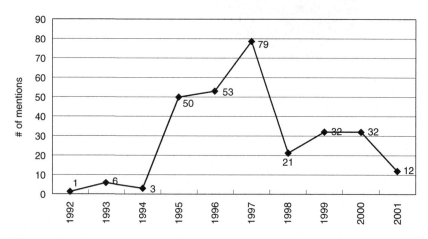

Figure 3.1.10
Media mentions with "child labor." Search words: Nike and Child Labor. Time frame:
previous ten years. Number of documents containing both words: 289.

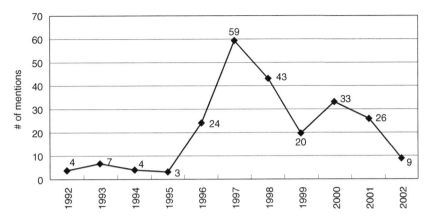

Figure 3.1.11
Media mentions with "exploitation." Search words: Exploitation Time frame: previous ten years. Number of documents containing both words: 232.

Figure 3.1.12
Unfavorable media mentions. Combination of three searches. Note: Articles may be repeated and some may contain all three search words.

Major Newspapers

U.S. newspapers must be listed in the top 50 in circulation in *Editor & Publisher Year Book*. Newspapers published outside the United States must be in English language and listed as a national newspaper in Benn's *World Media Directory* or one of the top 5 percent in circulation for the country.

Asian Wall Street Journal

Atlanta Journal and Constitution

Australian Financial Review

Baltimore Sun

Boston Globe

Boston Herald

Buffalo News

Chicago Sun-Times

Christian Science Monitor

Columbus Dispatch

Daily News (New York)

Daily Yomiuri (Tokyo)

Daily/Sunday Telegraph (London)

Denver Post

Dominion (Wellington)

Evening Post (Wellington)

Financial Times (London)

Gazeta Mercantil Online

Gazette (Montreal)

Guardian (London)

Herald (Glasgow)

Houston Chronicle

Independent and Independent on Sunday (London)

Irish Times

Jerusalem Post

Journal of Commerce

Los Angeles Times

Miami Herald

New Straits Times (Malaysia)

New York Times

Observer

Omaha World Herald

Ottawa Citizen

Plain Dealer

San Diego Union-Tribune

San Francisco Chronicle

Scotsman & Scotland on Sunday

Seattle Times

South China Morning Post

Southland Times (New Zealand)

St. Louis Post-Dispatch

St. Petersburg Times

Star Tribune (Minneapolis, MN)

Straits Times (Singapore)

Tampa Tribune

Times and Sunday Times (London)

Times-Picayune

Toronto Star

Toronto Sun

USA Today

Washington Post

Appendix D

List of Nike Interviewees

1. Oscar Cardona, vice president, human resources, USA

2. Marie Eitel, vice president and senior advisor, corporate responsibility

3. Fukumi Hawser, director of compliance

4. Jerry Hauth, director, corporate responsibility, equipment division

5. Dusty Kidd, vice president, compliance

6. Heidi McCloskey, global sustainability director, Nike Apparel

7. Mary Roney, global employee involvement manager, Global Community Affairs

8. Josh Tomaselli, vice president, apparel sourcing

9. Patrick Werner, director, apparel compliance

10. John Wilson, director, contact manufacturing, equipment division

Appendix E: The Nike Code of Conduct

Nike Inc. was founded on a handshake.

Implicit in that act was the determination that we would build our business with all of our partners based on trust, teamwork, honesty and mutual respect. We expect all of our business partners to operate on the same principles.

At the core of the NIKE corporate ethic is the belief that we are a company comprised of many different kinds of people, appreciating individual diversity, and dedicated to equal opportunity for each individual.

NIKE designs, manufactures, and markets products for sports and fitness consumers. At every step in that process, we are driven to do not only what is required by law, but what is expected of a leader. We expect our business partners to do the same. NIKE partners with contractors who share our commitment to best practices and continuous improvement in:

1. Management practices that respect the rights of all employees, including the right to free association and *collective bargaining*

2. Minimizing our impact on the environment

3. Providing a safe and healthy workplace

4. Promoting the health and well-being of all employees

Contractors must recognize the dignity of each employee, and the right to a workplace free of harassment, abuse or corporal punishment. Decisions on hiring, salary, benefits, advancement, termination or retirement must be based solely on the employee's ability to do the job. There shall be no discrimination based on race, creed, gender, marital or maternity status, religious or political beliefs, age or sexual orientation.

Wherever NIKE operates around the globe we are guided by this Code of Conduct and we bind our contractors to these principles. Contractors must post this Code in all major workspaces, translated into the language of the employee, and must train employees on their rights and obligations as defined by this Code and applicable local laws.

While these principles establish the spirit of our partnerships, we also bind our partners to specific standards of conduct. The core standards are set forth below.

1. *Forced Labor.* The contractor does not use forced labor in any form—prison, indentured, bonded or otherwise.

2. *Child Labor.* The contractor does not employ any person below the age of 18 to produce footwear. The contractor does not employ any person below the age of 16 to produce apparel, accessories or equipment. If at the time Nike production begins, the contractor employs people of the legal working age who are at least 15, that employment may continue, but the contractor will not hire any person going forward who is younger than the Nike or legal age limit, whichever is higher. To further ensure these age standards are complied with, the contractor does not use any form of home work for Nike production.

3. *Compensation.* The contractor provides each employee at least the minimum wage, or the prevailing industry wage, whichever is higher; provides each employee a clear, written accounting for every pay period; and does not deduct from employee pay for disciplinary infractions.

4. *Benefits.* The contractor provides each employee all legally mandated benefits.

5. *Hours of Work/Overtime.* The contractor complies with legally mandated work hours; uses overtime only when each employee is fully compensated according to local law; informs each employee at the time of hiring if mandatory overtime is a condition of employment; and on a regularly scheduled basis provides one day off in seven, and requires no more than 60 hours of work per week on a regularly scheduled basis, or complies with local limits if they are lower.

6. *Environment, Safety and Health (ES&H).* From suppliers to factories to distributors and to retailers, Nike considers every member of our supply chain as partners in our business.

As such, we've worked with our Asian partners to achieve specific environmental, health and safety goals, beginning with a program called MESH (Management of Environment, Safety and Health).

7. *Documentation and Inspection.* The contractor maintains on file all documentation needed to demonstrate compliance with this Code of Conduct and required laws; agrees to make these documents available

for Nike or its designated monitor; and agrees to submit to inspections with or without prior notice.

Source: http://www.nike.com

References

Brummer, James J. 1991. *Corporate Responsibility and Legitimacy: An Interdisciplinary Analysis.* New York: Greenwood Press.

Cheibub, Zairo, and Richard Locke. 2000. "Valoures ou Intresses? Reflexoes sobre a responsabilidade social des empresas." Unpublished ms, Federal University Fluminense, Niteroi, Brazil.

Cone Inc. 1999. "Cone/Roper Cause-Related Trends Report: Evolution of Cause Branding." Boston: Cone Inc.

Friedman, Milton. 1970. "The Social Responsibility of Business is to Increase its Profits." *New York Times Magazine*, September 13, pp. 32–33.

Frooman, Jeff. 1997. "Socially Irresponsible and Illegal Behavior and Shareholder Wealth." *Business and Society* 36, no. 3: 221–249.

Paine, Lynn Sharpe. 1996. "Corporate Purpose and Responsibility." Boston: Harvard Business School. Case # 9-396-201.

Waddock, Sandra, and Samuel B. Graves. 1997. "The Corporate Social Performance—Financial Performance Link." *Strategic Management Journal* 18, no. 4: 303–319.

Weiser, John, and Simon Zadek. 2000. "Conversation with Disbelievers: Persuading Companies to Address Social Challenges." Report written through grant from Ford Foundation.

Zadek, Simon. 2001. *The Civil Corporation: The New Economy of Corporate Citizenship.* London: Earthscan.

www.bsr.org

http://europa.eu.int/comm/employment_social/soc-dial/csr/csr_whatiscsr.htm

www.mori.com/polls/1999/millpoll.shtml

www.wbcsd.org

3.2 Discussion

Sloan faculty members discussed the Nike case with alumni in small groups as they would teach it in the classroom. What follows is a sampling of the responses the alumni offered to the questions posed by the faculty.

Q. What's the problem in this case? Or, to put it more directly, what do you think keeps Phil Knight awake at night?

A. An alumnus started the discussion by expressing the view that perhaps what Nike was facing was a "power of the press" problem. That is, Nike had not considered the media to be as large and powerful a constituency as it proved to be. Taking this view further, the question arose, was Nike's problem actually a big problem or not? As another alumnus pointed out: "We know from the data in the case that Nike took a hit in 1998 at the peak of the criticism, but it wasn't a big hit. Do consumers care? Is it really a problem for Nike? Data from the case show that Nike earnings kept growing." An alumna from the United States voiced the view that the Nike case broadens the definition of the corporation: "We're talking about Nike's suppliers, and considering them as part of the corporation. Did Nike know what its suppliers were doing? They were incompetent if they did not, and it was bad business if they did. In either case, the question broadens the definition of the corporation."

Q. So, if corporations are to be held accountable for meeting some basic standards, whose standards should guide them? Those of the local country? U.S. standards? Some global standards? Internal standards set by each corporation?

A. This point was hotly debated. Some argued that the company should uphold U.S. standards and pay high wages.

To this point an alumnus who runs a company in Eastern Europe said that his company paid twice the standard average wage of the local standard, yet that wage was not enough to allow the employee to travel to America. But if he tried to offer a comparable U.S. wage, his company would go out of business.

Similarly, a Sloan alumna raised the point: "Would we as consumers pay for sneakers made at American labor wages?" Others, like an executive from the software industry, argued that personal standards, rather than global standards, may be the way to go: "The question is, are you doing something you are proud of or ashamed of? Are you doing something you wouldn't be embarrassed about if the press was writing about you? You can't hide behind the letter of things and say 'it's their country and their standard.' If you have caused harm, then you are doing wrong."

Along with several others, an alumna from India argued that for certain things like air quality, there must be a global standard, because air quality affects more than just the citizens of one country. She stated this view clearly and simply: "Clean air is a basic human standard."

Another alumnus working in the United States raised the issue: "Is Nike able to decide what is an international norm, what is morally good? It's easy to say 'don't poison the water or make an unsafe product,' but I'm not sure I want Nike to be making decisions on human rights."

The standards of the legal minimum age for employment were no easier to define. Some alumni raised the point that Nike should adhere to the U.S. standard of 16 as the youngest legal age for a worker. But an alumnus from Brazil pointed out the difficulty with this argument: "In Brazil, a 14-year-old is not the same as a 14-year-old in the United States. In the United States, 14-year-olds have the alternative of going to school. After school, maybe they play sports or take music lessons. In Brazil, it's better to be working a part-time job at 14 than to be on the streets and be offered drugs. Limiting the worker age to 16 makes sense for the United States, but not for Brazil. You have to think locally."

An alumnus from Pakistan agreed. He had interviewed boys in Pakistan who were making soccer balls for Nike: "In Pakistan, the reality is that the 14-year-old's father may be a drug addict or dead, and his mother may have 10 other children to raise. As a 14-year-old, he represents the family's best earning potential." To deny the 14-year-old the ability to earn wages to provide for the family is age discrimination, taking away jobs. Indeed, the company could be sued for age discrimination. The notion that a 14-year-old is "too young" to work and that working is "not in the best interests of the child" must be informed by knowledge of the local conditions and the true alternatives facing 14-year-olds in developing countries. Sewing soccer balls at 14 may be damaging to the eyes, but what if the alternative is selling one's body?

The alumnus from Pakistan suggested that if Nike employs 14-year-olds, it can have a policy of offering 1–2 hours of education at the start of the day for the youth. This provides education for the employee while making the employee more valuable to the company (increasing literacy and numeracy).

An alumnus from the Philippines echoed this, adding that in the Philippines, having a job at Nike was considered very good: "Nike pays a higher wage. It would be considered low by U.S. standards, but in the Philippines it is good pay, and Nike helps you for education for your kids. Even though the wage doesn't match the first-world wage, it's a job in the third world that people want to get."

An alumnus from Argentina offered the following advice to managers of global companies: "Most of the problems must be solved locally by looking at the local conditions. Many things in Argentina fail because they create corruption, so actions must be looked at from the local situation. Companies can evolve slowly to higher standards in each country as they evolve and grow in that country."

Q. *Assuming corporations should be held accountable for not just their own practices but also those of their suppliers and contractors, how should these practices be monitored and controlled?*

A. An alumnus from France described how his company, a distributor of bottled water, operates in third-world countries: "We realize that the more people consume water, the more money we make. But at low income levels, most people don't have water. So we have tried to get water to third-world countries, installing a tap. But we've found that we install a tap, and the next day someone steels the tap, and again there is no water. So what we have learned over the years is to work with local NGOs—to work with well-established people, people who are not political dreamers but work on practical issues and are dedicated. We work with them as our intermediary, and this mechanism has worked well for us."

An alumnus who runs a venture capital fund in Europe answered this question as follows: "We ask the question, 'does management of this firm have the capacity to take care of these issues or not?' If not, they simply won't get our funds."

Another participant's words captured the feeling that whatever standards and monitoring mechanisms are developed, they will have to be open to change over time: "Setting standards is not just a one-time event. It's an ongoing process, like quality, because values change, the community changes. The theme is one of transparency and an open process."

Professor Richard Locke summed up the case discussion: "As we can see, there are no simple answers to any of these questions—what standards we want to hold firms accountable to depends on our conception of the economic and social responsibilities of global firms. What specific standards should guide corporate practices is both a hard economic question and a hard political question. Effective and trusted monitoring will require substantial institutional innovation. Firms may need to learn how to work with NGOs, local governments, local labor organizations, and other groups. Regardless of how each of us answers these questions, it is clear that defining and meeting the global responsibilities of corporations are defining issues facing managers today, and tomorrow."

4

Human Capital and Twenty-First-Century Organizations

4.1 Navigating the Future: The Networked Organization

Phil Condit

Anniversaries are important milestones. They offer us a time to look back and to look ahead, to anticipate the future, to imagine "what might be." Today, I want to talk about the future, about "what might be," as the Information Revolution takes hold and produces dramatic changes in how we communicate, in how we make decisions, and in how we are organized.

I believe we are in a period of unprecedented change. The Information Revolution will produce social impact and disruptive change, just as the Industrial Revolution did when it changed civilization from a rural, agrarian, small economy to an urban, industrial economy. The Information Revolution will change us into a more global, collaborative, integrated economy. The impact on industry and institutions is going to be huge because in a network-centric world, information will flow to where it is required, and this will change decision-making, hierarchy, and bureaucracy as we now know it.

If you look for the roots of the way we are organized, the way every large company in the world is organized today, you will find the organizational lessons of the Greeks, Romans, and Mongols. Whether you were Alexander the Great, who rode in the front of the battle line to conquer a very large territory in a relatively short amount of time; or a general like Julius Caesar, with "legions of many," who added to the Roman Empire; or Genghis Khan, who united all Mongol tribes and organized his army by dividing them into groups of tens, hundreds, thousands, and tens of thousands so he could expand his empire of "all people who lived in felt tents"—if you were going to take "thousands and thousands of soldiers" on foot, or horseback, and march across Persia, across Europe, across China, you had to build both a communications and a logistics structure. You *had* to have a hierarchical structure because 20,000 or 50,000 people couldn't fit into the tent every morning for assignments. Even a legion of 3,000 to 6,000 was too big for that.

But you could get your top ten people into the tent, and give directions and orders on the plan to march on a city, or to feed the troops. Those top 10 people, in turn, could get their top ten people together to communicate the plan and hand out orders. The pyramid provided the logistics and communications structures. This same basic logistics and communications structure exists today in industry and institutions. Alfred P. Sloan, Jr., studied the military structure and applied it to his company—General Motors. It's the reason why business has "divisions" and "general" managers today.

We are moving into a network-centric world, where organizational structures will look radically different and direct communications will allow for better decision-making. Today e-mail, a graphic-rich environment, videoteleconferencing, and networks are part of a world that allows us to share data and connect, to make better decisions, to improve efficiency and effectiveness. In the future, we will get information directly to the person who needs it to do a job, who needs it to make decisions on the spot. We will routinely communicate messages directly to large masses of people, without going through a hierarchical structure. We have started to do some of that at Boeing, but we are in the very early stages of network-centric communications. I can send an electronic broadcast message over our network and communicate anytime, anywhere, to thousands of employees.

But this is only the beginning. I believe a network–centric world offers a great opportunity to radically change and improve decision-making. It will be able to collect data, process data into information, and structure it to allow people at all levels to make decisions quickly. It will allow leaders to move information to people who need to have it, who can turn it into knowledge, who use that knowledge to efficiently make the best decisions.

One simple example is library research. When I was at Sloan in 1974–75, I used the card catalog, the Dewey Decimal system. Created by Melvil Dewey at Amherst 130 years ago, the Dewey System has its own brand of well-developed, structured hierarchy, which was "divided into ten main classes, which together cover the entire world of knowledge."

My searches were often slow and tedious. Today, there are powerful search engines and online links. Today's students have tremendous access to almost limitless sources of material, from MIT libraries and non-MIT libraries, from online subject experts and huge databases, from virtual to brick-and-mortar libraries. A student today saves tremendous amounts of time by researching on a laptop anytime, from anywhere in the world, from an Internet cafe and soon with Connexion by Boeing on an airplane. But this is still just the first step.

Just think "What will it be like in 50 years?" Today part of management's responsibility is to talk to other managers, to go to meetings, to fix mistakes, to make decisions together, to resolve misunderstandings. Take, for example, the first-line manager. Almost everything in a first-level manager's life is driven by recent and current events. Most manage in a chaotic environment. They juggle parts and daily schedules, and make judgments on the best use of everyone's time in order to get the job done for the day. They rebalance work when the team is short a person because someone called in sick that morning. Other management levels have different responsibilities. They may audit the operational plan and communicate status. They ensure that the plan is getting done, just like the ancient empires.

In a network-centric world, that process will fundamentally change. Status will be available automatically online. I believe we will see a shift in roles and responsibilities as more teams work on projects around the clock globally to use time effectively and wisely. When I was an engineer, for example, we created drawings on Mylar that had to be moved physically. Today, we have the ability to work digitally and interactively so our employees can work with customers and colleagues across the world, with a collaborative environment systems tool. The 78,000 people in our new Integrated Defense Systems unit work in 33 states, with many working in a virtual environment on the same programs.

All this is improving our efficiency and ability to compete. Not long ago, we had an opportunity to bid for a government contract, but only had three weeks to write a proposal. We were able to compete and win because we could work 24 hours a day with a virtual team in the United States and Australia. Interactive network tools allowed our people to make it happen.

Historically, we have trained people to follow directions, to let others make decisions. Now, when data and information can be available to all, we must teach and encourage local decision–making. In the military, we have trained people to take orders and follow directions because situational awareness existed only at the highest levels of the pyramid.

Now, as the ability to process data and distribute information spreads widely to the lowest level, we will have the ability to allow people on the front lines to make decisions about what to do next in the battle. Information will be the ultimate "high ground." We saw that for the first time in Afghanistan, where a soldier on horseback used satellite communication to direct bombs from a B-52, bypassing the standard long and often slow command and communication structure.

The same applies to the business world. We have trained people to follow orders, follow rules, take direction. When the data and the information are directly available to them, what will that mean? What happens in a network-centric world when people are able to make their own decisions because they have the information to get the plan done, to make decisions to fix problems, to smooth the disruption of a team member who is out for the day?

What happens when the right information easily flows to the right people, in the right way, and not through levels of bureaucracy? What happens when you have fewer errors and mistakes that the complex bureaucracy and long communications paths create? I can imagine less structure, fewer people. I think the role of management will, and can, be significantly changed in a network-centric world. The leaders, fewer in number, will be coaches and teachers. They will focus on removing barriers. The efficiencies will be huge. We will be able to build products faster from design to market, with enormous benefits to customers and consumers. So what will happen when organizations and decision-making look very different? How will we reward employees?

Today, we have a reward structure that, for the most part, is based on how many layers are beneath you and where you are in the pyramid. We pay people based on where they fit in that hierarchy; but does that really make sense? If we no longer need that structure and can get a lot of information to flow through the organization, how do we pay the valuable people—sometimes individuals with no direct reports?

There will be tremendous hurdles to cross as we move toward a network-centric world. Remember, we have thousands of years invested in a hierarchical structure, and so this is not going to change overnight. We might start by asking questions: How can we build an organization that will quickly shift direction when new information, data, or circumstances change the business environment? How do we evaluate progress, skills, and people? What are the roles of management? How do we provide the social structure that is part of the fabric of everyday business?

If we have a network-centric organization where everyone has access to information at the same time, how do roles shift when the old axiom "Knowledge is power" applies to all? How do we get the right data easily to the right people in the right way? Will there be less middle management and more individual contributors? What does a world look like that allows us to achieve the massing of information versus the massing of people? Will these changes be phenomenally rapid or happen slowly? What education and training are required when we expect each person to act logically, with common sense, and make the best decisions?

All of these questions reflect my belief that a network-centric world will be about superior decision-making by those closest to the action. What will be very difficult for many people is that they will have to perform in a totally new and unfamiliar environment. It will not allow participants to sit on the sidelines and complain about those who lead.

I don't have all the answers. But I do know all of this is going to take a phenomenal amount of leadership. We must consider the implications for our industries and universities, for our government and military, for our managers, students, and employees of a network-centric environment. In business, we will need leaders who understand their roles in business, how they can move the company forward, and be willing to think about the future so their company will exist 20 or 30 years from now. My bet is that many companies aren't going to survive because they won't be able to make the huge transition.

It will take working against huge cultural and institutional biases that have been in place for thousands of years. But it is a journey with huge rewards, and thus one worth taking.

Discussion

Q. The future networked corporation will be smaller. How will society be different when many fewer people can aspire to work for larger companies like Boeing, GM, etc.?

A. I think the reality is that we will create jobs at a pretty amazing rate. The challenge is that they will be very different jobs than those there ten years earlier. That's the disruptive part. Boeing will do less bending of sheet metal and building of airplanes but do a lot of network development and tying of systems together. We are not the builder of platforms but the integrator of systems. There will be lots of jobs, but they will be ones that will change at a rate faster than in the past. When my father went to school, he said "I can do this job for the rest of my career." That is no longer the case. That's why continuing education will be so critical.

We have a tuition reimbursement program, and people can go to any school they want and take courses on anything they want. When we put this in place, some people worried that people would take courses on issues not related to our business. And sure some have done some of this. One person got a degree in mortuary science—but this was offset by two people who got degrees in divinity. But the point is, everyone is learning and they are developing, and we are playing a constructive role.

Q. *What is the view of Boeing on sustainable development?*

A. One of the fascinating parts of the global corporation today is the understanding of the social responsibility that goes with it. Toffler pointed out that corporations can move faster than government institutions. That puts a responsibility on corporations to address issues like sustainable development. All corporate leaders I talk to think about this. We have to look at our role and how we are doing it since that will determine whether we will be here in twenty years.

Q. *What kind of managers and leaders are required in the world you describe? How does Boeing create these leaders? Who will be running the future corporations and how?*

A. We have a leadership center outside of St. Louis that has graduated 11,000 leaders. I am there about eighteen times a year. That's where we talk about these issues. What will it take to be a good leader, a good coach? How do you employ those skills? Having a place and opportunity to discuss these issues is absolutely critical for leadership development. It also serves other purposes. We are a company that comes from McDonald Douglas, Rockwell, Hughes, Boeing, and others. This is where we mix people together and build their common skills. The most common e-mail I get is one that says our people are amazed at the range of experiences we have in this company.

Q. *What are the differences between being an American company operating globally and a global company?*

A. We have traditionally been an American company doing business globally. So when we first said we want to be a global company, some said we are already. We sell to 145 countries and have operations in 132 countries. But most have been there to support the products we have sold. I believe we have a responsibility to have our voice heard. To do this we must be present. We can't stand outside and yell—we have to be in the room. The diversity of experience that is brought by people from different countries is amazingly powerful, so we have to be on the ground in a lot of different countries. We have about 3,000 people on the ground in Australia. This allows us to do things we couldn't do otherwise. We run their secure radio network. We couldn't do this as an American company selling globally. I can sit down with the prime minister and express my view on where technology is going because we are there. To be a truly global company, you have to be on the ground and have a truly global management; and your leadership must reflect the diversity of that breadth.

4.2

Beyond McGregor's Theory Y: Human Capital and Knowledge-Based Work in the Twenty-First-Century Organization

Thomas A. Kochan,
Wanda Orlikowski, and
Joel Cutcher-Gershenfeld

Nearly fifty years ago, at the Sloan School's 5th Anniversary Convocation, Douglas McGregor launched a debate over how to manage "The Human Side of the Enterprise."[1] By comparing what he called Theory X and Theory Y perspectives, he challenged the management profession to reexamine its assumptions about the motivations employees bring to their jobs. The question was: Could employees be trusted and empowered to do good work, or did they have to be closely directed, monitored, and controlled to act in the interests of the firm? While McGregor's Theory Y sparked important innovations in human resource practices, it did not challenge fundamental assumptions underpinning the twentieth century organizational model. If, as is widely recognized, human capital and knowledge are the most important sources of value for the twenty-first-century organization, then fundamental assumptions about the relationship between work and organizations will also need to be challenged.

The approach that dominated organizational theory, teaching, and practice for most of the twentieth century looked at organizations from the top down, starting with a view of the CEO as the "leader" who shapes the organization's strategy, structure, culture, and performance potential. The nature of work and the role of the workforce enter the analysis much later, after considerations of technology and organization design have been considered. However, if the key source of value in the twenty-first-century organization is to be derived from the workforce itself, an inversion of the dominant approach will be needed. The new perspective will start not at the top of the organization but at the front lines, with people and the work itself—which

---

1. Presentation to the Sloan School's 5th Anniversary on "The Human Side of the Enterprise" by Douglas McGregor and later expanded into a book: Douglas McGregor, *The Human Side of the Enterprise* (New York: McGraw Hill, 1960).

Piore and Sabel on "The Second Industrial Divide" (1984)
Kochan, Katz, and McKersie on "The Transformation of American Industrial Relations" (1986)
Schein on "Culture and Leadership" (1988)
Senge on "Learning Organizations and Systems Thinking" (1990)
Bailyn on "Integrating Work and Family" (1992)
Orlikowski on "Use of Technology in Organizations" (1992)
Ancona, Kochan, Scully, Van Mannen, Westney on "Organizational Processes" (1994)
Walton, Cutcher-Gershenfeld, and McKersie on "Strategic Negotiations" (1994)
Orlikowski and Yates on "Collaborative Technologies" (1994)
Cutcher-Gershenfeld et al. on "Knowledge-Driven Work" (1998)
Osterman, Kochan, Locke, and Piore on "Working in America: A Blueprint for the New Labor Market" (2001)
Carroll on "Organizational Learning in the Midst of Crisis" (2001)
Sterman and Repenning, on "Nobody Ever Gets Credit for Fixing Problems That Never Happened" (2001)
Murman et al. on "Lean Enterprise Value" (2002)
Malone and Morton on "Inventing Organizations of the 21st Century" (forthcoming)

Figure 4.2.1
Selected Sloan faculty research reexaming assumptions about people, work, and organizations.

is where value is created. Such an inversion will lead to a transformation in the management and organization of work, workers, and knowledge.

We believe accomplishing this inversion is among the most important challenges facing organization and management theory, research, teaching, and practice today. In fact, these challenges have been at the forefront of the research of a number of Sloan School research groups (see figure 4.2.1). Furthermore, several Sloan faculty recently stated these challenges in the provocative form of a "Manifesto for the 21st Century Organization."[2] And, over the past semester, we have explored these challenges with a range of industry experts, Sloan School students, and alumni in our course on "Managing Transformations in Work, Organizations, and Society."

---

2. MIT 21st Century Manifesto Working Group, Sloan School of Management, "What Do We Really Want? A Manifesto for the Organizations of the 21st Century," November 1999.

This paper has its roots in an MIT course entitled "Managing Transformations in Work Organizations, and Society," which was first offered in the spring of 2001 and again offered in the spring of 2002. The course, which was developed under the leadership of Tom Kochan in partnership with Joel Cutcher-Gershenfeld, Wanda Orlikowski, and others, focused on all of the themes covered in this paper. From the outset, the course involved participation from Sloan and other graduate students on campus, as well as System Design and Management (SDM) students on rotation back in their home organizations. It also included lifelong learning participants from partner corporations such as the U.S. Air Force, Pratt & Whitney, Ford, Hewlett-Packard, Lucent, NASA, Otis Elevators, Polaroid, Qualcom, Saturn, Teradyne, Visteon, and Xerox. It involved both in-class discussion, remote video participation, and online discussions.

In honor of Sloan's 50th Anniversary, we offered Sloan alums the opportunity to participate directly in the sessions as well as the chance to follow the discussions and make contributions through the Internet. Over one Hundred Sloan alums signed up at the Web site and contributed comments or vignettes on the topics covered in the course. Students in the class drew on their own experience and interviewed some of the alums to generate additional vignettes on all of these topics. They also organized all of these data into integrative final papers that corresponded to the themes for the course. The analysis in this paper draws on independent research conducted by all three authors as well as the many vignettes, comments, and papers generated. Current Sloan student experience and the experience of Sloan alums are woven throughout the text (with the names of specific individuals and organizations deleted for confidentiality).

Figure 4.2.2
Methods and process in developing this paper.

In this paper, we build on these efforts to first contrast the twentieth and twenty-first century organizational models and then to examine how organizations are attempting to move toward a human capital and knowledge-based model of organizing (see figure 4.2.2 for our methods and process). Finally, we explore the implications of this alternative organizational model for the future of management education.

Contrasting Assumptions: Twentieth and Twenty-First Century Organizational Models

As evident in figure 4.2.3, the organizational model that dominated the past century embodied assumptions (about people, work, technology,

Assumptions about:	Assumptions characterizing 20th century organizations	Assumptions that may characterize 21st century organizations
People	Theory X: People are a cost that must be monitored and controlled	Theory Y: People are an asset that should be valued and developed
Work	Segmented, industrially-based, and individual tasks	Collaborative, knowledge-based projects
Technology	Design technology to control work and minimize human error	Integrate technology with social systems to enable knowledge-based work
Leadership	Senior managers and technical experts	Distributed leadership at all levels
Goals	Unitary focus on returns to shareholders	Multi-dimensional focus on value for multiple stakeholders

Figure 4.2.3
Contrasting assumptions in twentieth- and twenty-first century organizations.

leadership, and goals) that contrast with the model that may come to dominate the next century.

Like McGregor, we are counterposing two alternative models, each of which involves competing assumptions. Reality, of course, may involve a spectrum of choices between these extremes, but it is helpful to understand the way alternative choices will pull organizations in one direction or the other. In the balance of this section, we will examine the implications of each of these assumptions.

People: Labor Costs or Human Assets?

Conventional economic and organization theory views labor as a cost to be controlled. Moreover, since labor cannot be separated from its human motivation and free will, incentives are needed to ensure employees will commit their full energies and skills to the goals of the organization. Labor also brings its own interests and sources of power to the organization. Therefore, efforts on the part of employees to use their collective power by forming unions or other organizations to represent their own interests need to be discouraged or defeated.

A human capital, knowledge-based perspective understands workers as human assets who create the value of the organization. By joining and staying in the organization, employees invest and put at risk some of their human capital. By taking advantage of opportunities for continued learning and development, their human capital is deepened and expanded. Since employees have interests and obligations outside of work—to their professions, families, communities, and themselves—they cannot and do not wish to commit their full energies to the organization. Therefore, efforts are needed to integrate work and personal aspects of life. Employees also bring a variety of expectations to their jobs, including an interest in having meaningful influence and voice in matters that are important to them. At the same time, employers can reasonably expect employees and their representative organizations to contribute to the continued viability and effectiveness of the enterprise. Therefore, efforts are needed to engage employees individually and collectively in ways that simultaneously address organizational and individual interests and expectations.

Work: Industrial or Knowledge-Based Systems?

The early years of the twentieth century witnessed the gradual movement from agrarian and craft to an industrial model of work organization. The latter part of the century has witnessed efforts to continue the transformation from the industrial to a knowledge-based system of work organization. That transformation process continues today.

The industrial model created sharp legal and status distinctions between managers who conceived and directed how work was done and nonmanagers who executed their tasks as directed. Productivity was maximized by organizing tasks into well-defined jobs and functions. Efficiency gains were achieved through increased specialization and formalization of reporting relationships, promotion paths, and compensation rules.

The transformation in work systems underway today involves efforts to shift from industrial to knowledge-based work systems that blur the lines between managerial and nonmanagerial work. These systems assume that in a knowledge-based economy, high levels of performance can only be achieved by organizing work in ways that allow workers to use and deepen their knowledge and skills, while working collaboratively on multiple, temporary projects to accomplish flexible and innovative operations. As a result, there is an emphasis on horizontal interrelationships among diverse groups (both internal and external), and the coordinated use of teams, cross-functional task forces, and cross-organizational alliances and networks.

Technology: A Mechanistic or Integrative Perspective?

Technology is conventionally viewed as a physical asset—a piece of machinery or an information system—that is initially developed and designed by technical experts and then implemented for use by the workforce. This view emphasizes the mechanistic dimensions of the technology, while disregarding or attempting to eliminate the human side. For example, a major function of technology in this view is to reduce reliance on human inputs—both the quantity of labor and the variance (error) that can result from human judgment, fatigue, lack of motivation, or direct challenges or conflicts with management decisions or actions. Even today, the dominant assumption in much of the machine tool industry, for example, involves designing people out of the process—even at the expense of flexibility and innovation.

A human capital, knowledge–based view of technology is best captured by the saying that it is "workers who give wisdom to the machines."[3] Technology is understood to be simultaneously physical and social, and its capabilities are only effective when employed in practice by workers operating in a variety of social/organizational contexts. This relational view of technology recognizes that technological outcomes are highly contingent and emergent—depending on how the technical capabilities interact with human choices, political actions, cultural norms, and learning opportunities over time. In this view, benefits from technologies can only be realized when the technical and social dimensions are integrated through the design, implementation, and ongoing adaptation of the technologies employed in an organization.

Leadership: Exclusive Role of the CEO or a Distributed Capability?

Leadership is conventionally viewed as being vested primarily in the role of the CEO and other top executives. The CEO is to provide vision and broad strategic direction to the rest of the organization and in

---

3. Haruo Shimada and John Paul McDuffie, "Industrial Relations and Humanware," Sloan School of Management Working Paper, 1987.

doing so shape the culture and values of the enterprise. The search process for CEOs therefore focuses on identifying individuals in top positions in apparently successful organizations who appear to have these personal attributes. Wall Street analysts, the business press, and business school case studies often attribute organizational success (or failure) to the quality of the CEO's leadership, thereby perpetuating this image of what leadership is and where it resides in organizations.

A human capital, knowledge-based view of the enterprise envisions leadership as a distributed capability that involves multiple people and groups at all levels of the organization. To be sure, the CEO and other executives are critical players in leading a process which generates a clear and compelling shared vision for the organization. However, such action by senior executives is not sufficient unless and until it engages the aspirations and energies of all organizational participants. Leadership is thus more than a set of individual traits or abilities; it is a set of capabilities that extends throughout the organization and over time. In this view, a CEO would be seen to be effective if she/he creates the conditions that enable people at all levels in the organization to exercise leadership in their everyday activities. Performance in the twenty-first-century organization is a function of the quality of leadership capabilities in action throughout the organization.

Goals: Value for Shareholders or Multiple Stakeholders?

This brings us to a fundamental question: What purpose(s) do organizations serve? With the rise to prominence of the modern corporation, the answer that dominated American organizations and management education throughout most of the twentieth century was that business organizations exist to maximize shareholder value. This reflects a recognition of the role played by owners who provide and put at risk the critical resource—significant pools of financial capital—needed to build large corporations. As a result, the governance structure and processes are seen to be the exclusive domain of the financial owners and their direct agents, the CEO and other top executives.

Knowledge-based organizations depend on employees to invest and put at risk their human capital in joining and remaining with the firm. This places human capital in an analogous position in the twenty-first-century organization to that of financial capital in the twentieth-century corporation. Thus, employees could claim a legitimate role in shaping the objectives of the organization to be consistent with their interests and values. Other stakeholders can make similar claims. Suppliers, for example, are increasingly responsible for critical aspects of product design, inventory management, and other tasks that require long-term partnership agreements. Communities have legitimate claims to the social and environmental impacts generated by the products and processes of organizations. Governments today are more interested in long–term, public–private partnerships (government as "enabler" rather than "enforcer"). Even regulatory agencies are exploring more interactive relationships with the regulated community. Thus, processes of stakeholder—not just shareholder—governance assume strategic significance in the twenty-first-century organization. Viewed one way, these many embedded stakeholder relationships represent complex constraints on organizational flexibility and innovation. Viewed another way, these same stakeholder relationships constitute an extended enterprise capable of delivering value to the organization and to these many stakeholders in unprecedented ways.[4]

Today, organizations are connected to these many stakeholders in complex networks including strategic alliances, public-private partnerships, and other collaborative initiatives. In all cases, there are both common interests that bring these parties together and conflicting interests that threaten the viability of the cooperative venture. In many cases, individual organizations may come and go, but others will take their place in these emerging institutional arrangements. Therefore, organizations are called upon to take a longer view—ensuring today's actions do not make it more difficult for future generations of citizens and communities to realize their aspirations and objectives. Management and management education needs to take a longer-term, sustainability perspective and a broader, networked view of organizations. More emphasis is needed on developing professional standards, ethics, and norms that hold individuals and organizations accountable for their effects on multiple stakeholders, both today and in the future.

Taking Stock of Current Organizational Practice

The above distinctions between twentieth- and twenty-first-century organizational models are somewhat oversimplified. Few organiza-

---

4. Earl Murman, Tom Allen, Kirkor Bozdogan, Joel Cutcher-Gershenfeld, Hugh McManus, Debbie Nightingale, Eric Rebentisch, Tom Shields, Fred Stahl Myles Walton, Joyce Warmkessel, Stanley Weiss, and Sheila Widnall, *Lean Enterprise Value: Insights from MIT's Lean Aerospace Initiative* (New York: Palgrave/Macmillan, 2002).

tions could survive by completely ignoring some of the assumptions underlying either model. And, as noted, many organizations have been pursuing aspects of a human-centered, knowledge-based approach for some time. So the reality today is that organizations have implemented different sets of assumptions drawn from both the twentieth- and twenty-first century organizational models depicted above. Below, we draw on the data collected from our industry participants, students, and alumni to take stock of current organizational practices as experienced by the people in these organizations. These are the people who will collectively shape the organizations of the twenty-first century. In this section, we summarize their experiences and assessments of current practice, their visions for where they want their organizations to be in the future, and their ideas for what it will take to get there.

People: The Workforce of the Twenty-First Century

One word best captures the contemporary workforce: *diversity*. A second key word applies to the workforce of tomorrow: *scarcity*.

Diversity and Its Implications

Tomorrow's workforce, even more than today's, will depart dramatically from the twentieth-century image of the average (some would say "idealized") worker as a male breadwinner or organizational man with a wife at home attending to family and community affairs. Today, workers are more diverse in gender, race, ethnicity, age, nationality, and culture, just to mention the more obvious and visible features. The households that workers come from are equally diverse, with less than 20 percent fitting the old image. The majority have either both spouses/partners in the paid labor force or are headed by an individual who is a working, single parent. Work and family decisions are highly interdependent.

Leading firms are recognizing the importance of both the need to attend to demographic diversity and work and family issues, as box 4.2.1 illustrates. Our research and the views of our students and alumni suggest that most firms have internalized the legal and social responsibilities introduced by the civil rights movement and laws enacted in the 1960s and 1970s. For example, there is considerable training aimed at "valuing diversity." Today's workforce generally also shares these values, especially younger workers who have grown up in more diverse cultural and racial settings. Many of our students and alumni

Box 4.2.1
A More Diverse Pool of Future Leaders

"Over the past 20 years, the demographics of our company's professional staff have been changed dramatically. Female engineers today represent a large percentage of the population and a large percentage of its high potential future leaders. These are employees we desperately want to hold onto for the long run."
—Contribution to Sloan Student/Alum Dialogue in Course on "Transforming Work, Organizations, and Society" (Spring 2002)

Box 4.2.2
Learning Across Cultures

"As the number of Japanese sales staff was reduced, the local staff built good connections with Japanese OEMs and delivered the same quality services without the assistance of Japanese expatriates. To do this, the local sales staff needed to learn skills and know-how to build the relationships with Japanese OEMs. . . . This change did not happen naturally."
—Contribution to Sloan Student/Alum Dialogue in Course on "Transforming Work, Organizations, and Society" (Spring 2002)

therefore are more frustrated than supported by this type of training. They are ready for something more substantive.

The current challenge in managing diversity is to go beyond efforts to change attitudes to focus on building the skills needed to facilitate work in diverse teams and to learn from the variety of backgrounds and knowledge people bring to their jobs. This is how the diversity in our contemporary workforce can be used to add value to both workers and their organizations. Box 4.2.2 provides a vivid example of this opportunity, drawing on the efforts of Japanese managers teaching their U.S. counterparts how to relate and sell to their Japanese customers.

People are also highly diverse in the expectations they bring to their work and organizations. To be sure, as survey data and labor market behavior continue to demonstrate, good wages and benefits remain a high priority for all workers. But these, by and large, are taken as a given—a necessary condition for individuals to consider a prospective job offer. Beyond these essentials, as a recent survey supplied by

Table 4.2.1
What attracts employees by age

Top attractors	U.S. Overall	Age 18–29	Age 30–44	Age 45–54	Age 55+
Competitive base pay/salary	•	•	•	•	•
Competitive healthcare benefits package	•	•	•	•	•
Opportunities for advancement	1	1	2		3
Work/life balance	2	2	1	2	
Competitive retirement benefits package	3			1	1
Pay raises linked to individual performance	3		3	3	2
Learning and development opportunities		3			

Source: Towers Perrin Talent Report 2001: New Realities in Today's Workforce
Key: • Core rewards that rank at the top for all groups
      1–3 Top differentiators in rank order

Towers Perrin indicated (see table 4.2.1), jobs have to be tailored to the priorities of different groups. Young workers place highest priority on possibilities for learning and developing their skills; midcareer and midlife workers value the opportunity to integrate work and family life; and older workers assign highest priority to long-term employment and income security. Most workers, young and old alike, appear to have learned the lesson of the past decades' breakdown in the prospect of long-term jobs. Over 40 percent of those employed actively look at alternative job opportunities on a regular basis and few see it as their responsibility to stay with a given employer for any particular length of time.[5]

Clearly, the actions of organizations in the last decade have shaped the expectations of the current workforce. Few are ready to commit their loyalty and put their trust in any single firm to provide lifetime jobs and careers. This does not, however, mean that they all want to be "free agents." As these data and others show, employees still expect firms to manage in ways that offer learning and career development opportunities. Also, with age comes the heightened priority of and expectation for long-term security. Fairness in employment decisions—layoffs, compensation, and promotion opportunities—are just as much an expectation today as in the past.

Work–family integration serves as today's frontier workforce issue. Of all the issues we examined, it generated the most interest among

5. Towers Perrin, *Talent Report 2001: New Realities in Today's Workforce* (New York: Towers Perrin, 2002).

our alumni, students, and industry participants. They documented a wide range of "family-friendly" policies and procedures offered in their organizations today, including flexible hours, part-time options, assistance with domestic services, and back-up day care. They also indicated that these policies and procedures often remained underused and, consequently, were ineffective. This is not for lack of thought on these matters. As one individual observed, being a "married couple with dual careers requires a constant evaluation of [our] roles as parents and professionals."

Two factors stand out as constraints, limiting the use and effectiveness of work–family policies. In many professions and organizations, the use of part-time options is still interpreted as signaling less commitment to the organization and to one's professional career. This was brought home vividly by our expert panel from the legal profession. Beth Boland, a partner in the Boston law firm of Mintz Levin, Cohn, Ferris, Glovsky, and Popeo, P.C., reported that although over 90 percent of leading law firms in Boston now provide a part-time option for associates and partners, less than 5 percent of those eligible actually take advantage of the option. Moreover, more than one-third of lawyers believe doing so would hurt their careers.

Similar low rates of uptake on work–family policies are reported in other studies and by our students and alumni in their organizations, for comparable reasons. The importance of face time and full-time commitment appear to still permeate the culture of many organizations and professions, dominating the images of the ideal worker or high potential employee in the eyes of senior executives and even peers. As one student commented, "Unfortunately, there still does occur this notion of "face time" that seems to equate the number of times your face is seen to that of a higher performer." Box 4.2.3 from another student further elaborates on this issue and the overall gap between policy and practice.

The second constraint lies in the need to focus on changing the work itself, collectively among peers and supervisors. Our colleague Lotte Bailyn[6] has documented this in her work and suggests the need to design work collaboratively around a dual agenda: achieving high performance *and* allowing individuals to integrate their work schedules with personal and family obligations. In the legal community, for example, Beth Boland pointed out that the legal work itself is well

---

6. Lotte Bailyn, *Breaking the Mold* (New York: Maxwell Macmillan, 1993).

Box 4.2.3
Gap Between Policy and Practice

"All of the work-life programs, however, are in reality used by only a small proportion of employees. The reasons for this are:

1. Rarely do male employees ever use them. Female employees therefore don't use them because they don't want to be seen as different than other employees.
2. With today's culture of starting work earlier than required and working later than required, many employees are reluctant to leave the office before their colleagues.
3. As others in the class pointed out, face time is very important. Out of sight is out of mind."

—*Contribution to Sloan Student/Alum Dialogue in Course on "Transforming Work, Organizations, and Society" (Spring 2002)*

Box 4.2.4
Reflections from the Spouse of a Medical Resident

"In addition, in spite of the fact that she was putting in all this effort, the head of the program, coming from a time when surgeons were men, with wives at home taking care of everything, could not understand how this lifestyle was not maintainable for her. There were no support programs or other alternatives available. Surgeons were supposed to do their job, not complain, and stick it out."

—*Contribution to Sloan Student/Alum Dialogue in Course on "Transforming Work, Organizations, and Society" (Spring 2002)*

suited to part-time arrangements, because most lawyers divide their time among many clients. As a result, reduced time arrangements just mean a reduced number of clients, not a reduction of effort in support of any one client. This sort of thinking is at the core of the approach that Lotte Bailyn has advocated.

The difficulty and yet the potential for addressing the stresses associated with the long hours professionals put into their work was brought home vividly through a vignette offered in box 4.2.4 by the spouse of a physician-resident.

The biggest uncertainty and most interesting source of debate involves whether the next generation, the so called "Gen Y" cohort, will bring and maintain different values and expectations than those of their parents. After all, they will have observed the breakdown in the social contract experienced by their parents and experienced the increased number of hours their parents have been devoting to the paid workforce. There is some anecdotal evidence to suggest that this generation is deeply committed to building individual skills and capabilities, but highly distrustful of organizations and other workplace institutions. There are even some indications of an unwillingness to work long hours of overtime at the expense of personal and family matters. If these are indeed defining characteristics of this cohort—shaped by their experiences growing up during the eras of rightsizing, downsizing, reengineering, and outsourcing—then there will be significant human capital challenges for organizations and industries in the future. These challenges appear to be particularly acute in such fields as autos, aerospace, and NASA, all of which are facing a demographic shock with as many as one-third of the employees eligible to retire in the next five years.

The Coming Labor Force Scarcity?

Predicting future labor supply/demand balances is tricky because multiple variables—including the rate of economic growth, productivity, immigration, working hours, retirement trends, and global sourcing of work—all interact to affect this balance. Nevertheless, straightforward projections by the Bureau of Labor Statistics, using moderate estimates of these variables, suggested that by 2010, labor supply in the United States could fall approximately five to ten million workers short of demand.[7]

The challenge is clear: Workers will be a scarce resource and those with the most knowledge and skills will be among the most scarce, as box 4.2.5 illustrates. The organization that seeks to compete on the basis of human capital and knowledge will need to learn how to attract and retain these valued workers. Thus, if anything, the individual and collective power of the workforce will continue to increase.

The vision for the future that emerged from our discussions and interviews is one that addresses the frontier challenges—managing diversity and addressing the different expectations of the workforce—by letting the people solve these problems themselves. This is a refrain that will echo through the visions expressed not just for this challenge,

---

7. Howard Fullerton, Jr., and Mitra Toossi, "Employment Outlook: 2000–2010—Labor Force Projections to 2010: Steady Growth and Changing Composition," *Monthly Labor Review*, November 2001, pp. 21–38.

Box 4.2.5
Stress and Shortage for Technical Professionals

> "Having entered the workforce in 1949 has allowed a unique perspective. Several factors contributed to the present condition. In the late 60's and early 70's corporations became increasingly concerned with mergers, acquisitions, global considerations and the issues associated with high technology. As a result, pay scales for "in-demand" positions such as patent law and technology specialties increased to attract talent. However, as salaries increased there was also an expectation of 60–70-hour work weeks. Also, as pay increased many companies could not afford to continue adding staff, so they began loading people down to accomplish the work. This carries through to today where people in technical shortage categories are still expected to perform to their pay level. Also, where supply is an issue for these positions, it is easier to get one person than two so the one hired may end up being asked to do more than the work of one."
> —*Contribution to Sloan Student/Alum Dialogue in Course on "Transforming Work, Organizations, and Society" (Spring 2002)*

but for all those discussed in this paper. Young lawyers aspire to succeed in their profession just as much as their counterparts of an earlier generation. But they also want to attend to their family and personal lives and to rearrange work processes and caseloads to better meet their dual agendas. They recognize they cannot do this unless others in their profession and in leading companies work together to change the culture and norms of their profession. The same movement is underway among residents in the medical profession. They are ready to transform the way they do their work, and, in the process, gradually change the culture of their professions and organizations. Will those in power in organizations support or frustrate these efforts? The answer to this question will influence the way this transformation process plays out in the years ahead.

Knowledge-Based Work

The last quarter century has witnessed the gradual diffusion of what are called knowledge-based work systems among front-line manufacturing and service workers. The general consensus derived from a broad range of studies and the experience of our industry participants is that these produce higher levels of organizational performance and higher levels of learning and employee satisfaction than the industrial models of work organization they are replacing.[8] Yet, the best known examples of knowledge-based work systems are generally in what are termed "greenfield" facilities (literally, new facilities built in open, green fields). Most organizations fall into the "brownfield" category— existing operations with many of the legacy twentieth-century assumptions firmly in place.

Implementing the new work systems in these existing operations requires extended and continued effort. Leaders from one Pratt & Whitney facility participated in our class and cataloged their fluctuating efforts to implement team-based work systems and sustained labor–management cooperation. Successes were periodically set back by turnover of plant managers or union leaders, and by decisions to outsource work or lay off employees, which undermined the trust needed to build and retain employee support for these workplace changes and innovations. This is not an isolated example. The best estimates from our research and others are that about one-third of U.S. establishments have implemented some features of knowledge-based work systems in their operations.[9] Very few have achieved what might be termed a transformation. Whether these efforts will be maintained and whether further diffusion will occur depends on the actions of a variety of stakeholders—managers, workers, labor union representatives, Wall Street analysts, and government policy makers. The key issue is whether these stakeholders will recognize the value that knowledge-based work systems offer the workforce and the economy, and choose to work together to sustain the momentum already underway, or will short-term decisions by these groups limit or even undermine transformation efforts?

Alongside the implementing of new work systems is another key labor market development: the increased use of various types of contract, consultant, and project work arrangements. From the demand side of the labor market, these arrangements offer employers access to specialized knowledge from outside sources, flexibility, reduced headcount and associated labor cost reductions, and the opportunity to focus on core competencies. From the supply side, these arrangements

---

8. Casey Ichniowski, Thomas Kochan, David Levine, Craig Olson, and George Strauss, "What Works at Work?" *Industrial Relations*, 1996, 299–333.

9. Paul Osterman, "Work Organization in an Era of Restructuring: Trends in Diffusion and Impacts on Employee Welfare," *Industrial and Labor Relations Review* 53 (2000): 179–96.

can also offer opportunities to learn across jobs and organizational assignments, while also providing more options for integrating work with different stages of personal and/or family life, for example, combining work with further education, child or elder care duties, or as a bridge into retirement. The downside of these arrangements lies in the reduction of benefits, employment security, status, influence, and more variable earnings for contractors. The costs to the organization include increased coordination requirements, potential safety or security risks, and the potential loss of organizational knowledge or capability—all downsides that become more visible after the outsourcing decision.

Clearly, if managed well, there are potential benefits to both organizations and individuals from sensible use of contracting arrangements. Our students and alumni see both the benefits and the pitfalls of these work arrangements playing out in their organizations (see box 4.2.6 for one student's experiences with contracting). Their hopes and aspirations for the future are that they and their organizational peers will learn to use these flexible arrangements sensibly, to draw on the knowledge and skills of independent contractors/consultants or those in transition stages of their life cycle, and to not use this option as a short-term way to simply reduce headcount or compensation costs.

Integrating Technical and Social Dimensions of Technology

In the last quarter of the twentieth century, U.S. manufacturing industries learned about the need to understand technology as an integrated system of technical and social dimensions. That is, they learned that a return on their investments in hardware could only be realized if they were linked to complementary investments in education, work redesign, and cultural change. The U.S. auto industry learned this the hard way, by losing market share to Japanese competitors in the 1980s—competitors who were quicker to build this socio-technical principle into their production systems, employment practices, and work operations.

Our research has documented that the greatest returns to both manufacturing and information technologies come when the technical dimensions of technology are appropriately integrated with the organizational and human dimensions. Two Sloan students, John Krafcik[10]

---

10. John Krafcik, "Triumph of Lean Production," *Sloan Management Review* 30 (1988): 41–52.

Box 4.2.6
Mixed Results with Contracting

For many tasks and positions, a contracting arrangement does indeed provide a benefit to the government. After all, there is probably little difference with regards to maintenance workers, technicians, and other unskilled or low-skill support personnel as to whether they are government or private-sector employees. Tasks for these employees also tend to be better defined, and supervisory functions are limited to general personnel-related issues. My observation, however, is that when the jobs that are contracted out become more complex, requiring higher-level skills and increased experience, then the system breaks down and ceases to function properly. This leads to more waste, less productivity, and more frustration on the part of both the civil servants and the private sector employees. I believe that this is due to several interrelated causes:

• First, the structure of the contract is usually such that there is no incentive for the private contractor to hire the best-qualified candidate. Instead, the least-costly candidate that meets the minimum criteria as specified in the job description is the person that is hired. This is because if the contractor hired a more costly candidate, then he might exceed his proposed budget, which would count against him when profit is calculated or when the contract is up for renewal.

• Second, a weaker candidate that is available immediately is preferable over a stronger candidate who may be available in one or two months. The reason for this is that every month that the position goes unfilled will usually count against the contractor's performance or profit. So the private contractor has every reason to fill every position as fast as possible. Whether the candidate is the best or not does not really matter to the bottom line.

• Third, in positions requiring more experience or skills, supervisor, reporting, and chain-of-command-related issues become more common and more complex.

• Fourth, one of the reasons that is often used to justify the on-site contractor structure is that it allows government programs to be more flexible in adjusting personnel levels, since the theory is that private contractors can lay off people more easily than the government. However, while this is true for many low-wage, low-skill positions, my observation is that most of these on-site contracts have significant job-protection guarantees built-in. In one case, three-month notices are required before a lay-off can occur. These policies, while socially laudable, diminish the value of the on-site contractor arrangement, making the need for such arrangements, especially with regard to higher-skilled jobs, questionable.

—Contribution to Sloan Student/Alum Dialogue in Course on "Transforming Work, Organizations, and Society" (Spring 2002)

and John Paul MacDuffie,[11] demonstrated that world class productivity and quality performance were achieved in auto plants that integrated deployments of technology with the development of flexible, knowledge-based work systems, deep investments in training and development, and high levels of employee participation in problem-solving and decision-making. Plants that adopted this integrated approach outperformed plants that invested more in technology without corresponding investments in human resources and work system innovations, and plants that continued to operate with more traditional industrial models of production and work organization. Later, the same results were replicated not only in other manufacturing industries but with information technologies as well.[12]

The relationship between the technical and social dimensions of technology has been further elaborated by Wanda Orlikowski's research on the uses of information technologies in the workplace.[13] Her studies investigated the implementation of new information technologies in U.S., European, and Japanese firms. With a few exceptions, she found that these firms had failed to realize the benefits anticipated by their technological investments—not because of some failure in strategy, technology, or deployment—but because these firms had failed to manage the most critical determinant of technological effectiveness in organizations: how people actually use the technologies to get their work done. These findings suggest the importance of shifting management attention from one primarily focused on managing technologies as physical assets to one focused on managing the human and organizational *use of technologies*. Managing the use of technology requires recognizing the critical interdependence between technical capabilities and the human capital (knowledge, skills, motivations) and work systems (norms, incentives, practices) that realize the value of

11. John Paul MacDuffie and John Krafcik, "Integrating Technology and Human Resources for High-Performance Manufacturing: Evidence from the International Auto Industry," in *Transforming Organizations,* ed. Thomas A. Kochan and Michael Useem (New York: Oxford University Press, 1992), 209–27; John Paul MacDuffie, "Human Resource Bundles and Manufacturing Performance: Organizational Logic and Flexible Production Systems in the World Auto Industry," *Industrial and Labor Relations Review* 48 (1995): 197–221.

12. Timothy F. Bresnahan, Erik Brynjolfsson, and Lorin M. Hitt, "Information Technology, Workplace Innovation, and the Demand for Skilled Labor: Firm Level Evidence," in *The New Relationship,* ed. Margaret M. Blair and Thomas A. Kochan (Washington, D.C., The Brookings Institution, 1999), 145–184.

13. Wanda J. Orlikowski, "Learning from Notes: Organizational Issues in Groupware Implementation," *Information Society Journal* 9 (1993): 237–250.

Box 4.2.7
The Dilemma of What Knowledge to Capture

The constant turnover of personnel in our organization has made even assuring short-term knowledge continuity very problematic. . . . First we tried to capture the basics, without focusing so much on the step-by-step instructions. This proved to be unsuccessful. . . . There is an extreme reluctance on the part of the users (scientists) to assume anything that was not explicitly written down. . . . In response to these comments . . . we would write down every step, providing check-points, approximate times of completion, etc. The result was that the procedures grew from a single 30-page manual to an over 500-page book. . . . This approach was as unsuccessful as the first one. . . . Some people are asking for more detail, others are asking for less. No matter what we do, someone will be disappointed.
—*Contribution to Sloan Student/Alum Dialogue in Course on "Transforming Work, Organizations, and Society" (Spring 2002)*

---

those technical capabilities in practice. It also recognizes that use of technology will change over time—as requirements evolve, market conditions change, learning occurs—and thus resources need to be dedicated to enable workers to adapt and augment their technologies and their use routines, as appropriate, over time.

These same lessons are now being learned in the area known as "knowledge management." As box 4.2.7 indicates, there are many dilemmas associated with the narrow concept of "capturing" knowledge. Note that this example links issues of knowledge management with issues of labor turnover.

One of the pioneers in the area of knowledge management, Larry Prusak from IBM's Institute for Knowledge-Based Organizations, built on this point in his presentation to our class, as illustrated in box 4.2.8.

Building Leadership Capabilities

Most business school cases are written and discussed from the vantage point of the CEO or others positioned at the top of their functional areas or departments. This sends the signal that it is the brilliance or individual leadership of those at the top who solve critical organizational problems and which accounts for the success or failure of organiza-

Box 4.2.8
Information Technology and Knowledge Creation

It has been argued "technology's most valuable role in knowledge management is extending the reach and enhancing the speed of knowledge transfer." Information technology is indeed very useful in capturing, storing, and distributing structured and codified knowledge, therefore enabling other individuals in the organization to have access to it. However, IT plays a much more limited role in knowledge creation, which is very much a social process involving the exchange of hard-to-codify knowledge and personal experiences. Also, IT, by itself, cannot create a knowledge-based environment that promotes knowledge use and sharing. For any technology to be optimized, it must be augmented by strategy, process, culture, and behavior that support knowledge sharing and knowledge-based work."[1]
—*Contribution by Larry Prusak to Sloan Course on "Transforming Work, Organizations, and Society" (Spring 2002)*

---

1. Laurence Prusak and Salvatore Parise, "Information Systems as a Conduit for the Transfer of Knowledge." Paper produced by the IBM Institute for Knowledge Management, Cambridge, MA, 2002.

tions. The leadership model implicit (and sometimes explicit) in these cases is one of the charismatic, visionary, and powerful strategist alongside a top-down model of innovation and change. Some have argued that in the last decade corporate boards of directors have been seduced by the business press (a seduction possibly reinforced by business schools) to search for a charismatic CEO to be the "leader" who will provide the new vision and direction to transform organizational performance.[14]

At Sloan, we are in a process (led by Deborah Ancona) of developing an alternative view of leadership better suited to modern organizational realities.[15] We see leadership as a distributed capacity, exercised individually and collectively at multiple levels of the organization. This capacity is constituted by four interdependent capabilities: visioning, sensemaking, relating, and inventing. As organizations

---

14. Rakesh Khurana, *Searching for a Corporate Savior: The Irrational Quest for Charismatic CEOs* (Princeton, N.J.: Princeton University Press, 2002).
15. Deborah G. Ancona, Thomas W. Malone, Wanda J. Orlikowski, and Peter Senge, "Distributed Leadership," Sloan School of Management Workshops, Cambridge, Mass., 2001/2002.

Box 4.2.9
Linking Diversity Training and Leadership Skills

> "Diversity training is mainly to help employees better understand other employees who are different from them. Additional training would be valuable if it worked more on the group process and leadership necessary to translate diversity into positive organizational results."
> —*Contribution to Sloan Student/Alum Dialogue in Course on "Transforming Work, Organizations, and Society" (Spring 2002)*

decentralize and flatten hierarchies, engage in greater cross-functional teamwork, and participate in multiple, dynamic, network-like interactions, we believe that the capabilities of this distributed model of leadership become even more relevant and effective in practice. Moreover, as organizations form more cross-boundary strategic alliances and become part of larger networks, leadership capabilities must be shared across these boundaries. In this way, leadership and change are highly interdependent processes.

While the Sloan distributed leadership model continues to stress the importance of developing individual capabilities, it recognizes that leadership is a collective phenomenon that requires engaging the energies, interests, and aspirations of the many people that constitute the organization—those involved in doing the everyday work of the enterprise. In this respect, distributed leadership cuts across all of the topics covered in this paper. As box 4.2.9 illustrates, for example, diversity training can and should bridge into broader leadership capabilities.

Redefining Organizational Goals

One inevitable consequence of adopting a human capital, knowledge-based organizational model is that the voices of employees will become more influential in shaping the values, goals, and priorities of the twenty-first-century organizations. Judging from the level of interest exhibited by our Sloan Fellows students, high on the list of priorities of employees today are concerns for social and environmental sustainability. These leaders want to work in and lead organizations in ways that ensure their children and future generations have the same opportunities as they do. This is the vision they express in their thesis projects and comments. Thus, sustainability may be the frontier example of how the underlying objectives of organizations may change in human centered organizations.[16] (See box 4.2.10 for an example.)

A number of organizations have made highly visible commitments to managing from a sustainability perspective. This movement is farther advanced in Europe, in part because the European Community will shortly require companies to report outcomes related to what they view as their "triple bottom line," that is, people, profits, and planet. Shell and British Petroleum are among the leaders in emphasizing sustainability, as documented in a thesis by two recent Sloan Fellows, Clare Mendelsohn and Anirudha Pangarkar.[17]

In the United States, we examined the Ford Motor Company's highly visible effort to refurbish its River Rouge manufacturing complex following principles of sustainability. The result has been a bold rethinking of the relationship between a factory, its products, and the environment. Ford's CEO William Clay Ford has been an outspoken advocate of the River Rouge initiative and the corporation has even added "environment" to its traditional set of standard metrics on safety, quality, delivery, cost, and morale. Still, the concept of sustainability has not yet become deeply embedded in the values and beliefs of the company's managers or in the corporation's manufacturing processes and product development processes. A small staff and a handful of strong line leaders support Ford's sustainability initiatives, but it remains to be seen if the vision will continue beyond the current CEO. That is, is the commitment to sustainability itself sustainable?

Another area where managing multiple stakeholders is critical is that of strategic partnerships, including labor-management partnerships, public-private partnerships, customer-supplier partnerships, and even strategic alliances among competitors. In class, we observed that these strategic partnerships are characterized by constant tensions—such as the tension between the personal relationships between individuals in the respective organizations and the formal roles that these individuals have—which can lead them to withhold information, act unilaterally, and otherwise undermine the relationships they have built. Similarly, there is a constant tension between the pressure to deliver short-term results and the long-term process of constructing and

16. Peter Senge and Gören Carstedt, "Innovating Our Way to the Next Industrial Revolution," *Sloan Management Review,* January–February, 2001.

17. Clare Mendelsohn and Anirudha Pangarkar, "Case Studies of How BP and Shell are Approaching Sustainable Development." Master's Thesis, Sloan School of Management, Cambridge, Mass., May 2002.

Box 4.2.10
Social and Environmental Sustainability: the Athabasca Oil Sands Project

The objective of the Athabasca Oil Sands Project (a joint venture effort led by Shell Canada) is to mine the estimated 100-yr supply of oil. While this oil field had been discovered as early as 1956, two prior attempts to mine the oil had failed on technical and environmental grounds. A big concern was the large environmental footprint associated with the mine and the 300 miles of pipeline. It was only on the third attempt, begun in 1996, that a breakthrough was reached, and oil was successfully produced. This third attempt was uniquely steered by social and environmental sensitivities and community need for involvement. Shell Canada's success came from being able to demonstrate to all the critical stakeholders that the project could provide economic, social, and environmental benefits. Through a participatory, collective approach—including and engaging local communities, experts, and NGOs—Shell Canada was able to realize numerous advantages for the community of Athabasca:

• 1,000 permanent jobs were established within the local community with as many as 12,000 employed during the construction peak.
• The community benefits from substantial tax revenues.
• The project helped to build and augment the skills of the local people.
• Process water was recycled, thereby reducing demand on local rivers.
• A domestic supply of gas was developed, resulting in less dependency on oil imports.
• No chemicals were utilized in the oil separation process, and mine lands will eventually be restored to a natural condition.
• A groundbreaking climate change program was developed to address international concerns and to identify ways to reduce CO_2 emissions.
• An independent panel of experts continues to identify other means for carbon offsets as well as renewable energy alternatives.

—*Contribution to Sloan Student/Alum Dialogue in Course on "Transforming Work, Organizations, and Society" (Spring 2002)* sustaining a partnership. These and other tensions reveal that strategic partnerships are fundamentally unstable organizational forms, dependent on a constantly adapting agenda which continues to deliver value to all parties.

We examined one unique labor-management partnership on this issue: the Kaiser-Permanente health plan partnership, which involves eight unions representing 55,000 workers in 26 bargaining units across 18 states. We heard evidence of the way that these partnership efforts have helped to grow the business by valuing employee knowledge, as well as by constructing path-breaking joint initiatives on work-family matters, the reduction of medical errors, systems for conflict resolution, and even methods of compensation. At the same time, we also learned of the constant difficulties of incorporating innovative lessons into ongoing organizational operations, as well as the difficulty of addressing key stakeholders who are not part of the partnership, whether they are the doctors who have a separate organizational structure within Kaiser-Permanente or the other unions and bargaining units that have chosen not to be part of the partnership.

Beyond the issues of strategic partnerships, we also explored examples of innovation in local, state, and federal government. Here the issues involved not only mechanisms to value employee knowledge and capability, but also transformation around redefined outcomes, greater collaboration, and new roles for the "clients" being served by the agencies. In her thesis on social sustainability, Sloan Fellow Lynne Dovey[18] found that broader social systems change requires a new role for governments (whether local or national): a role where they engage in power-sharing and joint accountability with organizations and communities, enable valued outcomes rather than only enforce regulations, create incentives for collaboration with multiple stakeholders, participate in longer term, relational contracting, and practice distributed leadership.

Implications for Management Education

As business schools rose to prominence over the twentieth century, organization theory and education focused more and more on

---

18. Lynne Dovey, "Achieving Better Social Outcomes in New Zealand Through Collaboration: Perspectives from the United States." Master's Thesis, Sloan School of Management, Cambridge, Mass., May 2002.

management within the individual firm. Organizational control, autonomy, flexibility, and managing uncertainty became key issues. Priority was given to strategies for attracting and allocating financial capital, managing these and other firm assets in ways that return value to shareholders, and protecting the firm from the influence of agents, groups, and organizations that lie outside the firm's boundaries. Organizations were conceived as "going concerns" that survive indefinitely, so potential future liabilities or costs were discounted and incorporated into current decision making.

As we rethink assumptions around the nature and value of work and organizations, key adjustments to business school curricula are needed. Just as we inverted the analysis of work and organizations to reflect where value is created, so too do we need to revamp teaching to provide future managers and leaders with the perspectives, knowledge, and tools that enable organizations to realize the potential value from the workforce and their knowledge. Each dimension highlighted in this paper—workforce demographics, knowledge-based work, integration of social and technical systems, distributed leadership, and expanded organizational goals—will need to be integrated in the curricula and supported with practical tools and experiences.

We need, for example, to prepare business leaders to address high priority, sensitive workforce issues such as diversity and fair treatment, as well as career development and work-life integration. The management skills and tools needed here are straightforward: engaging, listening to, negotiating with, and facilitating different forms of individual and collective employee voice. Whereas twentieth century workforce management focused on command and control, in the twenty-first century the workforce is directly engaged in the management process. Skills in negotiations, problem-solving, conflict resolution, and coordination of horizontal, cross-boundary interactions need to become the standard tools of the trade.

Similarly, knowing how to implement and sustain mechanisms for knowledge creation and application is essential in the knowledge-based organization. This requires an understanding of the needed knowledge, skills, and abilities at every phase of what is sometimes termed a value stream in an organization. Most efforts to manage value streams effectively are focused on mapping the flow of products or services from conception to ultimate customers—looking for constraints and improvement opportunities. Our analysis would call for training next-generation managers to be able to do a parallel mapping of knowledge and capabilities—looking for constraints and opportunities along the dimensions of knowledge and human capital.

In the domain of technology, we would call for deeper and more explicit attention to the interdependence of social and technical aspects of business operations. The MBA degree grew to prominence in the twentieth century as a specialized profession, separate from the disciplinary training of other university departments. This reinforced the view that issues of training, development, teams, and even leadership should be treated separately from efforts to design, implement, and innovate with various types of new technology. Managing the twenty-first-century organization will require integrating state-of-the-art knowledge and skills that cut across traditional disciplinary boundaries. The implication here is clear: management schools need to be better integrated with their physical and social science and engineering counterparts, and vice versa.

As we educate next-generation business leaders, we must better understand and appreciate the leadership development that has occurred over the past decade. Even if the so-called Internet bubble has burst, what still remains is a cohort of young, talented people who have developed valuable insights and capabilities in this concentrated e-business crucible. Already there is anecdotal evidence to suggest that this cohort is less interested in traditional business cases centered on large, multidivisional corporations and more interested in learning that incorporates what they now know, as well as the kinds of organizational settings to which they aspire. Leadership, as Robert Thomas and Warren Bennis emphasize,[19] is often best learned through experiences of failure. The lesson here is obvious: we simply have to work with our students to help them and us to reflect on and learn from the rich experiences they bring into our classrooms.

The basic assumption of a shareholder- and customer-driven, profit-maximizing organization is woven throughout business school education. Much less common is attention to the multiple stakeholders associated with any business operation and the objectives or metrics relevant to these other stakeholders—whether they be the workforce, communities, regulatory agencies, strategic partners, or suppliers. Our challenge is to build on and go beyond such initiatives as "the

---

19. Warren Bennis and Robert J. Thomas, *Geeks and Geezers* (Boston: Harvard Business School Press, 2002).

balanced scorecard,"[20] "stakeholder value,"[21] reciprocal contracts, and related mechanisms for attending to outcomes for multiple stakeholders. We have found the best way to do this is by bringing representatives of these different stakeholders into our classes—to hear directly about their perspectives, interests, and the value they can add to organizations and to build cases and simulations that put students in these different stakeholder roles and hold them accountable for addressing these multiple criteria.

Conclusion

We draw three broad conclusions about the diversity of practice in organizations today, the process of transformation, and the leverage associated with broader assumptions on work and organizations. First, the differences between the two organizational models outlined at the outset of this paper are reflected in organizational practices today, where organizations are seen to be positioned at various points along the continua characterizing these two organizational models. Many organizations are currently trying to transform themselves as they recognize the importance of human capital and knowledge to their future effectiveness.

Second, there is no guarantee that such a transformation process will continue or succeed. It is not guided by some invisible hand or market imperative. Indeed, we have encountered many "disconnects" between rhetoric and reality. Organizational change is a highly political, contested process involving individuals and groups with different, often conflicting, interests, beliefs, and power. Therefore, whether the various transformations currently underway will result in organizations more suited to the demands of the twenty-first century will depend on management's willingness to challenge fundamental assumptions about organizations and the quality of the negotiated change processes they engage in with various stakeholders.

Third, we have outlined a broader set of assumptions about work and organizations that represent a powerful set of levers for transformation. Yet to put this larger set of assumptions "on the table" for discussion and change will require opening a dialogue with the various stakeholders who share an interest in and commitment to building

---

20. Robert Kaplan, *Strategy Focused Organizations: How Balanced Scorecard Companies Thrive in the New Business Environment* (Boston: Harvard Business School Press, 2001).
21. Murman et al., *Lean Enterprise Value.*

effective twenty-first-century organizations. The implication here is simple but blunt: the future of management (and management education) is too important to leave to managers alone! Employees from the front lines through middle management and the executive ranks, professional associations and unions, families and communities, partner organizations, as well as nongovernmental organizations and government policy makers are all part of the network of leaders who need to be engaged and involved in shaping the organizations of the twenty-first century.

McGregor asked us to rethink our assumptions about people. Now our task is to examine an even broader set of assumptions around the very nature of work and organizations. The choices we make will determine whether the rhetoric around the twenty-first-century organizations will become a reality.

Acknowledgments

Invaluable assistance in this research was provided by Natasha Iskander, Jen Fabas, Lynn Dovey, Carolyn Corazo, and many other participants in the Sloan seminar 15.343 on "Transforming Work, Organizations, and Society." Support for this paper was provided through MIT's Sloan School of Management and the Cambridge-MIT Initiative (CMI).

4.3　　　　Discussion

Meg O'Leary, senior manager at PriceWaterhouseCoopers, exemplifies the rising class of virtual knowledge workers of the future. Rather than commute to an office, Ms. O'Leary does her job from her home and has done so since 1998. Figure 4.3.1 illustrates a typical day in her life.

The new style of work environment described by O'Leary affords both better and worse work-life balance. On the one hand, it is easy to have lunch with the family and never miss dinner. On the other hand, the tenuous boundary between work and home means longer hours and a feeling of never being far from work. Being a virtual worker means never having to face an ugly commute in snarled traffic, but it also means never having a reason to leave the house for days on end. O'Leary also lamented her dependence on technology—one of Boston's infamous Nor'easter storms can knock out telecommunications and disrupt her work.

Ms. O'Leary's work schedule also shows an important point about globalization: working in multiple time zones forces workers to expand their workdays to overlap with the workdays of global colleagues. Boeing CEO Phil Condit had noted how important round-the-clock, round-the-world knowledge work has become for his company. Boeing uses such practices both for design work and for rapid response to project proposals. Because of telecommunications, knowledge work has the potential to bring people together in ways that the industrial revolution never did. Global knowledge work practices bring people from different countries to work directly with each other. While the industrial revolution brought the people from the country into the cities, the information revolution will bring the people of all countries together.

Working in globally distributed teams makes face time difficult even for workers who don't telecommute. Nonetheless, telecommuting

•	5:00–6:00	Arise and prepare for global teleconference call
•	6:00–9:00	Participate in global teleconference call
•	9:00–11:00	Read, listen, and respond to e-mail and voice-mail
•	11:00–12:00	Write proposal with team from NC, CAN, and DC
•	12:00–12:30	Have lunch with daughter
•	12:30–2:00	Test conference software with vendor and clients
•	2:00–3:30	Join all-hands call re: IPO/merger and forecast
•	3:30–5:00	Debrief with colleague and prep for late-night
•	5:00–8:00	Spend time with family
•	8:00–10:00	Call with Hong Kong and wrap-up day's business

Figure 4.3.1 A Day in the Life of Meg O'Leary

brings additional challenges to workers. "Being a high-performer doesn't require you to see and be seen," O'Leary said, "but it is isolating." She recalled a time where she realized that she had not left the home for an entire week as she moved from "downstairs" family time to "upstairs" work time throughout the days.

The autonomy and nature of telecommuting work also demands constant learning, but there is little programmed professional development time. "You're doing it on your own," Ms. O'Leary said.

Finally, working in virtual teams brings great opportunities to demonstrate leadership by stepping forward and managing projects, but there is little opportunity to interact with role models or see them in action.

When asked what a company can do to enable work that promotes a work-life balance, O'Leary said that the key is for the company to create a culture that supports the balance. "It has to be the culture, not just paying lip service to the concept," Ms. O'Leary said. "There can't be a huge discrepancy between practice and philosophy. At PWC, working from home is not seen as a career-limiting move. It's not seen as not being committed to the organization. That is what has kept me with PWC."

Ms. O'Leary offered two additional suggestions to companies. First, companies should provide opportunities for growth and development, to keep employees engaged. Second, companies should focus on outcomes, not process. "I do project work and complete my projects. The company doesn't need to know when the work gets done, just that it gets done and that clients are happy." This approach requires to trust employers that employees will complete their work and exceed expectations on client service.

Thus, the employer-employee relationship is very different at PWC, going beyond McGregor's Theory Y. The company is based more on trust than on command-and-control. Workers are judged on their ability to fulfill the commitments that they make to each other. Colleagues and the company measure people by the quality of their results rather than the quantity of their hours on the clock. Complex, unscripted project work—in contrast to routinized piecework—requires a flexible work environment.

SAS Institute, the world's largest privately held software company, exemplifies a corporate culture based on trust and flexibility. The example of SAS illustrates how a $1.2 billion company can do well financially by doing right for its 9,000 employees. SAS CEO **Dr. James Goodnight** noted that when "95 percent of a company's assets drive out the front gate every night, the CEO must see to it that they return the following day." A trust-based environment, onsite healthcare, recreation facilities, and good equitable pay structures help get people to return.

For these efforts, SAS is ranked third on *Fortune* magazine's "Best Places to Work in America" rankings. With 3 percent employee turnover—compared to the 20 percent figure common to the software industry—SAS saves an estimated $75 million per year by not having to acquire replacement workers. "We would rather pay our employees than pay headhunters," Goodnight said. Such practices mean that new employees want to join SAS. The company enjoys first pick among the very best workers, getting some 200 applicants for each job posting. Finally, he stressed that strong employee loyalty drives higher customer loyalty. Workers that stay with the company form lasting relationships with the company's customers; retaining employees helps retain customers.

The low turnover ratio at SAS prompted an audience member to ask whether low turnover impeded innovation, thereby creating an inbred corporate culture. Goodnight answered that SAS uses internal mobility to create a strong flow of ideas, rather than using a revolving door of entering and departing employees. Workers at SAS work on a project basis, and they can move freely about the company. Unlike a traditional hierarchical manufacturing company, SAS lets workers move in and out of linear career development paths. Moreover, the company is still growing—getting fresh new workers as it expands. With its commit-

ment to the long-term, SAS is even hiring during the economic downturn in the software and technology sector. The company is foregoing
short-term profits to hire very skilled workers who were laid off in the
crash of the technology sector.

Dr. Peter Senge suggested that people should question their
assumptions about corporate and government practice and about the
developed world's entire way of life. Assumptions are embedded in
the language that we use. Under McGregor's transition from Theory X
to Theory Y, people shifted from being a labor "cost" to being a corporate "asset." Yet, Senge questioned even the language of calling
people "assets" or "resources." He noted that the definition of a
resource is "something standing ready, waiting to be used." Kofi Annan
spoke of the need to move from talking about balance sheets (with their
lists of categorized assets) to a more people-focused perspective. In
moving beyond McGregor's Theory Y, leaders need new ways of thinking about the unique relationship and mutual responsibilities between
employers and employees. This new model would move away from
the assumption that employees are assets that can be bought, depreci-
ated, and disposed.

Dr. Senge also suggested that, because of sustainability, the entire
industrial revolution is a giant bubble, not unlike the dot-com bubble.
We don't see it yet because the industrial revolution's bubble has not
yet popped. People do not see the bubble-like nature of current practice because of the most insidious feature of bubbles—they look so
good to those inside them, until they pop. Those inside see nothing
but growth and good times. Those outside see how the bubble has
overstepped rational bounds and is bound to pop. Just as the dot-com
bubble was not sustainable, the rapacious resource consumption patterns of the industrial revolution are not sustainable. Senge noted that
the average American needs, literally, a ton of resources per week to
support their lifestyle. Few believe that everyone in the world can reasonably attain the resource consumption patterns of the developed
world. Thus, he echoed Kofi Annan's concern about those outside the
affluent circle (or bubble) of the major industrial nations—"15 percent
of the people having 95 percent of the goodies" is not sustainable.

All three panelists commented on the need for education reforms,
especially at the lower educational levels. For Jim Goodnight, the issue
was that the old model of education presumed that the student was
destined for the manufacturing world. He noted that it is clear that the
U.S. will, and must, leave behind its manufacturing past and embrace

the world of knowledge work. Rote learning of preconceived answers will not work in the coming age. Toward this, both Meg O'Leary and Peter Senge noted the need for teaching thinking skills to twenty-first century global citizens. As the nature of O'Leary's telecommuting workstyle shows, managers and employees alike need a better understanding of work-life balance and how to work in cross-functional, cross-cultural teams.

In summarizing the panel, **Dr. Joel Cutcher-Gershenfeld** noted the classic dilemma of change: how do new practices prove themselves to the adherents of old practices while breaking the molds of those practices? Peter Senge noted that the transition beyond McGregor is but 5 percent complete and quoted Dee Hock (founder of Visa International) in foreseeing an era of massive institutional failure, filled with crisis and retrenchment. Fortunately, the engine of new venture creation provides a mechanism for transitioning to new practices (in the private sector, at least).

Dr. Cutcher-Gershenfeld also commented on the gap between policies and practices: many companies and civic leaders espouse enlightened viewpoints but fail to follow them with action. Unfortunately, the drive for short-term results outweighs the goal of long-term sustainability. Yet companies can bridge the gap between short-term results and long-term ethics. In her presentation, Hewlett Packard CEO Carly Fiorina argued that even without compassion, companies can see that it is in their long-term best interests to create a sustainable long-term future. Currently, only 10 percent of the world can afford HP's products. Thus, working toward a long-term better future for everyone presents tremendous opportunities for growth for all companies.

5   Marketing

5.1 Innovation and the Constancy of Change

Rick Wagoner

I want to talk about change, innovation, and the long-standing relationship between General Motors and the Sloan School of Management. The relationship between the Sloan School and GM is based on a rich history and solid results. GM and Sloan share a common heritage of cutting-edge research, real-time business applications, and bottom-line contributions in business and education.

Today, GM and the Sloan School remain, in many ways, reflections of the man who largely defined both institutions—Alfred P. Sloan.

At GM, Alfred Sloan set out to build a different kind of auto company—one that embraced his belief in, as he put it, "a car for every purse and purpose"—one that rejected the prevailing notion, in 1918, that customers could buy a car in any color they wanted, so long as it was black.

At MIT, Alfred Sloan had a vision of a different kind of business school, one that promoted a closer association between science, engineering, and industry. Sloan imagined a school that did more than just teach best practices—he foresaw a school that helped *define* them.

And I think we can all agree that it's no stretch to say that Sloan achieved more than even he thought possible, at both institutions. Under Sloan's direction, GM went on to become the world's most successful automaker. And under Sloan's influence, the Sloan School went on to change the paradigm of management education *forever*.

And yet, successful as GM and Sloan have been over the years, we're both in the process of reinventing ourselves today. Frankly, we have little alternative. As Sloan, himself, said, "There is no resting place for an enterprise in a competitive economy . . . no company ever stops changing." And that's as true today as it was in 1918, as true for MIT as it is for GM.

So, how do we deal with the constant changes that we find ourselves confronting every day? Let me offer a little story.

Last year, the city of Detroit marked its 300th anniversary, and one of the things the city did to celebrate was open a time capsule that had been sealed in 1900. In the time capsule were some 55 letters from prominent business and community leaders at that time, and it's interesting to note that not one of those letters represented the auto business.

In 1900, the auto companies were, in many ways, the dot.coms of their day. In fact, for most people in 1900, cars were little more than an expensive novelty. As Sloan put it, "many bright automotive ideas ended with a horse and a towline."

Consider the case of Billy Durant, founder of GM, whose single best decision may have been to bring Alfred Sloan into the company. From 1914 to 1920, when GM was just one of a number of speculative auto companies, investment capital poured into the auto industry. During that period, GM stock soared more than 5,500 percent.

In the early 1920s, however, the overcrowded automobile industry failed to deliver on expectations, and auto stocks plunged. In six months, GM lost two-thirds of its market value. In a panic, Durant began to borrow huge amounts of money and buy back shares, in a futile attempt to prop up the company's stock price.

To make a long story short—after a wild ride, GM eventually recovered. The upshot is that as uncertain and challenging as the auto industry is *today*, in some ways, it's really not so different from our industry of 100 years ago. History shows us—and the dot.com debacle is just the latest example—that one of the few constants in our world is change, and unless you keep up with it, you'll be history yourself.

At GM, we think the answer to keeping up with this change—or better, staying ahead of it—lies in innovation. GM built its reputation, and its position at the top of the global auto industry, primarily because of its commitment to innovation—product innovation and business innovation.

In fact, you could argue that Alfred Sloan's greatest contribution to society was his "invention" of modern business management. Under his leadership, GM was a pioneer in market research, retail and dealer franchising, cost accounting, the annual model change, vertical integration, and much more.

But, Sloan's GM built a great track record of product innovation, as well—from the self starter and electric headlights, to safety glass and the fully automatic transmission—technologies we don't even think about today, but which revolutionized the auto industry 50, 60, 70 years ago.

At GM, we're very proud of our innovation history—but, of course, we can't operate in the past. As Thomas Jefferson put it, "The past is a good place to visit, but I wouldn't want to live there."

My point is simply this—it's innovation that got GM where it is today, and it is *continued* innovation that will enable us to succeed in the years to come.

Of course, I should point out that not all of GM's past innovations have come out exactly the way we intended. From the ill-fated copper-cooled engine of the 1920s to the Corvair of the 1960s, from the Rotary Engine of the 1970s to our assembly-line robots that painted *themselves* in the 1980s—we've had a few miscues.

But that's part of the innovation process. We don't stop every time we swing and miss—we regroup, learn from our mistakes, and try again. In fact, my favorite quote from Sloan's famous tome, *My Years with General Motors*, is this: "Each new generation must meet changes—in the automotive market, in the general administration of the enterprise, and in the involvement of the corporation in a changing world. . . . The work of creating goes on." And it does go on. In fact, we've been doing a lot of "creating" at GM, lately—working hard to really turn our company around and get it back on the road to vibrancy and growth. And while we continue to face plenty of challenges, we're also making some good progress—in our quality, our cost competitiveness, our financial results, and most important, in our new products. This is the kind of innovation that Alfred Sloan would have expected of GM—just as he would have expected the kind of progress and innovation that you are driving these days at MIT and the Sloan School.

Long before the days of GM and MIT, the Greek philosopher Heraclitus pointed out that "Change alone is unchanging." As he put it, "You can't step twice into the same river." Of course, his words still ring true today, but that river he talks about—it seems to flow faster all the time.

The rate of change in today's world is extraordinary. At GM we work hard to keep ahead of it. And we want to recognize the organizations that work equally hard to *help* us remain ahead of it.

The Sloan School of Management is a great example of just such an organization; and at GM, we want to recognize the role it plays in preparing business executives who understand and value the need for innovation. I am therefore pleased to announce a gift from GM to the Sloan School of Management, to be used for the creation of a new award to honor excellence in marketing science theory.

The award will be called the "Buck" Weaver Award, in honor of Henry "Buck" Weaver, the first director of Consumer Research at GM—and, we believe, the first in the auto industry—in the 1930s.

Weaver pioneered many market research methods that we take for granted today. He had customers designing their own cars, helped link GM styles with designs outside the auto industry, and—truly radical—helped GM build cars with the features that customers said they actually wanted.

"Buck" Weaver was way ahead of his time—he was "delivering the future" in the 1930s, just as the Sloan School does today. The "Buck" Weaver award will be presented by MIT to an individual who has made significant contributions to marketing science theory and relevance over the course of his or her career. MIT will present the first award next spring.

At GM, we're proud to play a part in ensuring that the Sloan School continues to build on its extraordinary reputation for innovation and the recognition of innovation excellence.

5.2 Consumer Power and the Internet

David Gagnon, Susan Lee,
Fernando Ramirez,
Siva Ravikumar,
Jessica Santiago,
and Telmo Valido, under
the direction of Professor
Glen Urban

Although the Internet has not revolutionized the way consumers shop, it has brought more subtle yet equally important management implications. Among these implications is the marketing influence which consumers and suppliers have as a result of the Internet.

On the consumer side, customers have greater bargaining power through increased access to timely and accurate information about their product of interest. On the supply side, marketing automation technology allows targeted promotion and differential pricing. The two forces are generally opposing. Marketing automation supports push marketing and price discrimination, while customer power prevents manufacturers from practicing push marketing.

This paper explores three industries in depth—travel, new automobiles, and health care. For each industry, we examined the pre- and post-Internet industry structures, looked for changes in customer power, and analyzed the strategic responses by firms. From this, we infer which strategies companies should use to balance the forces between increased customer power and increased automation. On the one extreme is pure trust, or advocacy marketing, which entails full, honest information exchange with customers who are regarded as a community. On the other extreme is pure push marketing, which aims to isolate customers and extract the maximum surplus from each customer.

To understand the historical context of the shift in consumer power and its implications for the science of marketing, we look to Douglas McGregor and his impact on the science of management. As noted in chapter 4, in 1957 McGregor posed a new view of what motivates employees. The traditional view, Theory X, held that employees dislike work, avoid responsibility, and prefer to be told what to do. In contrast, McGregor proposed Theory Y, that employees are creative, willing to exercise self-direction and accept responsibility. Theory Y provided a new view of employees as empowered employees, and it led to innovations such as participatory management. Similarly, Theory Y can be applied to marketing. Theory Y marketing provides a view of empowered customers and leads to trust-based marketing. Under trust-based marketing, consumers are seen as imaginative and capable of making decisions. Rather than using one-sided advertisements to push products, companies following trust-based marketing principles provide unbiased information to consumers that helps the consumers make their own decisions.

One element in which all industries seem to be most equally affected by the Internet is in the expansion of the market structure to accommodate new entrants with a prominent online presence. The automotive industry, for example, has seen a massive proliferation of third-party infomediaries and buying services. These companies place themselves between the consumer and the dealer, providing a wealth of resources for the consumer to access, and often generating sales leads that can then be sold to dealerships. In the travel industry, online travel agencies have emerged to enable the consumer to conduct his or her own research and book travel arrangements. This growth has come largely at the expense of independent travel agents, who now find a customer base that is willing to perform the services traditionally managed by the travel agent. The healthcare industry has given rise to online health "super sites" that aim to provide consumers with access to health information previously accessible only to physicians. While the access to prescription medication is still in the control of licensed physicians, the process to determine which drug is most appropriate for a patient can be influenced by an educated patient. This new consumer power has an indirect effect in the pharmaceutical sales process.

Our research indicates that customer power in this Internet era is largely dictated by three factors: *more options*, *more information*, and *simpler transactions*.

More Options: Does the Internet create new purchase and distribution channels, or is it merely a resource for additional information? Industries that have accommodated the Internet as another option to purchase the product typically provide consumers with a greater degree of power.

More Information: How quickly and easily can consumers obtain timely and valuable information regarding the price, availability, and specifications of available products? The value of this information is enhanced when the consumer has online tools to make direct comparisons between the relevant choices.

Simpler Transactions: Simpler transactions translate into greater consumer power. The Internet empowers customers by facilitating transactions that are easier to evaluate and/or more convenient to execute. Conversely, complicated transactions like those that involve negotiating a final price, customizing an order, or bundling associated products/services tend to mitigate a consumer's power by raising the level of complexity in favor of the retailer.

While we have tried to separate these categories into unique entities, significant overlap often exists, and the three components are highly interdependent. The effect of any one of these components on the total consumer power is a function of the other two components, which becomes obvious in our industry analysis.

The nature of consumer usage varies widely across the three industries we studied in depth. In the automotive industry, the Internet is primarily still a research tool. Over 60 percent of new vehicle shoppers access vehicle information on the Internet before making a purchase, but only about 6 percent employ online purchasing services. In the travel industry, the Internet is a purchase tool that reduces the need for travel agents. Over 35 percent of leisure travelers use the Internet for research and 13 percent of all travel bookings are purchased online. The healthcare industry is more difficult to measure along these dimensions, but over 50 percent of the total active online adult population in the United States are "e-health consumers," meaning that there are approximately 46 million Americans who actively use the Internet to research personal health issues.

Our breakdown of the factors indicating which strategy (push marketing, full trust or partial trust) is most likely to be successful is summarized below in the weights-and-balance scale analogy.

At one extreme is the pure push business model, which involves virtually no trust. In a push-based business model, a company tries to manipulate customers into buying products and services. The goal is to get as many sales as possible, especially sales of high-margin items. Alluring, flashy ads create hype that drives sales—advertising and marketing emphasize form over substance. Fulfillment and after-sale support are minimal and very cost-oriented. Under the push business model, the goal is to get the next sale, rather than the sale after that.

In the middle is a business model based on partial trust. The company's sales strategy is one that honestly tries to match customers to the products offered by that company. Such a company offers extensive and honest information about its own products, although it will not necessarily provide any useful comparisons to competing products. A partially trust-based company has a value-based pricing strategy so that customers know that they are getting what they pay for. Because trust is one element of such a business model, companies in this middle category will have adequate fulfillment and support services that deliver the promised value to the customer (e.g., good quality products, adequate returns processes, and service guarantees). A partially trust-based company worries about customer retention, but may try to retain customers whose needs are no longer met by that company.

A fully trust-based business model seeks to create customers who trust the company to act on their behalf at all times. Sales, marketing, fulfillment, and support all work together to under-promise and over-deliver. In seeking to unconditionally serve and satisfy customers, a fully trust-based business will actually occasionally act against its own short-term interests (e.g., recommending a competitor's product or covering the cost of some extreme level of service). Because a trust-based company tries to build customers for life, these companies strive to create reputations for impeccable honesty. Although a fully trust-based business can lose customers (whose needs or circumstances change), the quality of the experience means that even ex-customers become delegates of that company's marketing department.

The most significant implication of this model is that the full trust strategy requires a more desirable market presence. This strategy is most successful for companies with the best products and an educated consumer base. These factors also tend to be more stable in the long run, which is another advantage of being on this side of the scale. An educated consumer is able to better validate any corporate claims of product performance, and thus one would expect this customer to be more receptive to the notion of an advocacy relationship with the supplier.

Push marketing, however, is successful in that companies are able to respond to information-enabling technology (such as the Internet) more quickly than consumers can. Therefore, companies can use marketing automation tools to capitalize on consumers that are not yet fully informed about the product/service features. These customers, in the absence of specific information, are more likely to emphasize how much of a deal they believe they are being offered. Since the seller often easily manipulates these perceptions of value, push marketing has the potential to be most effective in the short-term aftermath of new technology introduction. Eventually, consumers will gain access to the information they need to make better judgments, and the seller's marketing automation efforts will be offset by consumer knowledge.

Table 5.2.1 summarizes the impact that the Internet has had on the travel, automotive, and healthcare industries, as well as how those industries have reacted to the changes that the Internet has catalyzed.

Air Travel Industry

Industry Structure

Five years ago, 75–80 percent of all travel was booked through agencies. Today, billions of dollars of travel are booked online, which has changed the structure of the industry enormously. The Internet has created a vast repository of information as well as extensive marketing and service opportunities. This has led to the birth of large companies like Orbitz.com, which are now considered by airlines to belong to the same category as American Express.

Jeff Katz, CEO of Orbitz.com, believes that travel is one of the few industries that has truly succeeded in taking advantage of the Internet's resources, and in this particular case, "the Internet has increased consumer's power by 100 percent."

NFO Plog Research's *The 2001 American Traveler Survey* documents the tremendous effect the Internet has had on the trip planning and booking practices of the overall population of travelers between 1999 and 2001. According to the survey, fewer leisure travelers now use travel agents when planning their vacations: 28 percent, down from 33 percent two years ago. During the same period, usage of the Internet has grown by half. Today, 36 percent of leisure travelers use the Internet to gather travel information, up from 24 percent in 1999. Among heavy leisure air travelers (those taking three or more trips a year), 63 percent report using the Internet for research.

Among online air travelers—defined as air travelers who have an e-mail address—the switch is even more dramatic. Ninety-three percent of the online leisure travelers use the Internet as an information source,

Table 5.2.1
Industry Summary Table

Industry	Evidence of customer usage	Change in industry structure and leadership	Evidence of consumer power	Corporate response
Travel	>35% of leisure travelers use the Net for research. Over 50% of all airline tickets are sold via the Internet.	Consumers can research and purchase their travel without an agent, diminishing the role of travel agents.	Airlines discontinued commissions to agents. Over 2,000 brick and mortar travel agents have gone out of business.	Travel agents are trying to reposition themselves as personalized service providers.
Auto	>60% of new car buyers use the Net for research; 6% use Internet buying services.	Prominent emergence of third-party information and selling services. Dealer network still intact.	Online purchase transactions using an Internet buying service save an average of $450 per vehicle over the traditional buying processes —a savings of about 1.2%	Dealers purchase customer leads generated by Internet buying services. Many dealers offer sophisticated Internet buying tools directly.
Health Care	>50% of adults online conduct research via the Internet.	Comprehensive research sites on the Net empower consumers to research their health needs.	Customers select HMOs, research illnesses online, ask doctors for specific products.	Pharmaceutical manufacturers market directly to consumers, encouraging them to ask their physicians about specific products.

up from 57 percent just two years ago. The portion of online business air travelers who consult travel agents has dropped 17 percent since 1999, when 59 percent relied on agents as an information source.

Perhaps the more important question is how the Internet has changed travelers' booking practices. According to the survey, agents continue to see an erosion of market share. Currently, 23 percent of business travelers surveyed typically book through agents, down from 33 percent a year ago. One in ten business travelers now typically book through the Internet, up from 7 percent a year ago. On the other hand, 12 percent of leisure travelers say they typically purchase travel online, up from 9 percent a year ago. The percentage of leisure travelers booking their vacation through an agent dropped from 22 percent a year ago to 18 percent.

Although 87 percent of travel is still booked through traditional travel agents and direct-to-supplier venues, the Internet has enabled a new way of travel planning and has increased the leverage that consumers hold over the traditional travel industry players. As a result, over 2,000 independent travel agents have gone out of business in the past few years.

Evidence of Power

With the Internet, customers have more leverage when making decisions about their travel plans. Figure 5.2.1 shows ways in which the Internet has strengthened consumer power in the travel sector.

Before the Internet, small businesses had to rely on travel agents for their business travel needs, paying a combination of management and transaction fees. If they spent less than $10 million a year on travel, suppliers would not offer them discounted fares. Furthermore, small-sized businesses typically did not have dedicated travel managers to keep track of travel expenses. With the advent of B2B online travel agents that target small and midsize companies—such as GetThere.com, Yatra.net, Delta's MYOBTravel.com, and Continental's RewardOne program—these smaller businesses can now have more control than ever over one of their biggest expenses. The B2B online agencies not only provide standard travel management tools, such as customer profiles and real-time tracking reports, but they also aggregate purchasing power of multiple customers to negotiate deals with suppliers. As competition heats up in this historically underserved B2B

More Options:
- Online travel sites
- Online airline sites
- B2B online travel agents
- Traditional brick and mortar travel agencies

More Information:
- Online price quotes
- Online aggregation of flight details for multiple airlines
- Free online reviews of airlines, hotels, and other travel amenities

Simpler Transactions:
- One-stop shopping for flight, hotel, rental car
- 24-hour convenience for planning/booking
- Instant reservation confirmation

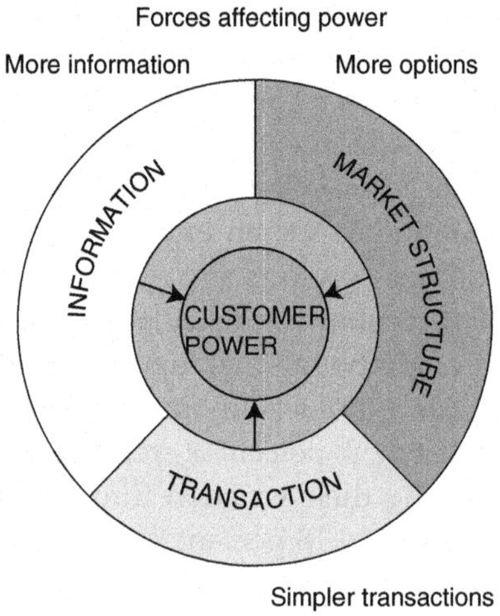

Forces affecting power

More information   More options

INFORMATION

MARKET STRUCTURE

CUSTOMER POWER

TRANSACTION

Simpler transactions

Figure 5.2.1
Forces affecting power in the travel industry.

travel market, suppliers are providing additional incentives for these small businesses to book directly through them. For example, MYOB-Travel customers receive a discount on the first, fifth, and 10th bookings through the site, representing 10 percent, 20 percent, and 30 percent off the published fares, respectively.

For most consumers, a key attraction of the Internet is the ability to save money by bargain shopping. Having price quotes available online allows consumers to price-shop when it comes to travel planning. Travel sites let consumers go beyond the price quotes from a travel agent and instead explore thousands of possible flights almost instantly. What's more, the cost of obtaining information is virtually zero for consumers with Internet access. Finally, the abundance of online information provides consumers with reviews on airlines, hotels, and other travel amenities that they may not have had access to in the past. Tourist information sites provide consumers with destination information on restaurants, sightseeing tours, and tickets to local events.

With the presence of online travel sites, consumers now have the ability to plan their travel any time, day or night. More travel sites are offering one-stop shopping. Through a few clicks, a consumer can do everything from purchasing airline tickets to shopping for concert tickets to renting a car.

Strategic Response by Industry

In response to emerging customer power, some industry players in the travel industry have decided to further empower consumers with a straightforward business model to build trust and loyalty; others have chosen to use the Internet as a tool to target different market segments. Traditional agents are going back to basics.

Southwest Airlines' Internet strategy is apparent throughout its website—direct and simple. No matter what the route is, the website offers nine standard fares (e.g., Refundable, Child, Senior Citizen, Roundtrip Fare Mon–Fri 6 AM–6:59 PM, Discount, etc.). Southwest also lets customers cancel reservations online or apply funds from a previously unused trip to a new purchase. According to Nielsen//NetRatings and Harris Interactive, Southwest Airlines is the top-ranked online travel site for customer satisfaction. The rankings for customer satisfaction include factors such as site ease-of-use, information availability, flight options, pricing, duration of shopping experience, and customer service.

While Southwest is determined to stay independent in their distribution, other airlines have adopted the strategy to push products to consumers via multiple channels.

According to Delta Airlines' CEO Leo Mullin, the Internet has enabled his company to generate incremental revenue by providing different value propositions to different segments of travelers.

• Delta.com designed for very loyal business travelers from larger corporations

• Orbitz.com, financed by American Airlines, Continental Airlines, Delta Airlines, Northwest Airlines, and United Airlines, targets the general leisure segment

• Priceline.com lures the price-conscious travelers

• Site59.com attracts those looking for last-minute deals

• MYOBtravel.com helps small companies take complete control of their business travel

By partnering with these other discount websites, Delta can better manage distressed inventory by selling off unsold seats. Furthermore, with the consumer data harvested through these sites, Delta migrates selected price-conscious travelers to become loyal customers by offering targeted promotions.

In the past, travel agencies were responsible for booking 85 percent or more of the airline tickets purchased, but in the last five years, airlines have drastically cut the commissions they pay to travel agencies. Delta and American Airlines, for example, eliminated travel agent commissions this year. The lack of commissions from airlines has unfortunately forced travel agencies to charge fees for their services.

Despite this negative impact on travel agencies, agencies can offer the advantage of speed—often agents can find in minutes fares that take consumers hours to locate. In addition, the Internet is a valuable tool for travel agents themselves. Agents can access resort, cruise, and tour websites, which provide information that agents can then tailor and pass on to their clients.

Since its debut in March 1996, Travelocity has gone from being the 33,000th largest U.S. travel agency to the sixth largest in terms of gross travel bookings. Travelocity's business model is to provide travelers with choices and control at the best price, but not necessarily the lowest price. "We provide our customers savings in terms of time, as well as money, by offering great choices, deals, 24/7 customer service and convenience, such as FareWatch emails," says Mike Stacey, director of loyalty at Travelocity.

As the leading online travel agency, Travelocity is much more than a website that sells plane tickets. In the wake of airlines' zero-commission policy, Travelocity is diversifying its revenue mix to rely less on transactional air-ticket sales and more on high-margin products like cruises and vacation packages. Although airline tickets remain the biggest segment of Travelocity's business, much of Travelocity's growth has come from other travel needs. According to Stacey, the website experienced a 1,000 percent growth in cruises between February 2001 and February 2002. Having realized that consumers look for more personal interactions when it comes to purchasing complex products like cruise packages, Travelocity recently added call centers in Pennsylvania and Virginia that focus strictly on cruise and vacation sales. Shoppers can now call Travelocity's trained agents seven days a week for information or even to book via the phone. "We are not defining ourselves as an online travel site, but more as a travel agent," says Stacey.

To further reduce reliance on air commission, Travelocity recently agreed to buy Site59.com Inc., a last-minute travel company, for $43 million. Site59.com, named for the 59th minute in an hour, sells

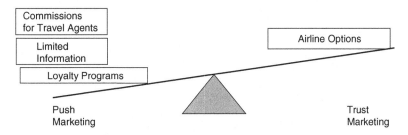

Figure 5.2.2
Balance between push and trust marketing before the Internet.

bundled vacation packages through partnerships with hotels, rental-car companies, and airlines. Acquiring Site59 will enable Travelocity to expand its high-margin merchant business, in which it buys hotel rooms and airline seats on consignment at a discount, and then sells them for profit.

As is evidenced by the diagram in figure 5.2.2, prior to the Internet, the travel industry was dominated by push marketing. The airlines held most of the power and were able to manipulate consumers through the use of loyalty programs, limited information, and by paying travel agents commissions to act as distributors. Although there were multiple airlines, price comparison information between airlines was not easy because it required phoning numerous airlines.

After the Internet (figure 5.2.3), we see that loyalty programs are still an aspect of push marketing, and some websites and travel agencies still choose to highlight certain airlines instead of being unbiased. The bulk of the weight, however, has now shifted to trust marketing. With the Internet, consumers have the luxury of more options, more information, and simpler transactions. In addition, because many airlines have stopped paying commissions to agents, agents can be unbiased when locating low fares for their customers. All of these changes have resulted in the development of an industry in which consumers hold a significant amount of leverage.

Global Power and Responses

Whereas the United States has led the way in moving travel booking onto the Internet, an increasing number of non-U.S. industry players have entered the market as consumer advocates.

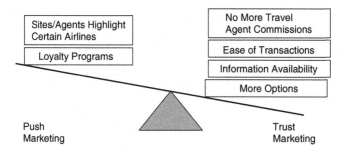

Figure 5.2.3
Balance between push and trust marketing after the Internet.

Europe

According to Jupiter mmxi, the European online travel market generated euro 4.3 billion in 2001. Unlike in the United States, where major online agencies outrank most airline websites in terms of sales, budget supplier websites dominate the online travel market in Europe. However, the same trust-based online strategy seems to be working in both markets.

Since its launch in 2000, ryanair.com has quickly become the largest travel website in Europe. Ninety-one percent of seat sales are sold via the Ryan Air website, while the rest is booked through call centers. The formula for success seems to be its special homepage promotions and its guaranteed lowest Internet fares. Ryanair.com "guarantees all Internet users that the air fares purchased at www.ryanair.com are the lowest available on the Internet."

To stay in the Internet game, nine European airlines launched a web-based travel agency in December 2001. The website, Opodo, targets leisure customers who surf websites looking for bargain fares. Besides airline websites, travel aggregation sites such as Expedia, Travelocity, lastminute.com, and ebookers.com are among the top travel sites in Europe.

Asia

For the most part, Asian consumers use the Internet to gather information, rather than to make purchases. Unlike the United States, where most airlines are fairly homogeneous and most travel is done within the country, travel in Asia is usually outside the country of origin, entailing visa and passport issues that require an agent's personal service. Many are betting, however, that simpler online transactions and price comparisons will encourage more Asians to buy more travel over the Internet. U.S. companies, such as Priceline, are forming joint ventures with Asian conglomerates in order to offer travel in Asia. Also, similar to the U.S.-based Orbitz, Japan Airlines, All Nippon Airways Co., Japan Air System Co., and major U.S. and Asian airlines have launched a Japanese one-stop online travel Web site called Tabini. Similarly, 11 Asian airlines have established agreements to launch Zuji.com for the Asia-Pacific market.

Forecast for Industry

Travel agencies, both big and small, are here to stay. Online and offline boundaries will disappear. Empowered customers will push airlines to simplify their pricing structures.

Delta, American, and Continental airlines have eliminated commissions for most travel agencies in 2002. Following the lead of the airline industry, Hertz Corp. announced elimination of commissions to travel agents handling negotiated corporate and government accounts in the United States and Canada. We believe that travel aggregators will continue to play the important role of consumer advocate, via the Internet or other future technology platforms. Nonetheless, not all agencies will survive. The small online-only agencies will likely face major consolidation. Large agencies will survive because of their negotiation power. For example, travel agencies like Travelocity and Expedia have sealed marketing partnerships with most major airlines to replace the eliminated transactional commission fees. Furthermore, major online players are becoming wholesalers—buying discounted seats and rooms from airlines and hotels, and making money by marking up and bundling extras such as theatre tickets or dinner reservations. Currently, only one-quarter to one-third of Expedia's revenue comes from airline commissions, and Priceline does not rely on commissions at all. Large corporate travel agencies redesigned their businesses to rely on customers to pay transaction fees, rather than relying on commissions from suppliers. According to American Express's 2001 Annual Report, 70 percent of AmEx's travel revenues came from customer fees and only 30 percent came from suppliers.

We predict that small, independent agencies will form a "super agency" to negotiate for incentive commissions. The survivors will be niche and specialized agencies that work closely with popular vacation destinations, such as the Caribbean and Jamaica. These agencies provide value to consumers by offering trusted expert advice (perhaps certified by the destination tourism authority) that is richer than the static information posted on travel websites. To better serve travelers' needs, they will form alliances with local entertainment and tour providers to create customized vacation packages. They will likely charge both suppliers and customers fees to cover the higher expenses.

The boundary between "click" and "brick" will disappear as companies serve different customer segments. Travelocity customers can place orders online or call trained agents by phone for advice. Priceline is considering adding call centers and retail kiosks to its Asian operations to overcome potential online skepticism from Asian consumers. Likewise, "bricks" travel industry veteran Thomas Cook added e-commerce capability to its website and became the fourth most visited travel site in the U.K.

As our data has shown, the Internet has become a critical channel to sell travel products, but it will not be the only channel. We predict that the distinction between online and traditional travel agents will disappear, and companies will use multiple channels to meet consumers' needs in whatever manner is most appropriate.

The Internet empowered travelers by providing them with easier transactions, more information, and more options. Because of the intense competition for travel dollars, consumers can now choose from a variety of ways to buy travel: through a traditional agent, through an aggregator site, or by booking directly with the supplier. As we mentioned, instead of fighting this rising consumer power, travel industry players are embracing it by offering simplified fare structures (Southwest), low-price guarantees (Ryanair), easy and unbiased price comparisons (Orbitz) and convenient transactions (Travelocity). Is this a paradigm shift or simply an aberration? We believe it is a paradigm shift, because companies with a trust-based approach will be the only ones that empowered consumers accept.

The Automotive Industry

Industry Structure

The Internet is having a tremendous impact on consumer behavior in the U.S. automotive industry, which measured 17.4 million vehicles sold in 2001.[1] Although Internet sales account for only about one out

---

1. *Automotive News*, January 7, 2002.

Table 5.2.2
Increases in Internet use in vehicle purchase process

	1998	1999	2000	2001
Percentage of customers who use the Internet for research purposes in the new-vehicle shopping process	25%	40%	54%	62%
Percentage of new vehicles that are sold through an Internet channel	1.1%	2.7%	4.7%	6.0%

Source: JD Power and Associates. An online buyer is defined as a new-vehicle buyer who purchases their vehicle from the same dealer to whom they are referred by an online buying service.

of every twenty new vehicle purchases, more than 60 percent of all new vehicle buyers research their vehicle online before purchase.[2] Those who use the Internet visit 6.8 websites on average and focus on two types of websites—original equipment manufacturer (OEM) sites and the third-party independent sites. Seventy-eight percent say they visit at least one OEM site. Table 5.2.2 shows the increase in Internet use in the vehicle purchase process.

The majority of Internet shoppers first visit a third-party site to compare vehicle specifications, narrow their consideration set to a few models, and then review detailed information for each model at the manufacturer's site. Next, the consumer returns to a third-party site and/or an Internet Buying Service (IBS) to perform detailed comparisons of pricing and financing. At this point, it appears that a majority choose to purchase offline, although inadequate responses from dealers to online inquiries may contribute to this decision. Interviews with dealers confirmed that they perceive Internet consumers to be more informed about features and pricing than non-Internet shoppers. These customers usually have more realistic views of fair pricing, which shortens the time spent selling a vehicle and negotiating a price. One dealer reported that it was not uncommon for a customer to bargain with a computer printout of a competitor's price or some assessment of fair market value.

For those who attempt to buy through an Internet buying service, the Internet has a mixed impact on consumer power. On the one hand, only 12 percent of new-vehicle leads sent to dealers through an online buying service actually result in a sale. Most leads are either not adequately served or are not serious leads.[3] A customer submits

2. JD Power and Associates 2001 New Autoshopper.com Study.
3. JD Power and Associates 2001 Dealer Satisfaction with Online Buying Services Study.

information detailing their vehicle of interest along with other basic personal information (i.e., zip code and contact information). The IBS uses this information to group leads by profile and then distribute them to the dealers awarded exclusive territories or, in some cases, to sell to the dealer who bids highest for that category of lead. In the latter case, rather than being based only on inventory and geography, the inquiry goes to the dealer with the highest interest and presumably greatest capability in servicing that customer profile. This matching process can benefit both the dealer and the customer, because it potentially introduces a greater efficiency to the shopping process for all parties. The dealership saves money on marketing and customer acquisition costs compared to the traditional recruiting process, and the customer saves time in the shopping stages while also having the convenience of beginning the shopping process from home.

The current industry structure is mostly an extension of the pre-Internet structure. The primary difference is that information and resource players, who were once a minor influence, have developed into a major influence in the industry. This is due to the emergence of the Internet as a high-quality source of information for consumers, to which some OEMs and dealers are scrambling to respond.

The first movers into the Internet space were third-party information providers and vehicle purchasing referral services, although the distinction between these two entities has been blurred over the past several years through alliances, acquisitions, and joint marketing agreements.

Although some of the most popular sites are Internet extensions of brick-and-mortar companies like Kbb.com of Kelly's Blue Book or edmunds.com of Edmunds, many of the popular third-party information sites provide services only on the Internet, such as Carpoint.com, AOL Auto, and AutoVantage.com. These companies strive mainly to provide information and impartial recommendations.

Another type of entrant is the Internet Buying Service (IBS), such as Autobytel.com, CarsDirect.com, and AutoNation's etailNetwork. These firms forge marketing relationships with dealers and serve as intermediaries to help consumers reach purchase agreements with dealers in exchange for a commission. The generation and sale of customer leads via the Internet has rapidly developed into a complex, multilevel distribution system. There are agents who sometimes serve as wholesale middlemen aggregating this demand information and selling it to dealerships. The high customer acquisition costs that dealers incur through the traditional marketing process (generally on the order of several hundred dollars per customer) allow great potential for improvement through Internet lead generation. The consumer also benefits, because many of these services offer a combination of no-haggle pricing and convenience.

Another segment of third-party information providers is aggregators such as Automotive Information Center (AIC), which is part of Autobytel Inc., and Autofusion. These companies are more shielded from the public's attention, and their main role is to aggregate vehicle detail content and sell access to other website providers.

Not to be left out of the Internet action, manufacturers and dealerships have made varied levels of effort in their online presence. Most manufacturers have introduced websites that are aimed at providing and collecting information, much like an interactive brochure. FordDirect.com and GM BuyPower connect consumers to their dealer networks with access to inventory, vehicle configuration tools, and current incentives.

Dealer websites vary widely, from being basic online advertisements to having many advanced capabilities such as a virtual showroom, updated inventory status, and online vehicle service scheduling. Inconsistent response by dealers to sales inquiry e-mails from customers demonstrates this variation among dealer websites. One study found that only 42 percent of such inquiries received responses, and less than half of the responses received included all the information requested.[4] In contrast, two dealers we interviewed who are focused on developing online sales have succeeded in attaining significantly larger market share through online sales.

Evidence of Power

Customer power seems to derive from three sources: more purchase options, more valuable and timely information, and the degree of transaction simplicity. That is, car buyers can search among a greater number of dealers, are better informed, and can simplify the negotiation process with no-haggle and online fixed pricing (figure 5.2.4).

Customers can now choose between the traditional buying process and the online process, or some hybrid of the two. In addition, the Internet enables customers to cross-shop among dealers over a larger geographic area and increase the set of competing dealers. Although a relatively low percentage of consumers actually commit to making a

---

4. JD Power and Associates 2001 Dealer E-Mail Responsiveness Study.

More Options:
- Traditional Dealers
- Online Dealers
- Internet Buying Services

More Information:
- Free Access to Specification and Pricing Information
- Online Buying Guides
- Interactive Comparison Tools

Simpler Transactions:
- Online Dealer and IBS Quote Requests
- Online Fixed-price Quotes

Figure 5.2.4
Forces affecting power in the auto industry.

vehicle purchase online, the IBS and Manufacturer Referral Sites (MRS) have nevertheless increased customers' geographic access to dealers. Recent evidence shows that buyers who use the Internet for price quotes typically drive 10 miles farther to purchase a vehicle than those who do not.[5]

The Internet has provided broader and lower-cost access to high levels of information, and usage statistics show that greater numbers of customers are accessing this information. In particular, studies cited that access to detailed information on dealer invoice pricing, online buying guides, extensive comparison tools, and dealer inventories is improving the convenience and quality of information for a great number of consumers. The consensus among the dealers we interviewed is that customers are more informed about what they want, what they are willing to pay, and what their purchasing options are.

The obvious manner in which the Internet has helped simplify the purchase process for customers is the no-haggle, fixed-price offerings by the IBS. Once a customer selects a vehicle, these online services provide a convenient means to complete most of the transaction by computer. Less apparent is the effect of the increased access to data. Many websites provide tools to help manage all the data—from basic vehicle comparison tools to sophisticated interactive decision advisors. Anecdotally, the evidence points toward a shorter purchase process at the dealership for customers who have researched online. That is, dealers report that the transaction process was shorter with well-

---

5. L. Jackson, "Web Influence on Automotive Retailing," HoustonChronicle.com, 2001.

informed customers because they tend to have more knowledge about vehicle specifications and a better understanding of fair pricing.

These changes in the purchase process lead one to expect that if customers have access to more information, lower search costs, and easier access to a larger number of dealers, they are experiencing increased bargaining power in the form lower prices. Indeed, one study comparing prices paid by online purchasers to offline purchasers found that IBS customers are in fact realizing lower purchase prices.

Strategic Response of Participants

Vehicle manufacturers have taken advantage of the Internet effect to cultivate a better relationship with consumers. The Internet has proven to be a powerful point of contact that enables two-way communication with the consumer. One recent initiative, which aims to expand the role of the manufacturer, is Auto Choice Advisor, created by General Motors (GM). This website service provides impartial recommendations from a database of over 300 vehicles, most of which are non-GM products. The consumer enters a variety of preferences for major attributes, and the website applies an algorithm to rank order the "best" vehicles based on the individual preferences. GM hopes this tool will provide meaningful insight into which vehicle attributes customers value most. The success of this website depends largely on how much trust the consumer is willing to place in GM as a source of advice, which GM is attempting to bolster by partnering with trusted sources such as JD Power and AIC.

Manufacturers are also experimenting with Internet sites that support dealer sales operations and connect consumers with local dealerships. However, simultaneous efforts by manufacturers to acquire an ownership stake in some dealership operations has overlapped with these Internet efforts and created confusion and skepticism within the dealer community. Both Ford and General Motors have experienced resistance from their dealer networks in their attempts to strengthen the Internet link from consumer to dealer via the manufacturer website. Some dealers see this as part of a larger strategy by the manufacturers to assume control in the selling process, a power that dealers will not voluntarily surrender.

Once heavily threatened by the potential of the Internet as an alternate purchase channel, the dealer network has responded with its own Internet tools. The response, however, has been slow owing to the federal franchise laws that require all new vehicle sales be made through an authorized dealership, thus reducing the perceived threat from the Internet entrants who cannot sell directly to consumers.

The Internet has presented dealers with an opportunity to redefine their relationship with the consumer. The task is not easy, though, because the industry suffers from a long history of strong distrust between consumers and dealership sales representatives. The most progressive dealers have responded by establishing a customized sales process to cater to Internet-savvy consumers. Since many consumers now walk into a dealership with full knowledge of invoice pricing and vehicle availability, there is higher potential for a trust-based sales process, with more emphasis on matching a customer with their desired vehicle, and less effort on trying to manipulate the customer's opinion.

In terms of the "push versus trust" scale, dealers find they have elements on all three areas of the scale. The fact that there are a substantial number of buyers that focus exclusively on the bottom-line price means that dealers should not abandon the push process with these customers, as there is little chance to make a sale with a full-trust, upfront price disclosure sales approach. Early recognition by sales representatives of which buyers are in this deal-prone segment is important in being able to effectively employ the push strategy without alienating the rest of the customer base that might be more receptive to a trust strategy.

As more customers rely on the Internet for research in the shopping process, the scale clearly tips toward the trust side. The customer armed with Internet information is able to quickly verify dealer claims about invoice pricing, options content, and even regional availability. Thus, the Internet presents a breakthrough opportunity for dealers to change the mindset of many customers in how they perceive the trustworthiness of the dealership. As the role of the Internet continues to expand in the automotive sales industry, the effectiveness of trust-based strategies is expected to increase. Although dealers are caught in the middle between push and trust today, the industry appears to be steadily progressing towards the full-trust model in the long term.

Internet companies, which positioned themselves between consumer and dealer, are beginning to find themselves squeezed from all directions. The Internet space is crowded. Advertising revenue models have proved unsustainable, so many of these online companies are forced to find alternate sources of revenue. This struggle has prompted the beginning of "Super Sites," which aim to provide full-service capability from one source. These services range from information, ratings, recommendations, buying services, financing referrals, and even insurance referrals. The best evidence of this trend is seen in Autobytel Inc., which in 2001 acquired a host of smaller companies such as Autoweb.com, Carsmart.com, Autosite.com, and AIC.

Third-party information providers find they have an advantage over dealers and manufacturers in that consumers trust these independent sites the most, as confirmed in many surveys. However, there is no evidence that consumers are willing to pay for information, especially since they are accustomed to accessing it for free. In order to stay in business, many of these companies rely on sales-lead generation and sale to dealerships. In this regard, these companies face an enormous challenge. They must maintain consumer trust when providing accurate information, convenience, or efficiency in the shopping process. At the same time, they must generate high-quality leads that can be sold to dealerships in order to secure a source of revenue.

Therefore, the Internet companies must expand their services to continue luring customers without compromising the perception of trust. For example, Edmunds.com provides consumers with a TMV (True Market Value) for any major make and model, new or used vehicle. Since most consumers view Edmunds as an unbiased and trustworthy source of information, it is no surprise that Edmunds's website commonly ranks as one of the most useful sites in consumer surveys. A strong brand name, impartial position, and leading-edge features are critical to staying in the Internet domain as a third-party service provider. Ultimately, there are only a small number of companies with these resources, and so the wave of proliferation in websites that occurred in the 1990s is expected to quickly reverse through a period of consolidation, alliances, and failure.

The unflattering stereotype of the pushy car salesman is one that is familiar to anyone who has purchased a vehicle from a dealership. Unfortunately for consumers, it exists for good reason. Before the Internet, dealer sales representatives could be pushy because it paid to do so. Consumers generally had little knowledge of invoice pricing and were unfamiliar with what inventory they could expect the dealer to have. Furthermore, finding out what inventory other dealers had typically meant visiting those dealerships—an inconvenient, time-consuming process. Consumers found themselves relying on the dealership for almost all of the vehicle information, a scenario that rewarded pushy sales tactics (figures 5.2.5–6).

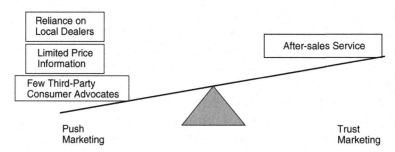

Figure 5.2.5
Balance between push and trust marketing before the Internet.

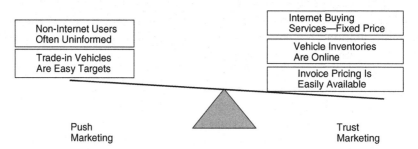

Figure 5.2.6
Balance between push and trust marketing after the Internet.

With the Internet, consumers have as much information as they want, including pricing and even dealer inventory. As a result, educated consumers can walk into a dealership and tell the sales representative exactly what vehicle they want, how much they are willing to pay for it, and where they will go for the next best alternative in the event that negotiations at the first dealership fail. The major factor that keeps the scales from tipping further in the direction of trust-based marketing is that there are still about 40 percent of consumers that do not conduct research on the Internet, and so the dealerships that are quick to identify these consumers are still able to rely on push marketing.

Global Power and Responses

Outside of the United States, the impact of the Internet on automotive shopping has been most prominent in Europe, a market largely similar to the United States. European markets have also seen the emergence of rapidly growing automotive websites that provide research tools for pricing, specifications, options, and availability.[6] This market is experiencing a lag of about one year compared to the United States in terms of percentage of new car shoppers that use the Internet in their search process. This effect is due primarily to the overall lag of Internet adoption in Europe compared to the United States.

One major impact of the Internet in the European market has been on unofficial imports across national borders. Owing in large part to highly variable tax structures in different countries, the prices of automobiles can vary by 30 to 50 percent from one country to another. Britain, the most expensive new-car market in Europe,[7] has seen a surge in vehicles that are imported into the country by individuals purchasing in lower-cost countries such as the Netherlands. More than 5 percent of new car registrations in Britain are now from unofficial import purchases. Figures for Germany, Austria, and France are also on the rise.

The Internet is a major enabler to this import process, giving broad access to pricing and availability in other countries. In fact, importing intermediaries, which operate primarily through a website, are providing shoppers with nearly all the vehicle information as well as transaction logistic details needed to make a purchase. In contrast, dealers in low-price countries are taking a cautious approach to selling cars for export. They have avoided overt promotions of this business, citing contractual arrangements with the manufacturers. However, by law, any EU citizen can freely purchase a car in any EU country. Empowered by pricing and logistical information, British customers are finding it easier to import cars and can even schedule a "Car Cruise" journey for the round-trip journey to select their vehicle.[8]

Forecast for the Industry

Manufacturers have opportunity and ample resources to build powerful, sophisticated Web sites with convenient tools to enhance the shopping and ownership experience. Manufacturers also have the

---

6. Clare Saliba, "European Auto Sites Enjoy Traffic Surge," *E-Commerce Times*, April 25, 2001.

7. Marjorie Miller, *Los Angeles Times*, July 23, 1999.

8. Brandon Mitchener, "Tax Arbitrage: For a Good Deal on a British Car, You'll Need a Boat," *Wall Street Journal*, July 19, 1999.

advantage of strong brand names which consumers are more willing to associate with trust and honesty in information. We expect that the presence and appeal of manufacturer websites will grow steadily in the coming years.

Dealers are currently still on the opposite end of the trust scale, but they benefit from the tremendous potential which the Internet provides in building trust-based sales strategies. Although the learning process has been slow, dealers are beginning to better understand how to segment the customers who will respond favorably to trust-based marketing. While the dealer network as a whole has a long way to go in this regard, the startling success of a few savvy dealers who aggressively use the Internet to reach a wider customer base is an indication of the future. That is, those dealers who have used the Internet to lower costs, like customer acquisition expenses, are able to enhance market share and increase profits even when selling at lower prices. The transparency of successful Internet tactics encourages imitation, and so it is just a matter of time before best practices are common throughout the dealer network.

The outlook for third-party Internet companies and buying services looks difficult assuming that manufacturers and dealers move toward trust-based marketing. Although the Internet information providers are currently rated as the most useful and most trusted sources for the research process, generating revenue while maintaining this image presents a challenge. Charging consumers who are accustomed to free information looks less than promising, and relying on advertising too much could threaten the image of impartiality. The most promising source of revenue for these Internet companies is the sale of customer leads that they can generate through buying services. However, as manufacturers enhance their dealer referral online tools, and dealers expand their ability to generate their own leads, the strategic advantage of third-party sites dwindles rapidly.

The extent to which one considers the Internet to be a paradigm shift in the automotive industry depends on one's initial vision of the Internet. For those that saw the Internet as a new way to purchase cars that would obsolete the existing dealer network in favor of virtual dealers, the Internet has been an aberration. Consumers have shown a preference for "kicking the tires" prior to making a purchase, and dealer franchising laws protecting the traditional process for completing a sales transaction have been upheld.

From the standpoint of reaching customers in the research process, the Internet has indeed created a paradigm shift. The business of marketing to consumers in the automotive industry is undergoing a radical shift in reaction to the increase in consumer power. The ability of customers to aggregate information, compare brands, and shop across dealers of the same brand is increasing in scale and scope. Because early evidence indicates that dealers who respond with "trust-based" marketing are showing success, we believe that they will be positioned best for taking advantage of the Internet to develop customer relationships (table 5.2.3).

The Healthcare Industry

Industry Structure

Pharmaceutical companies face new challenges to their business model with the emergence of Internet infomediaries. Today's business model is not a one-dimensional supply chain, but a supply web with new links in the traditional chain. Internet infomediaries are these new links. Internet infomediaries are Web sites that allow buyers to bypass traditional sales and distribution links. They provide a more direct conduit between pharma companies and patients. This emerging link in the supply chain puts patients in touch with pharma companies in an easier, faster, and cheaper fashion.

Infomediaries such as online pharmacies are more efficient because patients don't have to drive to a drugstore and wait in line to fill prescriptions. The online option is often cheaper because it eliminates several layers of overhead. In addition, infomediaries provide not only products but also information on drugs, doctors, hospitals, counseling, and other services—one stop shopping at its best. Infomediaries are empowering patients to become better informed and more active in managing their own health.

The number of American e-health consumers (i.e., all Internet users that access health information) in the first quarter of 2001 was 45.8 million, 52 percent of the total active online adult population. Internet and e-health users are forecasted to reach 81.6 million in 2006. The growth of e-health and the momentum provided by the empowered healthcare consumer is strong, with a positive outlook for continued growth.

Table 5.2.3
Internet auto industry players

Name of Web site	New car information	New car buying process
Information aggregators		
Kelly Blue Book (KBB.com)	car reviews, car and option pricing, buying advice, interactive decision guide	provides a choice of clickthrough to IBS, MRS, local dealer if available
Cars.com	car reviews, car and option pricing, buying advice	provides a choice of local dealers for requesting price quote
Internet buying services (IBS)		
AutoVantage.com/ AutoNation	car reviews, car and option pricing, buying advice	Provides quote request form for AutoNation etailNetwork
Carpoint.com	car reviews, car and option pricing, buying advice, interactive decision guide	forwards quote request to network dealer
CarsDirect.com	car reviews, car and option pricing, buying advice	provides fixed online quotes
Manufacturer referral sites (MRS)		
Ford.com/ FordDirect.com	car and option pricing, interactive decision guide	provides access to dealer inventories and forwards quote requests to dealers
GMBuyPower.com	third-party comparison reviews, car and option pricing	provides access to dealer inventories and forwards quote requests to dealers
Dealer sites		
DriversSeat.com (NADA)	car reviews, car and option pricing, links to manufacturers	provides choice of local dealers to request price quote, some access to inventory
Autonation.com	car reviews, car and option pricing	access to inventory and quote request

(JD Power 2001 New Autoshopper Study, 1/02)

Historically, pharmaceutical companies have operated in a patent-protected vertical integrated market, where they dominated the whole supply chain from early stage development to manufacturing, marketing, and distribution. Their goal was to educate doctors on the benefits of their drugs and create high incentives for them to prescribe the drugs.

The pressure of Healthcare Management Organizations (HMOs), however, coupled with the development of generics, the increasing demystification of the doctor role, and the increasing flow of information, has made pharma companies shift their focus to the patient. Regulatory changes now permit pharmaceutical companies to advertise directly to consumers, which can create brand awareness and build trust and loyalty. While the upstream value chain remains unaltered, the underlying assumptions of marketing and distribution have changed significantly. Nowadays, patients are much better informed about their diseases, and they ask their doctor about what medicine they want to take. Medical doctors find that "patients now come to the clinic better prepared and able to discuss the issues related to their illness. They ask pertinent questions and they look for second opinions."[9]

The Internet accelerates consumer power because it provides an easy-to-find space for information to flow rapidly and allows new infomediary business models. Websites like WebMD, Yahoo!Health, and AOL Health play the customer advocacy role in the industry to attract new visitors to their networks.

Evidence of Power

Although it is clear that the power of the health consumer is increasing, the potential to change is far from being met. Analysis was performed on three dimensions: more information, more options, and simpler transactions (figure 5.2.7).

About 52 percent of the adult American population has already used the Internet to search health information.[10] A lot of information is available: from drug manufacturer corporate websites, product-specific websites, disease management programs, online pharmacies and

---

9. Interview with Dr. Arnold Epstein—same point of view was provided by Melanie Kittrell and Melissa Moncavage.
10. The Coming Battle for the Hearts and Minds of the *Cyberchondriacs*, Harris Interactive, February 19, 2001.

More Options:
- More Treatment Options (different drugs, different options)
- Increased Rivalry of Generics
- Tiered Co-pays Offered by Insurers

More Information:
- Increase in Direct-to-Consumer Marketing
- Emergence of Online Information
- FDA Regulations Require More Disclosure

Figure 5.2.7
Forces affecting power in the healthcare industry.

PBMs, managed care organizations, federal and state agencies, mass media, and generic portals. Consumers see the Internet as a way to seek information about health for themselves or others and to get a second or third opinion in an anonymous way. According to a Cyber Dialogue Inc. Survey in 2001, two-thirds of adults view the Internet as a potential solution to reduce medical errors.

However, the information is still difficult to find, hard to trust, and hard to use. Irrelevance of information and concerns about trust and privacy are the main problems with health websites today.

Information about drugs is not easy to quantify and, therefore, drugs are difficult to compare. Regulations allow drugs to be compared,[11] as long as companies provide adequate evidence of the claims made. But, this evidence can be very costly,[12] because it often has to be built on drug-to-drug clinical trials. Drug-to-placebo data could not support drug-to-drug comparisons. None of the above-cited players has a tool that compares therapies for a disease or drugs within the same category.

The process of purchasing a drug remains complex because of the number of players involved. Consumers must have prescriptions from their doctors, and HMOs have a say in which medications are reimbursable at which levels.

Nonetheless, these relations might change as more information becomes available and health expenses increase on household budgets. Patients with chronic diseases, like asthma, tend to both know everything about their disease and be more concerned (or otherwise be pressured by HMOs or health insurers) about the cost of therapy. They

---

11. Interview with Melissa Moncavage, FDA.
12. Interview with Ernst Berndt, MIT Sloan.

are therefore more involved in the transaction. Consumers who are subject to chronic diseases, or have relatives who are, show a higher tendency to purchase products online (33 percent) compared to those consumers who have no history of chronic illness themselves or in their families (27 percent). This effect may be caused by a higher price elasticity of demand and higher predictability of the needs from the chronic patients. The use of lifestyle drugs (like diet-related therapies) or the presence of children also increases the tendency to purchase online.

Strategic Response by Industry

Big pharmaceutical companies seem to be trying different approaches to reach the online consumer, running tests on several Internet business models. The different responses made by pharmaceutical companies can be categorized into four groups:

Drug manufacturing companies have built large corporate websites. As well as in other industries, some of these websites broadcast corporate information for investors, industry experts, or job seekers. However, for some of these companies, the corporate website is integrated with e-strategy and works as a marketing tool. These websites offer a variety of services like medical publications, software, etc. For example, Merck offers an interactive version of its well-known "Merck Manual" at its corporate website.[13]

One of the most common Internet approaches is to build product websites for branded drugs. Merck's Vioxx.com and Pfizer's Viagra.com are good examples of proprietary sites that build brand loyalty with consumers. These websites help companies build and support communities around a product or therapy, providing useful technical information both for consumers and healthcare professionals and, sometimes, lifestyle counseling. Product websites are aimed at consumers and at healthcare professionals. The success of these websites is not easy to measure. Little is known about how many visits to Vioxx.com can actually be transformed into a visit to the doctor about arthritis.[14]

Another successful model is the disease education website. Drug manufacturers provide information about diseases on websites, without mentioning their specific therapy or product. The goal of these

---

13. Merck website http://www.merck.com
14. Interview with Melanie Kittrell, Merck.

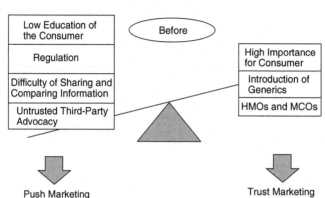

Push marketing was a characteristic of the industry.

Figure 5.2.8
Balance between push and trust marketing before the Internet.

websites is to educate the consumer and increase the number of visits to the doctor about a certain disease. Drug manufacturers expect conversations between doctors and patients about the disease to increase and to be more efficient. Doctors sometimes find that consumers know too much, but they like the fact that information can be easily updated.[15] Merck's thinhair.com or GSK's iBreathe.com are examples of this type of site.

Merck is also providing health services to healthcare professionals—through merckmanual.com and merckmedicus.com—and to patients, through mercksource.com.

The options of trust versus push marketing differ in their approach to the customer. Product websites, for instance, seem to be oriented toward one-time transactions and focus on giving information about the product and educating the consumer on the need to visit the doctor and have a smarter conversation about the disease. Community websites and medical information websites look forward to a longer relationship and try to build trust with the consumer (figures 5.2.8–9).

Pharmaceutical companies have moved to building their brands within the consumers, creating awareness of their products and knowledge about the diseases. This is recognition of the increasing power of the consumers.

---

15. Interview with Dr. Arnold Epstein, Harvard Medical School.

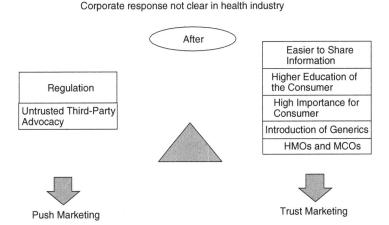

Figure 5.2.9
Balance between push and trust marketing after the Internet.

Global Power and Responses

As Amazon.com allowed books to be sold globally—and thereby par-tially put an end to local monopolies—the same is happening with drugs. Before the Internet, some Americans would travel to Canada to fill their prescriptions in order to save money. Now, with the Internet, the process is even easier and other companies around the world might enter this global business. This poses high threats to some countries' debilitated national healthcare systems and raises ethical issues about monopolistic pricing policies, participation of the government, length and extent of patent protection, and level of competition allowed in these markets.

Another interesting shift towards globalization is the possibility that patients have better access to a second opinion from a doctor and may search for the world expert in the matter.

Forecast for Industry

Regulations play a major role in the healthcare industry. On the one hand, politicians feel the pressure of increasing costs of health care, especially those related to prescription drugs, and they might be com-pelled to foster competition among different companies. Similarly, HMOs and MCOs are working to have generic drugs on the market as soon as patent protection periods end. On the other hand, politicians still have to protect pharmaceutical companies to the extent that they are the source of innovation in the drug development area.

So far, it is not clear which player will be a customer advocate and gain the trust of consumers. The doctors were the source of trust in the past, but the pressure of both pharmaceutical companies on one side and HMOs on the other has recently created some mistrust. It should be noted that in the early days, HMOs presented themselves as the future customer advocates and ended up focusing too much on costs and less on benefits for consumers.

Insurers could be customer advocates for healthcare services. Insurers have incentives to take a long-term view and establish a relationship rather than a mere transaction, which could make them move toward trust. However, insurers will end up paying for variable healthcare costs against the fixed fees paid previously, which will make them hard to trust.

Pharmacies have high interaction with customers and have an incentive to focus more on the relationship than on the transaction. In a business model that takes a fee out of each product sold, pharmacies have to trade off possibly higher revenues today with higher trust and possibly more loyal customers tomorrow.

The Internet is not, as many once believed, a mere diversion for small groups of doctors who are technophiles. Rather, the Internet is widely used by doctors to increase their knowledge. Also, large pharmaceutical companies have realized the importance of the Internet in conveying the right message about a disease and the drugs to cure such diseases. This vehicle is also a key way to reach the doctors who regularly see a large number of patients. Pharmaceutical companies and MCOs have spent billions of dollars to reach these targets through offline channels.

From this study, we feel strongly that healthcare industries as a whole are slowly moving toward trust-based strategies through the Internet as a medium. The industry—which has been very closed in its approach over the centuries, highly regulated, and closely monitored by governments—will not quickly break away from the traditional push-based way of doing things. Pharmaceutical companies protect their revenues through whatever legal channels are possible. They have slowly begun to realize the importance of gaining consumers' confidence, respect, and loyalty not just for their brand products, but also for their company as a whole. Thus, we have seen increased spending by these players in direct-to-consumer marketing online. This spending is still far less than the traditional channels, but we see a slow shift that is critical on a long-term basis. We also see a strong trust-based approach in the online sites for health advocacy groups. Some of the sites are sponsored by large pharmaceuticals, which suggests that on one hand they are pushing their drugs to the consumer and on the other hand they understand the importance of trust creation among the consumer group. Also, we see a strong effort being made by the intermediaries to create neutral sites to help doctors and consumers in making the right choice of drugs.

Although we cannot say the behavior is a paradigm shift at this stage, we predict that in the next five years a strong shift is going to be evident. It may not match the timeframe of other industries like travel or automotive, but it will eventually catch up as more and more healthcare players see their ROI increasing through use of the Internet.

Conclusion

Our research has found evidence across industries of growing consumer power. The Internet makes it easy for customers to learn about products and services, to compare offerings between companies, and to read third-party evaluations of product/service performance. The Internet also provides a new channel for buying products and services, which gives customers more options in buying a given product or service. Finally, the Internet makes transactions simpler, removing the need for haggling or automating them via online auctions.

Companies across industries are responding to the changes brought by the Internet. Leading companies are creating comprehensive websites that not only provide depth of information and enable transactions, but that seek to build ongoing relationships with customers. Although push-based marketing strategies still work in situations where customers are relatively uninformed, we're seeing a shift toward trust-based marketing. The premise of trust-based marketing is an honest sharing of information with the customer—being an advocate of the customer. In some cases, being an advocate of the customer means recommending a competitor product, as we saw in the case of GM's Auto Choice Advisor, which recommends either GM cars or competitor cars based on the each customer's specific needs. Although such marketing strategies seem counterintuitive at first, trust-based businesses can extract themselves from margin-killing price competition by proving to customers that they deliver true value. Trust-oriented businesses have high customer retention and more stable revenue streams. Ultimately, we predict that trust-based businesses will have higher sales volumes and lower marketing costs than push-based businesses.

Our research, and the evidence presented here, suggests two major implications for management education. First, we suggest making trust the focus of basic marketing courses. Second, we recommend that advanced marketing courses provide a deeper view into the trust-based strategies associated with marketing, including trust-based product development, trust-based selling, trust-based pricing, and trust-based advertising and promotion. Each aspect of marketing has a trust-based component, and an emphasis on trust changes the traditional approach to each of these marketing activities.

Acknowledgments

We want to express our appreciation to the managers at the following organizations that were instrumental in our understanding of industry dynamics. Their insightful comments proved helpful during our research process. We would like to thank AMR Corporation; Autobytel, Inc.; AutoNation, Inc.; Aventis Pharmaceuticals Inc.; CVS Corporation; Federal Drug Administration; Ford Motor Company; General Motors Corporation; Harvard Medical School; Herb Chambers Companies; JD Power & Associates, Inc.; Lee Travel; Massachusetts Office of Travel and Tourism; Merck & Co., Inc.; Millennium Pharmaceuticals Inc.; Orbitz; Pfizer, Inc.; Travelocity.com L.P.; and Yatra Corporation.

5.3   Discussion

The marketing panel began with each panelist sharing his or her view of consumer power and how their company is responding to this power.

For example, GM is embarking on trust-based marketing with its new Auto Choice Advisor. **Mr. Vince Barabba**, General Manager, Corporate Strategy and Knowledge Development at General Motors, explained how the Auto Choice Advisor (ACA) works. The ACA is an online trust-based advisor. It is designed for people who are shopping for a new car but who are not sure which makes and models might suit their needs. At the ACA website, potential car buyers answer a few questions, such as how they plan to use the car, what features they want, and how much they are willing to spend. Based on their answers, GM shows them which five car models match their needs best (out of 150 makes and models available from all manufacturers). What is unusual is that GM cars do not show up on the recommended list unless they meet the consumer's criteria.

For GM to offer such an unbiased recommendation service (using impartial data from JD Powers) is surprising to many companies.

Isn't GM possibly sending potential customers to the competition? But offering unbiased information is the heart of trust-based marketing. In addition, by providing trustworthy information, GM hopes to establish a dialogue with customers. Personal communication with customers is an important part of trust, Mr. Barabba said. The ACA establishes a dialogue with customers, a dialogue that complements the market research data which GM gathers.

For example, in the dialogue with consumers, GM learns consumers' true preferences. If GM does not already have cars that meet those preferences, then GM learns about that gap immediately with ACA. Finding out early gives GM the ability to respond to that need. It also gives GM the opportunity to modify an existing vehicle in a way that meets those emerging requirements. As soon as the car is available, GM can make its presence known on the ACA. Thus, consumers find out about the new product very quickly.

For **Mr. Jeff Katz**, CEO of Orbitz, providing unbiased, trustworthy information is imperative. Orbitz is a completely Web-based business and was formed by five competing airline companies (United Airlines, American Airlines, Delta, Continental, and Northwest). Katz shared evidence of the growing power of consumers. He explained that the average travel shopper visits 3–4 websites before making a travel purchase. The amount of travel purchased on the Web in 2005 is projected to be $50 billion, with the industry reaching $25 billion in 2002.

Orbitz, in business since 2000, sold $3 billion in travel and has 1 million customers each month. "If you can offer unbiased information in the delivery of the product, and offer customer care while the consumer consumes the product, you will have a trusting relationship," Katz said. Orbitz offers a customer care program that includes highway information and air systems alerts to customers, warning them of any potential delays or developments that will affect their travel (such as air traffic controller strikes in other countries.) The importance of the customer care dimension is increasing. Orbitz offers not only low fares, but adds a dimension of service that eases some of the hassles of travel. That service differentiates Orbitz from the competition.

Dr. Melanie Kittrell, executive director of eBusiness Strategies and Solutions at Merck & Company, Inc., provided further evidence that demonstrated the growing power of consumers. Some 70–100 million people in America are going online to find health information, she said. "People search for information about treatment options, and that information impacts their decision-making. The appetite for healthcare information is compelling pharmaceutical companies to move online and provide a rich source of information about their products. Many pharmaceutical company sites started as brochureware, but now they are much more interactive. Consumers now get a more personalized experience and receive information that they can use with their doctors."

Merck has created websites targeted to consumers, and it has also created websites for physicians, such as Merck Medicus. The goal is to provide evidence-based information in an advertising-free environment, which builds trust and credibility. As Merck provides this information, it must also be vigilant because pharmaceutical companies operate in a very regulated environment. Providing robust information but respecting the regulations is especially important.

Finally, Merck is moving away from a product-centric approach toward a more customer-centric approach. That is, instead of using the web to inform customers about each of Merck's products, Merck is creating sites that support interaction and dialogue. In this customer-centric view, the goal is to match customers with products, moving away from brochureware toward enriched medical information sites that help people make decisions. Kittrell showed a slide illustrating the move from brochureware to customization to personalization and finally toward the highest level, which is characterized by high trust and high value.

Questions posed by the audience provided a lively discussion among the panelists:

Is trust-based marketing a paradigm shift or an aberration?

Mr. Barabba saw trust as always having been important. Mass advertising created the separation between producer and consumer, but technology is restoring that connection and bringing producers and consumers closer together again. Dr. Kittrell agreed that trust was a paradigm shift that was here to stay, because of the volume of information that is available to consumers now. "The Web makes the information available, and it brings a transparency about the various treatment options that individuals have. Companies can't create mistrust and survive long. The Web is providing a new opportunity to develop more trust in doctors. We went through a period of mistrust of doctors. Now patients look up information on the Web and discover that the information is exactly what the doctor told them. So they feel confident that they have explored all the treatment options."

How can firms that have a reputation for being push-marketers move to trust-based marketing?

Mr. Barabba shared that his company made the move to trust-based marketing because the old way of working wasn't working. "It took soul-searching on the part of management to make sure we had the right products, and then how to let consumers know we had the products that they wanted. Mass communication is not effective because all the car makers are saying the same thing. So you need to find new ways to communicate with customers. We looked at the new trust-based advisor technology and took advantage of it. With the ACA, we act as an intermediary. As an intermediary, you don't promote one car over another—intermediaries have to be unbiased in order to be trustworthy," Mr. Barabba said.

Orbitz also takes a no-bias approach, and that nonbias is written into the bylaws of the organization. "Any change from push marketing (or 'torment marketing') to trust marketing has to start on the inside," Mr. Katz said. "You can't be a schmuck and be trustworthy. Trust has to start on the inside, and the organization has to believe in it."

Dr. Kittrell agreed, "Trust has to flow through the whole chain. In the pharmaceutical industry, customers can't order medicine themselves. They have to talk with their doctors, take their doctor's advice, and feel confident in that, as well as the opinions of the pharmacist, payors, and providers. The way to move from 'push' to 'trust' is to look less at individual products and services. Instead, companies need to take a more customer-centric approach. The goal is to get information tools to the consumer so that the consumer can make a good healthcare decision—not just about the features of a single product, but about their whole needs and how various products fit those needs."

Does using a trust-based strategy mean that your company will have lower margins?

Mr. Barabba said, "No. If you really believe that you will make the right product for the customer and put resources into it, then a trust-based strategy will actually improve your chances of getting higher margins. At GM, we have the phrase, 'a gotta-have product.' That means knowing that the cars meet customer needs. ACA is a tool that can do a better job of matching customer needs to products and identifying those requirements. Perhaps you thought you had what the customer wanted, and then find out that you did not. The ACA technology is a tool that tells you they want something else, and you can respond quickly to that, having a competitive advantage in that faster response."

Dr. Kittrell agreed. "Customer decision-making won't impact margins as much as help match the right products to the right customers. It will identify when products are right for customers. Customers may in fact choose a company's products more often if they have the tools available to help them decide when they need those products."

6   Governance

6.1

Corporate Governance

Stewart C. Myers

I'm proud to represent finance at the Sloan School's 50th anniversary celebration and in this volume. Finance is a *much* more important and sophisticated field than it was 50 years ago. I'm proud because many of the most far-reaching changes in finance during that half-century can be traced back to Sloan faculty and graduates. If you studied finance at Sloan, you had a head start on most of the rest of the world.

This paper[1] focuses on corporate finance, specifically governance and financial management in Europe and China. The hot word today is *governance*, of course, and I know what you're thinking: Why talk about governance in Europe and China, given the mess we seem to face at home?

Two answers to that question. First, we have exceptionally bright and hard-working M.B.A. students at Sloan, but they couldn't tackle the whole world at once. The most notorious examples of unsound finance and governance in the United States had not come to light when the students' projects started up a year ago. Second, when something seems broken at home, it doesn't hurt to seek advice from thoughtful senior executives from other countries. It helps to see ourselves as others see us.

So we invited two distinguished international business leaders, Dr. Rolf Breuer and Dr. Victor Fung, to comment on governance and financial management in the United States and their own countries.

I will introduce this topic with a few extra words on governance and finance in the United States and then note three general lessons to keep in mind in reading the material that follows.

---

1. These remarks by Stewart C. Myers were presented at Sloan's 50th Anniversary Convocation. They have been edited to provide cross-references to other parts of this book.

Why are we now so concerned about the recent state of American corporate finance and governance? The concerns can be traced to revelations of two general types. Either type of revelation would be a disappointment. Taken together, they are much worse.

The first is waste. Hundreds of billions of dollars were lost, especially in the telecom and dot-com meltdowns. I'm not just referring to falling stock prices—of course investors lost when the bubble burst. That was especially painful where retirement savings were at risk. But the $60 billion of market value that disappeared when Enron fell wasn't really lost. It wasn't there in the first place.

For the economy overall, the more important loss is the hundreds of billions of dollars of capital invested in real assets, both tangible and intangible, that are now nearly worthless. The loss also includes the human capital that could have been productive elsewhere, and is now looking for new employment.

The second revelation has to do with ethics. We have seen so many examples of egregious behavior by CEOs, CFOs, accountants, security analysts, investment bankers, and others. We've seen examples of dirty tricks, concealment, manipulation, lying, and top management compensation that amounts to looting.

Although there is no shortage of bad guys, please note that the stock market bubble created the space for the bad guys to operate. Investors must share the blame. They were driven by infectious greed to exploit the irrational exuberance of investors. (Double apologies to Alan Greenspan.)

The bad guys do serve a useful role, however, because they personalize the specific problems that need action now. The bad guys' behavior exemplifies what needs to be fixed. Thanks to them, we will get more transparent accounting, more independent and diligent boards of directors, more credible security analysts. We'll get more effective diversification of pension investments, and top management compensation schemes that are fairer and better aligned with stockholders' interests. We may even get expensing of stock-option grants, which should have been a no-brainer all along.

We'll achieve these things partly through tighter laws and regulations, but largely because investors will demand them. The present value of a reputation for competence and fair dealing has just scored a very healthy capital gain.

Tighter laws and regulations, designed to prevent the bad guys or gals from "doing it next time," are important now for investor confidence. So far these legal and regulatory changes—for example, the Sarbanes-Oxley bill and the New York Stock Exchange's new rules—are on balance positive. (I would say that about 50 percent of the specific changes are positive, 30 to 40 percent nearly harmless, and only a small minority dangerous.)

But it's about time to take a longer view, lest the dangerous changes multiply. We *don't* need new laws and regulations that penalize risk taking or impede the free movement of capital. Forgive me for stating the obvious, but the first task of the financial sector is to move capital to all the companies that can invest at superior risk-adjusted returns.

Some of that capital flows from fresh saving, some flows out of mature companies that exhaust their positive-NPV investments. (At least it *should* flow out of those companies. A financial system that restricts outflows of capital to investors—for example, by prohibiting share repurchases or blocking takeovers in declining industries—is just plain wasteful.)

How does this relate to governance? Again, I state the obvious. Capital flows only if it is protected. It flows through public equity markets only if public investors are protected.

The size of the stock market, relative to GNP, say, is a good rough measure of how effective investor protection is. The United States and other Anglo-Saxon countries score high on this market capitalization-to-GNP ratio, compared to most other developed economies. That may reassure American investors. I admit, however, that a positive year's return from the stock market would be even more reassuring.

You see my first general lesson: the main goal of improving corporate governance is not to catch or deter the bad guys, satisfying as that may be. It is to protect investors so that capital can flow in or out of the right companies at the right times.

I hasten to add that complete protection of investors is *neither feasible nor desirable*. It is not feasible because outside investors cannot know what employees and managers are doing or why they are doing it. One can write a law, regulation, or contract that specifies what a manager can't do, but no team of lawyers can write down what the manager should do. It is not just a problem of divining an uncertain future. We do not know what the future could be, much less what it will be.

Managers must be given discretion to act. Having discretion, they will consider their self-interest as well as investors' interests. The most that investors can do is to monitor and control through intermediaries, such as a board of directors. They can check that managers' and investors' incentives are reasonably congruent, and hope that laws, regulations, and the threat of takeover will keep management on the right track, more or less.

Complete protection for investors is not desirable, even if it were feasible. It would require too much of a power-shift to investors. I like to think of a public corporation as a kind of partnership between its insiders—its employees and managers—and the outside investors who finance the firm. A corporation requires *coinvestment* of human capital and financial capital. If you give the financial capital too much power, the human capital never shows up.

The second general lesson is this: An optimal system of corporate governance would ensure that human and financial capital are deployed with maximum joint efficiency.

The third general lesson is again obvious when you think of it. There is no single optimal system of corporate governance. Governance has to adapt to the nature of the business and to the legal and institutional environment. For example, the financing and governance arrangements that have evolved in U.S. private equity markets would not work in public markets, nor would the public markets' rules work for private equity.

Since we see different governance systems operating inside the United States, it should be no surprise to find that financing and governance have evolved differently elsewhere. When the student teams started their projects a year ago, there was no presumption that Anglo-Saxon finance should be exported to Europe or China. The only presumption was that corporate finance in Europe and China will change. The challenge was to understand how and why. The student reports and the comments of Drs. Breuer and Fung show how these governance systems are likely to change, and identify the most important issues of financial management in Europe, China, and the United States.

6.2 European Corporate Governance: A Changing Landscape?

Giovanni Carriere,
Andrew Cowen,
José Antonio Marco,
Donald Monson,
Federica Pievani, and
Tienko Rasker

This paper focuses on the evolving landscape of European corporate governance. Effective governance supports the stability and efficiency of the corporate sector. Countries with clear, accurate, formal, and widely accepted business practices are more successful in attracting global capital flows and creating economic prosperity. Companies with greater transparency have better access to capital, and thereby obtain a competitive advantage.

There is an ongoing debate on governance in the major industrialized countries. This paper describes where the countries of continental Europe stand in this debate and identifies possible future developments. We do not judge any particular country's governance practices, nor do we advocate changes. We review recent developments, highlighting key issues for the future.

First, we look at the sources and flows of capital that fund companies. We examine three areas: *stock markets, debt financing*, and *venture capital*. We begin with a look at the London stock market, which is more liquid and provides better access to capital than its continental competitors. This does not mean, however, that "Anglo-Saxon" governance practices will—or should—prevail on the continent. Next, we look at debt financing, which plays a crucial role in capital allocation in Europe. European banks often lend on the basis of long-standing relationships and government influence. Banking reform measures are under discussion, but progress on banking reform may be slow. Finally, we examine venture capital. European entrepreneurs face a shortage of seed funding. Relatively few high net-worth individuals in Europe invest in start-ups, preferring safer investments. This is an important issue for Europe, since innovation and growth are often fueled by start-up companies.

Second, we look at corporate governance from the perspective of control, examining the role of *boards, corporate takeovers,* and *institutional investors*. European boards of directors are becoming more influential. The current power of the CEO over nominations and the influence of cross-shareholdings among companies may change. The failure of the European Commission's European Takeover Directive and the prevalence of defenses against hostile takeovers mean that the market for corporate control is not well developed in Europe. Finally, pension reform is increasing the importance of institutional investors in Europe. The professional managers of new funded pension plans will strengthen the role of institutional investors in corporate governance.

Stock Markets

The London Stock Exchange and the London-Continent Connection

The European corporate and investment community considers the U.K.—not the U.S.—as their model for capital markets. The U.S. and the U.K. markets are similar in many respects, including accounting, exchange reporting requirements, corporate structure, and laws surrounding events such as takeover. The U.K.'s membership in the EU, however, and its proximity to the rest of Europe move the U.K. closer to the continent and apart from the U.S., particularly with regard to laws, taxation, the recent move to deregulated/privatized national industries, and dual stock listings.

Although the U.K. is under common law and the continental law is based on Code, the regulations affecting securities create a similar environment. For example, violations of insider trading are subject to criminal—not civil—standards in the U.K. and in continental Europe. Therefore, prosecuting violators of insider trading laws is just as difficult in the U.K. as it is in continental Europe. Unlike in the U.S., corporate officers in the U.K. and Europe face little or no risk of monetary loss for breach of fiduciary duty.

Tax laws in the U.K. and in continental Europe are also similar, particularly regarding corporate compensation and capital gains. For example, in the U.K., taxes equal to 17 percent of the value of a stock option have to be paid upon issuance. While options haven't caught on as much on the continent, similar tax policies exist surrounding them.

Enforcement of governance laws is another shared trait between the U.K. and the continent. In the United States, although exchanges enforce certain requirements, the Securities and Exchange Commission (SEC) is the main watchdog of companies and their officers. In the U.K. and the continent, the exchanges themselves are the main watchdogs.[1]

The Big Bang

Lack of liquidity and access to capital is what historically attracted European companies to dually list their shares domestically and in London. The U.K. had started a privatization move in the 1980s that had enormous implications for capital markets. When the largest companies in a country or region are not publicly traded, the affected capital markets lack liquidity. With reduced liquidity comes less investment and fewer investors, making it more difficult for other companies to access the capital markets. This situation characterized continental markets. In contrast, access to capital markets is a hallmark of the Anglo-Saxon (i.e., U.K. and U.S.) business model.

A 1986 law called the "Big Bang" opened up the London exchanges. The Bang had a massive effect. First, ownership of member firms by foreign companies became permissible. American and continental European investment banks established a beachhead. This development, along with more liberal commission schedules, increased the competition for brokerage business and caused a surge in trading volume.

The increased volume, along with the establishment of the Stock Exchange Automated Quotations (SEAQ) system, enhanced London's capital-drawing powers beyond what anyone anticipated. For example, over 60 percent of all Swedish stocks were traded in London at one point.

London has continued to draw trading volume. Daily trading grew to $24 billion by 2001.[2] Just over $3.3 billion were traded daily at the Deutsche Börse, the next largest continental exchange.

1. This situation might change in the U.K., however, with the establishment of the Financial Services Agency (FSA) in September 2001. The FSA is the result of the combination of all of the governmental agencies with securities industry oversight. It is still too early to gauge the FSA's effectiveness, but increased governmental vigilance in enforcing securities laws may result.
2. London Stock Exchange Historical Statistics.

London is also the world's largest center of equity assets under management. As of 2000, almost \$2.5 trillion was managed from London. New York was second with just under \$2.4 trillion. Paris ranked as the largest European center with less than \$500 billion.[3]

These developments were catalysts for the change of European corporate governance. First, companies who list their shares in London must comply with the U.K. reporting and accounting standards, regardless of the requirements in their home countries. This means quarterly reporting of operating income, balance sheets, and statements of cash flow. Second, dual-listed companies can expect to be plied for data and pushed in new ways by the English and American investment community. Many management teams got their first taste of Anglo-Saxon investment community requirements when they listed in London.

Addressing these requirements was the price of admission for access to the U.S. and U.K. capital pools, access which European companies looking to grow quickly wanted. Continental Europe was almost devoid of large equity pools until very recently. Governments on the continent controlled most of the largest companies and thus the largest pension funds. These pension funds usually invested a minority of their assets in equities. In Italy, for example, the pension laws almost entirely precluded pension investment in equities.

The London Stock Exchange still leads in overall trading, with over \$4.5 trillion of annual volume compared to the Deutsche Börse's \$2.1 trillion.[4] In order to retain volume and compete against larger exchanges, the smaller and regional exchanges have either consolidated or gone public to raise their profile. For example, Paris, Belgium, and Amsterdam merged to form Euronext in the spring of 2000. Euronext had \$1 trillion of annual volume in 2001.[5]

Introduction of the Euro Brings Convergence

The euro's introduction has had major implications for reporting and capital markets. Total European securitization has surged from just under 40 billion euros in 1996 to almost 154 billion euros in 2001. Although the U.K. has historically accounted for the bulk of these issues, the market for new asset-backed and mortgage-backed

3. Thomson Financial, International Target Cities, Report 2000.
4. "The Battle of the Bourses," *Economist*, May 3, 2001.
5. Ibid.

securities is growing robustly in several countries on the continent.[6] Naturally, a larger marketplace around a unified currency attracts capital. Companies have found it much more efficient to issue debt via these larger capital markets than from banks. Companies using the capital markets need to have better public disclosure of operating results and capitalization than companies using bank debt.

Accounting Standards

The European Union has issued a directive for the implementation of International Accounting Standards (IAS) by 2005 by companies in all member countries.

One reason why the IAS was favored over something closer to the U.K. Generally Accepted Accounting Principles (GAAP) is the lack of prescriptive requirements. Both U.K. and U.S. GAAP call for specific treatment of specific issues. IAS allows more flexibility in reporting methods. Investors need to guard against being forced into a false sense of security by companies that claim strict adherence to IAS.

A nonshareholder-friendly version of IAS emerges from tax policy. Most continental European countries do not allow companies to keep two sets of accounting books—one for the government tax authorities and one for the markets. Therefore, in situations where CEOs feel more pressure to pay the least in taxes rather than book the most earnings, the shareholders could lose out.[7]

Summary

Recent developments on the continent suggest an apparent embracing of the Anglo-Saxon model of corporate disclosure and structure of capital markets. However, although there have been many changes—specifically in terms of reporting standards, capital mobility, and the role of outside shareholders—there are still many differences.

For example, the majority of continental countries have a history of universal banks, acting as holders of equity and providers of debt. Many of the largest banks—including Deutschebank, Societé General, BNP Paribas—have purchased U.S. and U.K. investment banks, and they appear to be evolving into more pure investment banks. But

6. *ESF Securitisation Report* (Spring 2002), pp. 1–3.
7. Peter Joos, professor of finance and accounting, MIT Sloan School of Management.

considerable equity ownership of borrowers by continental lenders continues. Given the structure of boards, the state of capital markets, the structure of tax laws, and the training of management, the continental country systems may be the most effective for those countries.

Each country also retains its own standards in almost every facet of capital markets, accounting, and disclosure. Differences can exist even within the newly consolidated exchanges. Euronext came out of a merger between the Paris, Brussels, and Amsterdam stock exchanges. However, French companies listed on Euronext have far weaker reporting standards than their Dutch counterparts. French companies do not have to report quarterly or even semi-annually. In another example, retroactive adjustments to earnings announcements are forbidden in London and Holland, but they are permissible in Germany (even though Germany is leading the move to IAS on the continent).[8]

The relationship between London and the continent has a long and complicated history. All indications are that this relationship will continue to evolve with the nature of financial and operational disclosure and the structure of capital markets in both places. While it is impossible to predict exactly what will happen, all signs point to an increased alignment of systems both within continental Europe and between the U.S., the U.K., and the continent.

The Neuer Markt

Less than ten years ago, access to capital markets in Europe was restricted to well-established companies with real assets and reliable cash flows. The advent of new markets, formed in the image of NASDAQ across Europe, shifted the balance of power and fueled the technology boom of the late 1990s. In Germany, over 300 companies went public on the Neuer Markt between 1997 and 2000, compared to a mere 49 public offerings in the previous three years. The STET developed a platform for young, innovative companies to reach the public market, and many investors quickly realized extraordinary returns on the Neuer Markt during the Internet era.

The "new market" renaissance that started with AIM in London (1995) and Nouveau Marche (1996) in Paris quickly spread across Europe to include, by the end of 1999, the Nuovo Mercato in Milan, Nuevo Mercado in Madrid, SWX New Market in Zurich, NMAX in

---

8. Communication from Damien Horth, European airline analyst, ABN-Amro, London.

Amsterdam, EURO.NM in Brussels, and pan-European EASDAQ. The Neuer Markt, with its pure growth and technology focus, transparent standards, wide analyst coverage, and ability to attract private investors, became the premier European growth market in terms of market capitalization, with about half of the total capitalization of all of Europe's new markets.

The Neuer Markt experienced phenomenal growth in the late 1990s as the technology sector blossomed and a cadre of venture-capital-backed start-ups gained access to the capital markets. High-profile successes like MobilCom and EM.TV triggered widespread enthusiasm for equity investments in Germany. Private and institutional investors scrambled to accumulate shares of new public offerings. The Neuer Markt's early adoption of market regulations in adherence to international standards, coupled with corporate governance guidelines, made it an attractive platform for high-potential companies and international capital.

When the Internet bubble burst, the Neuer Markt suffered a severe market correction and lost 90 percent of its value. Without the cover of inflated returns, high-profile cases of insider trading, regulatory violations, and management negligence contributed to widespread erosion of investor confidence in Neuer Markt companies. Capital markets depend on corporate governance and market regulation to ensure efficiency and liquidity. Neuer Markt companies had to obey regulations in accordance with private law; but with no strong central regulatory body similar to SEC, the Deutsche Börse (a private institution) was left to create, monitor, and enforce market regulations.

One of the forefathers of German venture capitalists, Rolf Dienst of Wellington Partners admitted that lax enforcement of securities regulations contributed to the collapse of investor confidence. Insider trading and lock-up violations tarnished Neuer Markt IPOs. The six-month lock-up regulation, which restricts existing shareholders from selling their equity within six months of the public offering, was frequently broken. Intertainment, Buecher.de, and EM.TV are examples of companies whose founders faced charges for selling large blocks of personal shares, often with insider information, before lock-up periods expired.

The problem of the insider trading and lock-up violations stems from Germany's reliance on a private institution, the Deutsche Börse, to establish and enforce Neuer Markt regulation. In contrast,

NASDAQ establishes listing requirements and market regulations subject to SEC laws and minimum requirements. In Germany, Neuer Markt companies adhere to regulations in accordance with private law.

Ultimately, the Börse announced plans to close the Neuer Markt, but as a European capital market innovation, the Neuer Markt provides some useful lessons.

Regulatory Alignment: The Need for Regulatory Body Consolidation

The NASDAQ has developed into the paragon for growth markets, and its regulatory oversight body, the SEC, deserves much of the credit. The SEC, a U.S. federal agency, serves NASDAQ at all levels—rule formation, monitoring, and enforcement. Thus, the SEC ensures the transparency and credibility of the exchange. One investment banker we interviewed contended that, given the Neuer Markt's youth in comparison with NASDAQ, it regularly explores new territory not wholly contained in its guidelines. Such was the case with early violations of insider trading and loopholes in lock-up period trading. The multiple institution involvement makes Germany's regulatory regime comparatively less responsive and often unprepared to handle emergent violations and ensure market efficiency.

The legal and regulatory framework of the Neuer Markt, like other European growth markets, was subject to a complex market surveillance regime that spanned private and public institutions. In contrast to the regulatory sovereignty of the SEC in the United States, the involvement of multiple institutions in rule formation, monitoring, and enforcement hindered the development of the Neuer Markt as a wholly transparent marketplace for international capital.

Germany has a three-tier supervisory system for monitoring German securities markets. The first layer for regulation is the Deutsche Börse AG, a private organization, which manages the Frankfurt Stock Exchange (FWB). The Deutsche Börse oversaw regulatory adherence on the Neuer Markt, where it set listing requirements, monitored trading regulation compliance, and imposed fines for rule violations. Much of the regulation was established in accordance with private law, legally equivalent to a private contract between a listed company and the Deutsche Börse.

The second layer of supervision came at a state level from public quasi-regulatory bodies, including the FWB, which monitored the various Deutsche Börse market segments, and from the stock trading authority of the Economics Ministry of the state of Hessen, which assumed further responsibility for legal and market supervision.

The third layer, the Federal Supervisory Office for Securities (BAWe),[9] conducted overall surveillance of the German markets with a specific focus on public information disclosure and insider trading violations. Because the Neuer Markt regulation was largely a matter of private law, the role of the BAWe in the case of the Neuer Markt remained opaque.

Market transparency and liquidity are two crucial criteria that determine the success of a stock exchange. The Neuer Markt had ostensibly taken great measures to ensure transparency with stringent regulatory guidelines (RWNM)[10] created in accordance with private law that are augmented with exchange laws and orders (BörsG and BörsO)[11] established by the FWB as well as securities law (WpHG)[12] set at a federal level.

Market Enforcement: Cracking Down on Securities Violations

A structural disconnect between monitoring and enforcement of securities laws in Germany had contributed to insider trading, sloppy reporting, and management negligence, which in poor market conditions exacerbated the Neuer Markt downturn. Until recently, disclosure of insiders' holdings (director's dealings) had not been required. Without one clearly defined body for securities law enforcement, insider trading grew from a couple of isolated cases to an epidemic in late 2000 and 2001.

Once considered a management perk in Germany, insider trading has dealt a severe blow to the perceived transparency of the Neuer Markt in the eyes of international investors. Case in point: EM.TV, an Internet start-up that went public in 1997 on the Neuer Markt, triggered concerns when they lowered 2000 earnings from $250 million to $24 million. EM.TV went on to lose more than 98 percent of its value. State market regulators accused founders Thomas and Florian Haffa of falsifying midyear reports in 2000. Further investigation into Thomas Haffa revealed that he sold $18 million worth of shares within six

---

9. Bundesaufsichtsamt für den Wertpapierhandel (BAWe).
10. Regelwerke Neuer Markt (RWNM).
11. Börsengestz and Börsenordnung (BörsG and BörsO).
12. Wertpapierhandelsgestz (WpHG).

months of EM.TV's November 1999 capital increase, which appears to violate the Deutsche Börse lock-up guidelines. Haffa claimed he received clearance for the transaction from investment bankers and violated no criminal law. Prosecution of such cases in Germany is difficult because it is deemed a matter of private law and not a criminal offence.

The Deutsche Börse can threaten to delist violators and even levy penalties up to 100,000 euros, but ultimately the enforcement must carry criminal charges and as such must involve the Federal Supervisory Office for Securities (BAWe). The BAWe is an understaffed, weak federal office. To act on specific cases, the BAWe needs the cooperation of local authorities to seize documents and conduct an investigation. The result is that many violations fall through bureaucratic cracks and managers go unpunished. In fact, no one has ever gone to jail for insider trading in Germany.

Likewise, crime and punishment were not sufficiently aligned to deter reporting inconsistencies in companies. Until recently, the fine for publishing quarterly data late was 25,000 euros, a small sum for a company wanting to delay bad news on the market.

On May 1, 2002, the German parliament passed a law integrating three federal supervisory bodies—securities (Bundesaufsichtsamt für Weltpapier, BAWe), credit (Bundesaufsichtsämter für das Kreditwesen, BAKred), and insurance (Bundesamt für das Versicherungswesen, BAV)—under one federal financial services supervisory body, the Bundesanstalt für Finanzdienstleistungsaufsicht (BAFin). The final step was to empower BAFin as a powerful government watchdog, which sends insider traders to jail and demands corporate governance guideline adherence.

On September 27, 2002, the German stock market council voted to restructure the German stock market, which will result in the abolition of the Neuer Markt by the end of 2003 at the latest.

Debt Financing

In Europe, where professional investors have long tended to avoid equity as an asset class, debt plays a crucial role in the capital allocation system. Bank managers offering credit to their customers channel scarce capital toward the best investment opportunities. Managers of bond portfolios make decisions guiding Europe's capital to where it can work the hardest. A number of recent incidents have raised serious doubts as to whether European financial institutions have the capabilities, and the desire, to perform these functions effectively.

Europe has too many banks, and banks sometimes issue debt on the basis of standing relationships and under government influence—often at the wrong interest rates to the wrong companies. A spectacular recent example of poor judgment was the failure of the Kirch Gruppe in Bavaria. German banks lent the company billions of euros to make dubious investments in a variety of media ventures, including Formula 1 motor racing. The company declared bankruptcy. Financial experts finally had publicly doubted Kirch's creditworthiness, and there were serious accusations of meddling in some of the bank's decisions by the prime minister of Bavaria, Edmund Stoiber. German banking regulators have subjected the transactions to review. A comparable lack of judgment can be perceived among investors in the fledgling high-yield bond markets in Europe, which are showing large negative returns. Experts comment that too many European debt investors lack due-diligence skills.

The Reform of Banking Regulations: "Basel 2"

Traumatic events, such as the near-collapse of Long-Term Capital Management in September 1998, highlighted the need for reexamination of current frameworks for risk management within the financial system. The international Basel Committee on Banking Supervision launched a review of banks' risk management and capital reserve requirements. It has published a detailed proposal for setting banking capital requirements, known as "Basel 2." Basel 2 will revolutionize the way capital requirements are set, adjusting them to the banks' own measures of the risks they run. The new rules were intended to come into effect everywhere in the EU in 2004 and to replace Basel 1, which has been in place since 1988. Progress on finalizing the proposals has been slow. At this time, commentators predict that the proposals will not come into effect before 2006.

The intention of Basel 2 has been to stimulate banks to put in place more sophisticated schemes for risk assessment by offering a reward in the form of reduced capital requirements. However, the rules must not give advanced banks too great a competitive advantage over less sophisticated, perhaps smaller, competitors, or else they will be perceived as unfair. Getting the balance right has been a serious challenge and has delayed the finalization of proposals.

Apart from the emphasis on improved internal risk management by banks, another novel aspect of the Basel 2 proposal is the intended use of market discipline—rather than regulatory supervision—as a means of enforcing good practice. As the Basel committee writes, "The new framework aims to bolster market discipline through enhanced disclosure by banks. Effective disclosure is essential to ensure that market participants can better understand banks' risk profiles and the adequacy of their capital positions."[13]

Basel 2's focus on promoting good risk management through lower capital requirements and enhanced disclosure is designed to improve the economic rationality of banks. So far, it seems to have been reasonably successful. The *Economist* comments: "There is no doubt that the Basel 2 exercise has heightened awareness of risk among banks. It has prompted them to overhaul their credit-scoring methods and to tighten up their operations."[14]

The Banks

Current lending practices in Europe have raised eyebrows. "Risk is underpriced," comments a London fund manager. "In a smaller German bank, a manager could get fired if he loses business from a company like DaimlerChrysler, even if the rate he has to offer is unattractive." In some countries, relationships between the banks and their clients have become so close that, rather than providing critical supervision, the financial institution starts to "go native." In Germany, long-term bank lending to large corporations is a crucial part of the funding system. Banks gradually grow together with their corporate clients. The proposed Basel 2 arrangements give incentives to promote short-term rather than long-term lending. It is not surprising that Germany has lobbied for the removal of these incentives.

Political pressure to help certain companies, for example when job losses threaten, is another major source of bad credit decisions. This behavior is not financially irrational: a bank with strong backing from its government need not worry as much about possible losses because the government can bail it out. A common example of banks enjoying government backing, and acting accordingly, are the publicly owned German Landesbanken, which are backed by explicit state

---

13. Secretariat of the Basel Committee on Banking Supervision, "The New Basel Capital Accord: an Explanatory Note," Bank for International Settlements, 2001.
14. "The Good Tailors of Basel," *Economist*, February 21, 2002.

guarantees. Several of these banks were involved in the Kirch Gruppe debacle. The Bayerische Landesbank—50 percent owned by the Bavarian state government—injected more than 1 billion euros into Kirch in 2001. This funding decision was probably made by the bank, even if it was good politics for the Bavarian prime minister. The general perception is that the bank was routinely used to provide capital to companies favored by the government as part of Bavarian economic policy.

In 1999, competing European banks launched a formal complaint about the unfair advantage the German regional banks have in raising cheap funds. A deal has now been struck between the European Commission and the German government. The deal will lead to a dismantling of the guarantee system starting in 2005. Of course, the dismantling of state-backed banks also has disadvantages. A very large share of small-company lending in Germany comes from public-sector savings banks. It is feared that tighter credit controls will inevitably lead to decreased access to credit and higher interest rates for some. There may well be a significant number of bankruptcies and a wave of restructuring. This is the pain caused by the financial discipline being forced through the system. Regarding Basel 2, German chancellor Gerhard Schroeder said that only an accord that is friendly to small companies (the "Mittelstand") will win Germany's approval. Very tight Basel 2 rules on lending to small and medium-sized companies have already been relaxed through a variety of adjustments.

The Markets

The attempt to introduce greater market discipline on banks through better risk disclosure may lead to a more efficient economy in the long run. Whether the European markets are currently sophisticated enough to impose that discipline, however, is not known. For instance, in recent years the junk bond market in Europe has seen significant increases in liquidity. But early experiences suggest that investors have not done a very good job of valuing these securities. Average investor returns in some classes of high-yield debt have been negative in the double digits. A trader comments: "Of course everyone was suffering from irrational exuberance the last few years, but it is certainly fair to say that some European investors in high-yield securities have lacked the necessary due-diligence skills." Another trader mentioned: "Within half an hour of putting an issue, we get calls from buyers, without even looking at the prospectus. They just go by the credit rating and are not able to do any due diligence themselves."

It is ironic that European investors are ill-equipped to handle high-yield debt. Some believe that here lies the solution for some of the German Mittelstand. As one trader put it, "Corporate Europe is not yet issuing junk, even though this is the source of capital for middle America. Family businesses can use junk to raise capital without losing control." The negative returns on high-yield debt have scared many of the investors who were pioneering this market, and it will take time before they return.

Conclusion

In Europe, regulators wishing to reform the financial system are fighting a tradition of government interventionism and relationship-based banking. It is perhaps reasonable to expect reform in Europe to take substantially more time than it did in the United States following the savings and loan crisis.

Venture Capital

An important aspect to corporate finance is early-stage venture funding. Although the amounts of capital transacted are relatively small, the economic importance of funding start-ups is enormous. These new enterprises keep the economy young and create jobs. Over the last decades, the importance of early-stage financing has become widely accepted and the European business community—often with government support—has taken active steps toward creating a venture capital industry which can provide funding to small private companies, filling the so-called "equity gap." There is now a sense in most European countries that the availability of venture capital funding is adequate. This has highlighted two other weaknesses of European venture funding.

The Shortage of Seed Funding in Europe

It is often said that the hardest round of funding to get for a new company is the very first seed capital injection, which allows the business to grow from an idea into a proper business proposal. Would-be entrepreneurs, who are excited about setting up a new business, need to convince a family member, a friend, or a colleague to give them a small amount of money so they can quit their job, plan the new business, and assemble a founding team. A recent study by the Global Entrepreneurship Monitor (GEM)[15] consortium—a large international consortium of academics collecting data on entrepreneurial activity in different countries for comparison—suggests that this kind of informal investment is a major engine of the economy. In the 29 countries included in the survey, informal investment made up as much as 1.1 percent of total GDP. This kind of informal funding normally exceeds funding from professional venture capitalists by a large margin.

Professional venture capitalists in Europe are selective investors. They will only invest in a business which has outstanding growth potential. Although they are willing to endure substantial risk, they will usually not consider a venture until its products are fully developed and the first customers have been won. The funding provided by informal investors in the very early stages of a company's development is therefore a key first step in the process of business creation.

It seems as if European entrepreneurs should have no trouble finding an informal "angel" investor to back their plans. A recent study published by Merrill Lynch and Cap Gemini Ernst & Young[16] says that in 2000 there were 2.3 million high net worth individuals (HNWI) in Europe. Together, they held assets of $7.2 trillion, no less than 27 percent of all wealth held by HNWIs worldwide. This puts Europe only slightly behind the United States. Although one would think that a large chunk of this private capital is invested in would-be entrepreneurs, this does not appear to be the case. The European HNWI prefers conservative investments. Aggressive investment strategies such as private equity, venture capital, and hedge fund investments are left to the Americans, who invest roughly six times as much in these types of assets. The GEM report concluded that there is no mature business-angel culture in Germany. Across Europe, the pattern seems to be the same: the GEM study indicates that in most European countries, informal investors are far fewer in number than in the countries of the new world, namely New Zealand, Canada, the United States, and Australia. According to the GEM study, it was New Zealand that had the most

---

15. P. Reynolds, S. Camp, W. Bygrave, E. Autio, and M. Hay (2001), "Global Entrepeneurship Monitor—2001 Executive Report," available at www.gemconsortium.org
16. Merrill Lynch/Cap Gemini Ernst & Young (2001), "World Wealth Report 2001," www.cgey.com, www.ml.com

angel investors in 2000, just over 6 percent of all adults, whereas the highest European country came in at less than 4 percent.

Recognizing the problem, European governments have sought to intervene through creative funding schemes. The U.K. government, for instance, created the University Challenge Fund, which allowed universities to compete for money to set up university seed funds. The initiative proved popular with the universities, and there are now dozens of university seed funds. However, the funds are rather small. In total, about £60 million was made available in the first round, with minor top-ups in later rounds. Total informal investment in the U.K. comes to many billions of pounds. Furthermore, the university funds can only invest up to £250,000 per deal, a very small amount for someone wanting to set up a laboratory. Therefore the initiative, though useful, can scarcely be considered a full solution to the problem.

Another very interesting attempt was made in the Netherlands. The Netherlands government created a government-backed incubator, Twinning, which aims to make funds available to entrepreneurs in the information and communications technology sector. Twinning not only offers seed funding, but it also makes available office facilities, provides counseling, and even participates in the first round of venture capital investment, though not as the lead investor. As part of its service, Twinning maintains intimate relationships with local venture capitalists, and Twinning also maintains a presence in Silicon Valley to allow their ventures to make the leap to the U.S. market. There has been serious concern that the Twinning is going the same way as the plethora of commercial incubators that rose with the Internet bubble and have now mostly disappeared. Recently, Twinning had to close one of its offices because they were simply unable to generate enough quality deals. Attempts by the Dutch government to privatize the unit have not been successful. In the current market, the model does not appear to be sustainable without continued government support.

Perhaps a more promising way in which governments are trying to stimulate seed investment is through tax relief. In the U.K., the Enterprise Investment Scheme gives HNWIs an attractive package of tax breaks if they invest directly in unquoted companies. Notably, the scheme gives the investor an exemption from the capital gains tax. However, the scheme can only be used for small investments, up to £150,000. Furthermore, the company has to trade in the U.K. This makes it difficult to use the scheme to finance technology companies, which want to trade internationally.

One weakness with all these attempts is that, arguably, government schemes are no substitute for a healthy angel investment climate. The best angel investor is an experienced entrepreneur who knows how to put together a solid business, with the right foundations for later growth. Tax breaks may make the affluent more interested in investing in start-ups, but it will not make them more skillful at guiding a start-up through the early stages. As one veteran Bavarian angel investor remarked, "There have always been angel investors in Germany, but they invest in a person, not a business. Though lately things have become more professional."

It is rare for a business to get venture capital funding. According to GEM, fewer than 20,000 businesses received venture capital world-wide in 2000, while more than 150 million persons were involved in start-ups or new ventures. If the corporate structure put in place in a company in the seed stage is not sound, the company will struggle to attract venture capital later. Venture-capital-backed companies are a mayor source of wealth creation in the United States. A study by Wharton Econometric Forecasting Associates, supported by the National Venture Capital Association, concluded that in the United States, venture-capital-backed companies accounted for 3.3 percent of all jobs and 7.4 percent of GDP in 2000.

The Difficulties with Going Public in Europe

Suppose the hopeful European entrepreneur manages to secure seed capital, and suppose that he also manages to attract venture capital. He will now want to grow his business quickly. In Europe, that means that relatively soon he will have to start operating internationally. As the business grows, he will usually require ever-increasing amounts of capital, especially if he is to expand internationally aggressively, as he must. Where should this capital come from?

In the first instance, the company will go back to its original venture capital investors, who will provide additional capital and try to put the firm in touch with other venture capitalists who can join the backing syndicate. European venture capitalists quickly run out of steam, however. Few European venture capital houses can invest more than 10–20 million euros in any one company. In the United States, it is not unusual for a venture to attract funding of well over 100 million euros. To raise that much, European venture capitalists would have to invest in large syndicates, but complications increase rapidly with the numbers of different parties involved. There are few venture capital houses in Europe that can supply that much money out of their own pocket, and often these are large private equity funds that do start-ups on the side. A recent study by KPMG[17] highlighted the fact that European Private Equity houses do relatively poorly when it comes to managerial support of their portfolio companies. Although many funds are addressing this need by hiring more staff with industry experience, they often lack the skills internally to react quickly to operational crises.

What else can a start-up needing a significant amount of growth capital do? One solution is to go public earlier. Recent years have seen the creation of a number of stock markets, including the Neuer Markt, NASDAQ Europe, and others, which will allow very new business to list their stock and gain access to the capital markets. However, a stock market listing constitutes a significant overhead for a company. The CFO of Morfosys, Germany's largest biotech start-up, told us: "The rules for [a public company] in Germany are a straightjacket." Regulations include the requirement to offer first refusal to current shareholders for major share offerings, which makes the process of raising capital that much more complicated. The rules also ban offering shares at a major discount to the market price, as is typically required for a PIPE, a process for selling publicly traded shares through private placement. One of the most frustrating rules is the requirement to hold a general shareholders meeting for almost every major decision. "Last year, we had to send 80,000 invitations to shareholders for the shareholder meeting. It cost us about DM 0.5 million. We hosted 700 guests. The rules disallowed us activities in the capital markets for months at the time of the meeting."

The raft of clumsy rules and regulations form a real problem: "The rules put you at a disadvantage with respect to your competitors." The CFO of Morfosys commented, "If I had to incorporate again, I would incorporate in the Netherlands." However, rules in the Netherlands are far from ideal. One Dutch venture capitalist told us that, although the law in the Netherlands is better than in most European countries, and many are deciding to incorporate there, the Dutch authorities are slow. "It takes months to create a Dutch corporation, especially if one of the founders is not Dutch. . . . In Delaware the process is much faster." The European venture, as it grows, will have to deal with more of these

---

17. KPMG, Manchester Business School (2002), "Insight into Portfolio Management—Private Equity Research Programme," www.kpmg.co.uk

kinds of complications earlier in its growth than its U.S. competitors. Will it be able to work with these regulations and beat more nimble U.S. competitors? Maybe, maybe not. In contrast to the problems with seed funding, these problems are not yet the topic of much public debate. Politicians give them little attention.

Conclusions

The financial infrastructure in Europe for supporting early-stage ventures is far from ideal. Start-ups face serious challenges when setting up and gaining seed funding. They face serious challenges again in the later stages, when they need large amounts of capital. Governments have tried to help the situation, but there have been few successes. It is hard to see what can be done about a perceived lack of skilled angel investors. A gradual cultural change may be required. Regarding the troubles European ventures have in the later stages, regulators should cut red-tape and streamline processes that are obstructive. Unfortunately, these issues are not widely debated, and there is little momentum behind the movement for change.

Boards of Directors

Within the different countries of Europe, companies' boards have special rules and structures which are hard for foreign investors to understand. A common perception is that directors are not always selected on the basis of how much value they can add to the company. Often, directors of listed European companies are not "independent." Individuals sitting on the board of large corporations routinely find themselves at the center of complicated webs of personal relationships and pressure groups that end up conditioning their behavior. Shareholder interests, especially minority shareholder interests, are not necessarily the first priority when making decisions.

Companies should have knowledgeable, well-informed, powerful boards because good boards create value for the company, the shareholders, the workers and, ultimately, for countries.

As is the case in all areas of the world, Europe does not lack examples of bad corporate governance. For example, a recent *Economist* article on French business[18] reported: "French bosses are particularly

18. *Economist*, March 21, 2002.

cozy with each other. . . . There is the tendency for top managers to sit on each other's boards. Mr. Messier [CEO Vivendi] sits on Mr. Arnault's [chairman LVMH], and Mr. Arnault sits on Mr. Messier's. The Vivendi boss sits on Alcatel's board, while Mr. Tchuruk [CEO Alcatel] is a director of Vivendi and three other big firms." Given these cross-relationships, there are strong possibilities that personal relationships could win out over the best interests of shareholders.

Germany provides another example. Each company has two boards: supervisory and management. An important quota of the seats (between 33 and 50 percent) on the supervisory board is reserved for workers.[19] The supervisory board can appoint and fire the members of the management board. There is no formal need to have a CEO: the chairman of the management board can be a strong leader. Often, however, the chairman is a mere spokesman. Value creation is, in the words of the chairman of a German company we interviewed in January 2002, "an academic goal" in such a complex environment. Shareholders who want to protect their interests cannot rely on independent board members to focus on value creation. Instead, they have to hold significant stakes. The phenomenon of "block sharehold-ing" is much more common in Germany than in the Anglo-American economies.[20]

More cases can be found in Italy and Spain. In Spain, recent research revealed that 50 percent of all listed banks of Ibex-30 do not comply with some or all of the provisions of the code of Good Corporate Governance (Codigo Olivencia) relating to boards' compensation. Banks do not frequently disclose the compensation of their directors, and they often fail to highlight the link between pay and perfor-mance. In the first months of 2002, a group of directors of BBVA (Spain's second largest bank) were found guilty of holding secret personal accounts in tax havens. The accounts were used to embezzle company funds.

Why Are Boards Relevant to Corporate Governance?

Boards are critical when a company seeks access to capital markets. Boards guarantee the protection of minority shareholders by supervis-

---

19. In companies with more than 500 employees. This practice is called "codetermination."
20. Gary Gorton and Frank Schmid, "Universal Banking and the Performance of German Firms," *Journal of Financial Economics*, 2000, 86–114.

ing management and ensuring they do not fall into the temptations generated by the principal-agent problem.

There are many studies that prove that boards matter to public shareholders.[21] At an academic level, it has been proven that investors are willing to pay a premium to own shares of companies run according to sound corporate governance principles. Having a good board is one of these sound governance principles. Furthermore, common sense tells us that the small investor giving his money to the managers of a corporation will sleep better at night if the managers have supervisors who make sure the money is put to good use. For this reason, it is worthwhile to worry about the effectiveness of the boards in Europe and their potential for improvement.

In our research, we performed a review of the economic literature to identify principles of practical relevance to identify what constitutes a "good board." Boards have been the object of extensive analysis in both the economic literature and the managerial literature. Although many questions remain unresolved, the studies point to some generally accepted principles with which boards should comply:

• Smaller boards will be more effective and create more value than boards with a large number of board members.

• Boards must be independent and members should be adequately compensated to create value.

• Practices of electing directors from lists prepared by the management have to be restrained.

• Boards have to include younger, active people, with time to spend in understanding the companies and their industries. Effective boards must be truly independent.

The results of our research show that true independence goes beyond what is usually required in most European governance codes.

Are European Boards Changing?

Despite some problems with continental European boards, one cannot say that the German two-tier system has proven ineffective or that the United Kingdom model has prevailed. No research has given obvious results on the greater "effectiveness" of either system. What is obvious,

---

21. Edward E. Lawler III, David Finegold, George Benson, and Jay Conger, "Adding Value in the Boardroom," *MIT Sloan Management Review*, Winter 2001, 15–23.

however, is that investors have started to put a great deal of emphasis on scrutinizing the corporate governance practices of companies and on the composition of the groups of people that represent their interests.

As a result, in the last two years, every European country seems to have issued some sort of Corporate Governance Code. In addition, in the last few months, the pace of change has accelerated. Deutsche Bank is undergoing one of the most important transformations of its history, shrinking the "management board" and creating an "executive group." BBVA has reduced the size of its board from 32 to 21 members, eliminating people with little experience in banking. A number of academic research institutions with a focus on corporate governance have been founded or revived in the last year. And Deminor Rating, a Belgian consultancy, created a website where investors can join a drive against the management and boards of European companies supposedly violating good corporate governance principles.

Stepping back from the daily flurry of news and opinions, we can see the big picture: the nature of boards in Europe is changing. In our research, we have found that changes across different countries and industries exhibit at least three patterns:

1. *European CEOs are acquiring more power in their boards.* There seems to be a shift to a more "American" style and status. Individuals are making an international name for themselves by rejecting the stuffiness of old-style business, prioritizing value creation, and speaking openly about it in and outside board meetings. CEOs like Jean Marie Messier, Francois Pinault (CEO Pinault Printemps-Redoute), Josef Ackerman (CEO Deutsche bank), and many more are reshaping the landscape of European boards and European capitalism in general.

2. *Boards are becoming more independent.* Among the most notable examples: In Germany, the private sector adopted two codes on Corporate Governance in 2001. One of the codes, adopted by a panel led by a former influential managing director of DSW (the asset management unit of Deutsche Bank), recommends that each board have a *sufficient number* of independent directors on the supervisory boards[22] and that boards have at least six board committees. In France, the National Assembly and the Senate are rumored to be close to approving a bill that would separate the solitary post of président directeur général

---

22. In Germany, retired members of the management boards usually move up to the supervisory board.

(equivalent to the chairman and CEO position) into two posts, unless shareholders explicitly vote for a different solution. In the U.K. in March 2000, the Department of Trade and Industry issued a *Report on Company Law Reform* with many recommendations aimed at strengthening the independence of the board and the chairman. In Italy, a new segment of the stock market, called "Star," was created. Companies that want to be listed in Star must comply with a set of guidelines, most of which relate to matters of board independence.

3. *Boards are becoming more "accountable."* The rise of an "equity culture" across continental Europe has led to an increase in shareholder activism. Shareholders, both individuals and institutions, are becoming able to bypass boards and voice their own interest. Board members are being called on more often to give reasons why they approved transactions that negatively affect minority shareholders. In 2001, minority shareholders: blocked the takeover of Legrand by Schneider Electric because it did not respect some preference rights attached to their shares; sued Deutsche Telekom because it wrote off some assets, implying that some of its acquisitions had been grossly overpaid; and blocked the board and management of Telecom Italia from converting all saving shares into ordinary shares at an unfair price.

Institutional owners cannot sell their shares without depressing market prices; and they prefer to increase their returns by fighting with management and replacing board members with their representatives. Financiers like the Swiss Martin Ebner and the American Wyser-Pratte spend their time looking for underpriced companies, buying minority stakes, vying for board seats, and fighting current board members and management. Board members can no longer sleep through presentations and cash their attendance check at the end. They are being called on for involvement.

Summary: Three Issues to Address

First, in our research and interviews, we found that CEOs in Europe are still the ones who choose the candidates to directorships that are presented to shareholders.

Second, CEOs and chairmen are the same person in most European corporations in many countries. If we add this feature and the fact that star European CEOs have become more vocal, we get situations close to "one-man corporations," which are often detrimental to shareholders.

Third, the main problem seems to be that European boards belong to a restricted "elite," defined by personal relationships and a web of cross-shareholdings among the major companies. Most students of European corporations would find it easy to identify who the most influential people are. The cadre of names from which to choose appears small. Also, changes in legislation can help eliminate the most obvious conflicts of interest As long as public European corporations are run by a lucky minority, the debate on independence will be largely moot. Instead, the debate should be about how new firms in Europe are created and how true meritocracy can be introduced across the business world.

Corporate Takeovers

There is increasing pressure on European managers to maximize shareholder value. This comes from three major sources.[23]

1. *Intense pressure from international capital markets to generate sustainable, above-average returns.* Growth and globalization have increased the demand and supply of equity worldwide. The shift to a savings culture based on equity, the change in demographics, and the increase in the volume managed by institutional investors (especially pension funds) have significantly increased the potential supply of funds to capital markets. On the demand side, an increase in the number of public companies (around 30 percent during the last decade) means more opportunities for investment. Furthermore, the intense pressure for high returns has increased trading volume (a 130 percent increase during the last decade). This higher trading volume, whether caused by an increase in the number of public stocks or by a decrease in the length of time of stock holding, shows that companies are more exposed to investor scrutiny. Private companies that went public are now compared against the stock market performance of their competitors. Investors looking for returns can get in and out of stocks easily.

2. *Activism and professionalism of shareholders; institutional investor ownership.* During the last decade, institutional investor ownership has increased significantly in Europe. Institutional investors focus on maximizing value because, unlike banks, they do not have conflicting incentives. While pension funds focus on generating future cash

---

23. M. Salter, "A Note on Governance and Corporate Control," Harvard Business School Working Paper no. 01-090, 2001.

flows to pay pensions, banks also consider the credit business they maintain with companies. CEOs consider institutional investors to be the most important investor class because institutional investors can significantly influence the market value of the firm.

3. *The winner-takes-all economy.* Hyper-mobile pools of capital search for firms with best practice in governance rules and super-normal returns. Today's winner-takes-all capital market signals a new era. Across sectors, a few players are creating most of the new shareholder value. A McKinsey study[24] highlights that 5 to 10 per cent of companies in a given industry create all of the shareholder value in that industry. Given these facts, investors are trading in and out of firms in continuous search of super-normal returns. In fact, McKinsey and Institutional Investor research[25] show that institutional investors would be willing to pay an 18 percent premium for the shares of a well-governed company[26] in the United States or the United Kingdom and a 20 percent and 22 percent premium for the shares of well-governed companies in Germany and Italy, respectively.

These three sources of pressure on corporate executives suggest that CEOs should give top priority to the design and monitoring of corporate governance systems, especially those related to defensive measures, because they have a direct and visible impact on shareholder value.

A Change in the European Way of Business: Telecom Italia's Takeover

One of the takeovers that greatly influenced the market for corporate control in Europe is the Telecom Italia (TI) takeover. Olivetti, with revenues one-seventh of TI's $30 billion and a market capitalization one-quarter of its target, created a turning point in the European way of business.

Legal reform in Italy made this takeover possible. The "Draghi" law, first proposed by and named after the former general director of the

---

24. D. Campbell and R. Hulme, "The Winner Takes All Economy," *McKinsey Quarterly*, November 2001.

25. P. Combes and M. Watson, "Three Surveys on Corporate Governance," *McKinsey Quarterly*, November 2001.

26. A well-governed company was defined as "one that has a majority of outside directors with no management ties on its board, undertakes formal evaluation of directors, and is responsive to requests from investors for information on governance issues."

Italian treasury, introduced two major changes that facilitated an active market for corporate control. First, it suppressed the rights of the Italian government to veto any acquisition of more than 3 percent of ordinary, voting shares if a formal offer was made for 100 percent of those shares. Second, once the formal offer was submitted to the Italian market regulator (Consob), no change in the capital structure of the target and no issue of new debt could be made without the approval of 30 percent of the capital. These two actions significantly limited the number of defensive actions that the target could take. Managers of undervalued or poorly performing companies were no longer secure in their jobs. Their companies could be bought from under their control.

The fight was very intense. Many international investment banks and the powerful Italian investment bank, Mediobanca, backed Olivetti. The takeover took the shape of an LBO in which Olivetti planned to use the cash flow of the target to pay the debt. A syndicated loan of 22.5 billion euros was arranged from 20 banks in three weeks, showing the corporate finance capabilities that had been developed in Europe. The number of banks, speed, and amount of the loan showed that European financial markets and bankers were prepared to facilitate an active European market for changes in corporate control.

Telecom Italia hired many investment banks as defense advisors, who presented many strategic, financial, and legal defenses, including a "white knight" takeover and a "pacman" defense. However, Franco Bernabe, CEO of Telecom Italia at the time, fought without considering the influence and power of capital markets: "I am not going to do anything I would not have considered in the normal course of business. I want to make a distinction between this highly leveraged, speculative bid, and a solid commercial strategy. Our defense will be our industrial plan." The CEO of Olivetti at the time, Roberto Colaninno, presented the acquisition as an opportunity to cut costs, create cell-phone alliances, invest in new services, and improve the domestic network.

The takeover resulted in a new paradigm for the European market of corporate control. Governance provisions protecting interests other than those of shareholders were fewer; now, the focus of the law was on preserving shareholder interests.

The Telecom Italia deal spurred similar transactions on the continent. In 1999, Vodafone completed the largest hostile takeover ever when it bought Mannesmann. One U.K. analyst qualified the logic of the deal as "impeccable, and . . . the value to be gained by both sets of shareholders of bringing these assets together is enormous."

For all of the progress from an investor perspective, there are still some barriers to mergers and to enhancing the majority of shareholders' interests. One high-profile case was the failed merger between the Spanish telecom operator, Telefonica, and the Dutch telecom operator, KPN. The discussions were not strictly focused on the shareholder value creation but on the degree of liberalization of the economy of both countries. On the one hand, Telefonica had already been privatized and the only right that the government had on it was a golden-share option. KPN was not privatized and its privatization process, according to the Spanish Finance Minister, was not starting immediately and did not have concrete milestones. Telefonica's board—directly influenced by the Spanish government—opposed the deal because Telefonica would have a state-owned partner, the Dutch government, while the Spanish government was actively liberalizing its economy.

Status of the European Market for Corporate Control

Presence of Takeover Defenses

A Corporate Governance Survey (2001) by Deminor, a consulting firm on corporate governance, analyzes the corporate governance behavior of companies included in the Euro STOXX 50. One area of analysis focuses on the presence and strength of takeover defenses. The results show that even the most internationalized companies maintain a significant number of takeover defenses. What are the major structural and capital defense mechanisms used by European companies in a hostile takeover?

1. *Capital structure*: because the voting power of the majority shareholder is very high (20 percent) compared to the second and third ones (6 percent and 3 percent, respectively), the majority shareholder can influence the balance of power in the shareholder base, thus being a significant takeover defense. Fourteen percent of the companies in this index have a majority shareholder.

2. *Board insulation*: in 42 percent of the companies that the report analyzes, shareholders have difficulties in removing board members. This takeover defense goes against some of the basic shareholder rights and breaks the most elemental principles of the agency theory: shareholders (principals) have the right to name and dismiss board members, including top management (agents) who run a business.

3. *Voting right distortions*: 60 percent of the companies have at least one voting right distortion. Voting right ceilings that cannot be waived represent an important takeover defense. For instance, Nokia and BBVA do not have this provision while TotalFina-Elf and KPN do have right distortions. The basic principle of "one common share, one vote" must be respected to ensure that shareholder interests are preserved.

4. *Authorized capital*: 35 percent of boards can authorize equity issues, waiving the preemptive rights during a takeover.

5. *Repurchases of own shares*: 65 percent of the Euro STOXX 50 companies can repurchase their shares during a hostile takeover.

6. *Targeted stock placement*: Other conversion instruments such as convertible bonds or warrants can be used for a capital increase during a takeover. About 14 percent of the studied firms are allowed to do so.

7. *Other takeover defenses*: 33 percent of firms can use golden shares and golden parachutes to avoid a takeover.

Recent Failure of the European Takeover Directive

On July 4, 2001, after 12 years of negotiations, the European Parliament rejected the proposed European Takeover Directive ("the directive"). Klaus-Heiner Lehne, a German member of the delegation who opposed the directive, felt that it would leave companies unprotected and open to hostile bids from, for example, U.S. companies.

The rejected directive aimed to preserve the following general principles (article 3):

• *Equal treatment*: all shareholders of an offeree company of the same class must receive equal treatment. This principle tries to preserve minority shareholders' rights.

• *Sufficient time and information*: shareholders need to know the views of the board and have time to make an informed decision.

• *Preservation of the interest of all shareholders*: shareholders of the offeree should be able to decide based on the merits of the bid. This principle tries to avoid defense provisions adopted by the board or by some shareholders.

• *No creation of false markets*: share price of the offeree should not be distorted for the purpose of the takeover.

• *Credibility of the takeover*: the offeror should ensure a minimum of guarantees required to execute the takeover (e.g., cash availability).

Investors had hoped that the directive would harmonize the rules on the conduct of takeovers across Europe. However,

• The directive aimed at setting the minimum standards and did not attempt to harmonize European takeover law except in limited areas.
• Each state had the legal power to implement this directive within a chosen timeframe.
• Very little detail was given in the directive. For instance, no principles were defined for determining the equitable price that must be paid if there is a mandatory bid.

Although it did not impose strict rules, the directive was not approved. The main opposition was to its defense provisions, the so-called "frustrating actions" provision in article 9. The directive, as a minimum requirement, required that after the announcement of the bid and until the bid has been made public, the board of the offeree should not take any action which may result in the frustration of the offer. The offeree could take some defensive actions if the shareholders in a general meeting authorized them.

Those who rejected the directive probably thought that undervalued companies in their country would receive hostile takeover bids by foreign companies. However, the directive left room for some flexibility on defensive actions. For instance, the board of the offeree company could increase its share capital during the period of the acceptance of the bid if prior authorization had been received at a general meeting of shareholders no earlier than 18 months before the beginning of the period of acceptance.

Finance practitioners reacted to the opposition of Germany to the new European directive and the new German takeover law. The new German law will probably not promote a focus on shareholder value. As a partner of the German law firm CMS Hasche Sigle put it, "The management board and the supervisory board of a company together can take whatever frustrating action they want as long as it falls under the normal running of the company." Furthermore, penalties from international capital markets to German companies owing to their poor governance would increase. One German investment banker said, "capital markets will punish Germany and we will learn the lesson. Germany will find it difficult to attract institutional investors."

The process and time that it took to reach a political agreement, more than 12 years, highlights the cultural obstacles that lie in the way of EU harmonization of legal issues, especially when national interests are at stake. A harmonized European market for corporate control will take longer than expected. Nonetheless, a new proposed directive is under revision now, and a number of factors continue to influence the market for corporate control in Europe: the increase in capital needs and the internationalization of the shareholder base are some of them.

Conclusion

Corporate governance systems in firms are more important than ever to facilitate shareholder value creation. In fact, defensive measures against changes in the control of a company are not well perceived by shareholders. Punishments to highly protected firms against changes in control have increased enormously during the last years. Furthermore, institutional investors are more professional and active than ever, and the volume of hyper-mobile pools of investors in search of above-average returns all over the world is increasing.

The Corporate Governance Survey (2001) shows that there is still a significant presence of defensive measures in firms within the European Union. Moreover, the European Commission's efforts to develop a common takeover law in Europe have not been fruitful. After 12 years of work on the European takeover directive, the directive was not approved because of opposition to the so-called "frustrating actions" provision.

Europe should meet two major future challenges. First, in the regulatory arena, financial regulators should develop takeover rules, at a European level, with high minimum standards. A homogeneous takeover law throughout Europe will help to develop a common shareholder focus such as that of the United States. If only a few countries adopt a takeover law favorable to shareholders, there will probably be significant differences in shareholder value creation among nations. In a winner-takes-all economy, with mobile pools of capital, nations that favor shareholder corporate governance systems will attract more capital, as the U.K. does compared to continental Europe. Second, in the corporate arena, top management and shareholders should work together to find an optimum in the separation of ownership and control through increased institutional shareholders—less concentration—and through an adequate equity-based compensation for top management.

Institutional Investors

Institutional investors (in particular life insurance companies, mutual funds and pension funds) own an increasing amount of equity. More and more firms are entering capital markets. As a result, a greater fraction of the economic base of a company is coming under the purview of institutional investors.

The volume of total financial assets relative to GDP (an indicator of the financial market dimension) has grown over the last 20 years, with a parallel increase in the proportion of assets held by institutional investors.[27] The high level of "institutional assets" as a proportion of the total financial assets has accompanied a decline in deposits held in household portfolios, a lower level of corporate loans, and a higher level of corporate equity. These trends are observed in all G-7 countries, with institutional investors growing in relative importance.

The emergence of large shareholders able to channel the investments of a large number of individual investors could offer a possible solution to the principal-agent problem in equity finance. Through the strategy of diversification, institutional investors would seek an optimal size of shareholding that justifies the costs of exerting their rights and of monitoring managers, without overriding the interest of minority shareholders.[28] The growing dominance of equity holdings by institutional investors, both in the Anglo-Saxon countries and in continental Europe, would lead to a new corporate governance model (the direct control via equity or shareholder value model). This new model would break down the traditional separation of the "Anglo-Saxon paradigm," in which the threat of hostile takeovers acts as a market disciplinary device against incompetent or fraudulent managers, from the "Continental paradigm" in which credit institutions are both the more important shareholders and the main providers of debt.

The Rise of Institutional Investors in Europe: The Role of Pension Reform

Institutional investors are likely to become even more influential in continental Europe, and the reason is developments in retirement financing.

---

27. E. Philip Davis, *Institutional Investors and Corporate Governance* (West London: Brunel University), 1995.
28. Ibid.

Demographic Trends and Public Pension Spending

Demographics will impact Europe's pension system and might cause corresponding changes in capital markets and corporate governance. Continental Europe, in particular France, Germany, and Italy, has the largest pure pay-as-you-go pension system in the industrialized world. Under these systems, payments to pensioners are funded by taxes on the working populations. These systems work at high, but sustainable, tax rates when the Old-Age Dependency (OAD) ratio (the ratio of people 65 and older versus those aged 20 to 64) is low enough to ensure a fully funded program. According to the ECOFIN Group, however, the German OAD ratio will increase from 26 percent in 2000 to 54.7 percent in 2040. The Italian OAD ratio will similarly increase from 28.8 percent to 63.9 percent.[29] As the population ages, the pay-as-you-go system (under which payments to pensioners are funded by taxes on the working population's incomes) automatically creates imbalance. The International Monetary Fund estimates that public pension spending in the countries listed above will increase to over 20 percent of GDP between 1995 and 2030. If this estimate is true, French, German, and Italian workers will pay, respectively, 38 percent, 41 percent, and 62 percent of their wages to the pension systems.[30]

Although the pay-as-you-go system also depends on the development in labor productivity, the high proportion of government spending on pensions relative to GDP suggests that the state pay-as-you-go models are already overstrained and have become a drag on economic growth. Indeed, in all the countries mentioned above, there have been pension reform proposals and reforms in recent years. These changes have not slowed system membership, however, nor have they stabilized contribution requirements. Academic research, particularly Boersch-Supan and Winter's advancement of Gruber, Wise, and Schnabel's studies on the negative incentive effects of public pension systems on labor supply,[31] suggests that workers who have grown up in a generous pay-as-you-go system tend to prefer early retirement or to take jobs that avoid social security taxation.

29. Axel Boersch-Supan and Joachim Winter, *Population Aging, Savings Behavior and Capital Markets,* "Working Paper 8561" (October 2001).
30. Chand and Jaeger, IMF Occasional Papers 147, "Aging Populations and Public Pension Schemes."
31. Boersch-Supan and Winter, *Population Aging.*

Structural Reforms of the Public Pension System

Many studies have been conducted on the structural remedies to the instability of the pay-as-you-go system. A common thread is the necessity of a funded component to augment the existing public system, in particular by encouraging occupational pension schemes that have the advantages to achieve a well-balanced risk mix, cost efficiency, and wide reach. Currently, the occupational pension component is underdeveloped in many European countries. In Germany, 82 percent of retirement income is paid from state resources, while occupational schemes account for 5 percent and personal provision 15 percent. Within Europe, only the Netherlands and Switzerland have a more balanced three-pillar pension system. Switzerland has 42 percent, 32 percent, and 26 percent of retirement income generated, respectively, by state contributions, occupational schemes, and personal savings. The European market per pension funds (meaning all pension products excluding life insurance, financed outside the sponsoring firm) was worth about US$2,750 billion in 1999, with the U.K. alone accounting for 50 percent. In contrast, Germany, the most powerful and most populous economy in Europe, accounts for just 5 percent of the European market.[32]

Germany has recently taken action to stabilize its pension system. According to a new law, the *Altersvermögensgesetz* (AvmG), all employees now have a legal right to ask for employee-financed occupational pension plans. Moreover, the new law introduces a new German-style pension fund (*Pensionsfonds*) as a new occupational scheme. These pension funds invest the assets outside the sponsoring firm, are financed by both employer and employees, and can offer either defined-benefits schemes or defined-contribution schemes with guaranteed minimum benefits. Italy now allows new pension plans only as externally funded, defined-contribution schemes. The contributions made by employers—and, in some cases, by the employees—are channeled into a legally independent pension fund organization, which calls on an investment fund to manage or invest them. Spain has taken a similar step. Since 1995, only external funding has been permitted as an occupational scheme. Companies must decide by mid-October 2002 whether to write back their book reserves and pay them out in cash or convert them into certified pension funds.

---

32. Deutsche Bank Research, Special Study: Europe on the Road to Pension Funds? June 15, 2001.

Essentially, we are witnessing the development of the private pension system in Europe. According to Deloitte Research and Goldman Sachs,[35] the impending shift from public to private retirement provision will create a private retirement market worth 4 trillion euros ($3.6 trillion) by 2010, rising to 11 trillion euros by 2030. Overall, the study estimates the market for long-term savings in Europe to be worth around 26 trillion euros by the end of 2010, up significantly from around 12 trillion euros in 1999.

The Forms and Effectiveness of Institutional Activism in Anglo-Saxon Countries

The empirical evidence from the Anglo-Saxon countries that institutional investors can improve the performance of the targeted firms can be useful to understanding the economic effects of an increase of the European private pension market.

Evidence from the United States

In the United States, institutional investors own 50 percent of the top fifty companies, and the top twenty pension funds own 8 percent of the stocks of the ten largest companies.

When U.S. institutional investors are dissatisfied with firm performance, they can choose to:

1. Follow the "Wall Street Rule" ('vote with their feet") by selling shares.

2. Take an active role in the corporate decision-making process through shareholder proposals and proxy fights.

3. Negotiate directly with management and, when a compromise can't be reached, sell shares with a public explanation of the reasons underlying the selling decision.

According to recent work by Parrino, Sias, and Starks (2000), "voting with their feet" by U.S. institutional investors significantly affects board decisions, and can force CEO turnovers, often replacing the CEO with an outsider.

The second alternative is often mentioned in the academic research as the only form of institutional activism. The definition is too narrow because it applies to just a small set of U.S. public pension funds, led

---

33. *Retail Banker International*, January 15, 2002, p. 12.

by CalPERS. The U.S. Department of Labor's 1989 "Proxy Project Report" requires pension fund managers (but not mutual fund managers) to regard proxy voting as part of their fiduciary responsibility.

Moreover, how effective this form of activism is in improving the financial performance of the portfolio companies is ambiguous. Wahal[34] analyzes activism by nine public pension funds over the period 1987–1993 and concludes that there is no significant evidence of increase in the long-term stock performance of targeted firms. On the other hand, Smith (1996, p. 251)[35] analyzes activism (proxy fights) sponsored by CalPERS from 1987 to 1993 and concludes that "there is a significant positive stock price reaction for successful targeting events and a significant negative reaction for unsuccessful events. Overall, the evidence indicates that shareholder activism is largely successful in changing governance structure and, when successful, results in a statistically significant increase in the shareholder wealth" (251).

The third way of activism is more "vocal" than the mere sell-off of shareholdings, and it is precisely what has been observed in recent years within the wide community of private funds. For example, the stock price of GE's dropped almost by half between October 2000 and May 2002 because of the strong sell-off by institutional investors. This sell-off raised valid concerns over disclosure and over GE's ability to pump out future profits.[36] GE's CEO, Jeffrey Immelt, was forced to take visible initiatives to regain investors' trust. The work of Wahal (1996) confirms that efforts by institutions to promote organizational change via negotiation with management are associated with abnormally high stock returns.

Institutional Activism in Europe

The Leading Role of Domestic Institutional Investors
The developments in the European pension market will gradually lead to an increase in the demand for equity by domestic (European) institutional investors, who will be acting as the depositors of occupational pension schemes. In this changing environment, domestic institutional

---

34. S. Wahal, "Pension Fund Activism and Firm Performance," *Journal of Financial and Quantitative Analysis* 31, no. 1 (1996) 1–23.

35. M. Smith, "Shareholder Activism by Institutional Investors: Evidence from CalPERS," *Journal of Finance* 51, no. 1 (1996): 227–252.

36. Diane Brady, "The Education of Jeff Immelt," *BusinessWeek*, April 29, 2002.

investors could play a leading role in pushing companies toward better corporate governance standards. In turn, a greater transparency in providing information and the direct threat to poorly performing management would attract new foreign capital.

Together with the crisis of the public model of social security, the reform of stock market exchanges and the advent of a single currency have led domestic institutional investors to change how they approach corporate governance issues. European investors are increasingly looking outside their national borders for higher returns, making comparisons on a pan-European basis. Until now, their performance was largely measured against that of other managers in the same country. Now that institutional investors have to compete internationally for investment capital, they are far more eager to make the most out of their assets. They put pressure on the managements of their portfolio companies to increase the shareholder value orientation.

Forms of Institutional Activism

1. *Collaborative investigations and public focus lists.* In a dramatic shift from the past, European fund managers have started to publicly voice doubts about bad corporate practices. They are joining forces to push change. For example, in March 1998, 15 Dutch pension funds with $42 billion worth of holdings in Dutch companies teamed up to investigate the corporate-governance practices of all the companies on the Amsterdam market index. At the top of their hit list was Royal Philips Electronics. Fund managers at the company's annual meeting openly protested a juicy options scheme (then worth $175 million) that Philips had put in place without fully disclosing its details to investors.

2. *Exerting voting rights.* Sometimes the decisions made by institutional investors at shareholders' meetings have led to formal investigations. For example, the Oslo Stock Exchange and the Norwegian securities started investigating insider trading in the stock of Kvaerner, an Anglo-Norwegian engineering and shipbuilding company, after the Norwegian investment company Odin Forvaltning asked for and got the resignation of Kvaerner's CEO, who had been responsible for the highly leveraged acquisition of Trafalgar House, a British conglomerate several times the size of the company.[37]

3. *New investment styles.* Besides public criticism and active participation in shareholders' meetings, European fund managers have started

---

37. "Bosses under Fire," *BusinessWeek*, November 30, 1998.

to approach corporate governance issues under a different perspective as well. For example, France's ABF Euro VA invests in European stocks and benchmarks itself against the FT Europe Index, but it favors holdings in companies that it expects will take actions to enhance shareholder value through good corporate governance practices. The strategy has turned out to be a winning strategy. The fund outperformed the market by 7.4 percent against a tracking error of 1.7 percent since its inception in 1998. This form of institutional activism disciplines management through markets, by timed buying and selling of target firms and by exerting voting rights when there are undervalued assets.

The Italian Case: Strengths and Weaknesses of the Investment Management Industry

The Italian system of institutional investing provides a representative example of the role of institutional investors in a continental corporate governance system. Analyzing the Italian case reveals positive signals as well as some limits of the current role of institutional investors. The case can be easily extended to other continental cases.

In the Italian financial system, the most common type of institutional investor is the investment fund (*fondo comune di investimento*), where the funds are invested in different financial activities and managed by a company (*società di gestione del risparmio*). In Italy, about 90 percent of money managers are affiliated with banking or insurance groups. Different oversight authorities regulate money managers according to the specific kind of client whose assets are under management (individuals, high-net-worth individuals, pension funds, or insurance companies).

With shareholdings amounting to about 35 percent of the Italian stock market capitalization, the Italian money managers system is ranked third after the United States and France. At the beginning of 1990 it ranked twelfth. The percentage of assets invested in corporate equities has moved from 12 percent in 1990 to 38 percent in 2001.[38]

According to some financial authorities,[39] Italian money managers have started to show a more active form of shareholding than foreign

---

38. Mr. Fabio Galli, secretary-general of *Assogestioni*.
39. Ms. Maria Pierdicchi, head of *Nuovo Mercato* and Mr. Fabio Galli, secretary-general of *Assogestioni*.

investors, who are more inclined "to vote by feet" in the Italian companies where they invest. The increasing awareness of corporate governance by Italian money managers is confirmed by the important role that they played in issuing the "Draghi" law *(Testo Unico della Finanza, 1998)*. In particular, they directly proposed the rule under which the board of directors cannot do anything to prevent takeovers unless two-thirds of the General Assembly approves the defense action. Assogestioni, the trade group for the Italian asset management industry, has recently started to take public actions against badly managed firms, thereby making it increasingly expensive (in terms of reputation costs) for firms to resist market forces. For example, in July 2001, through a formal communication to CONSOB, Assogestioni opposed SAI's acquisition of the insurance company Fondiaria because of the lack of information about the action and the inconsistency of the acquisition with respect to the expected development strategy of SAI.[40]

Despite these favorable signals, the evidence about the activism of Italian institutional investors is still sporadic. A study of Italian mutual funds by Bianchi and Enriques (2001) is useful for understanding the problems that might prevent the expected pension reform system from being an effective driver for corporate governance. Bianchi and Enriques's empirical analysis shows that Italian money managers could potentially play a more significant role in the corporate governance of Italian listed companies. Other factors limit the activism. Examining the number of shareholdings larger than 1 percent, among 221 holdings, about 60 percent is concentrated in the hands of five Italian fund managers, with an average of 25 relevant holdings each. However, ownership concentration in the targeted firms, dependence on banking groups, and competitive disadvantage with respect to occupational schemes are the main factors that tend to reduce the incentives for activism.

Conclusions and Open Issues

In Europe, the importance and number of institutional investors is expected to rise in the near future due to ongoing pension system reform. The development of the funded component of the pension system will lead to an increase in the demand for equity by domestic institutional investors, acting as professional money managers of the pension plans.

---

40. *Assogestioni*, Corporate Governance Committee. Acquisition of Fondiaria by SAI, Report published at http://www.assogestioni.it/novita/novita.asp

The discussion of the role of institutional investors as effective agents for change in Europe should address two issues:

1. *What is the optimal internal structure that new European pension funds should adopt?* The extent to which a plan is of defined-benefit or defined-contribution may affect the pension fund's investment horizon, thereby affecting the fund managers' interest in active corporate governance. Most of the U.K. pension funds are run according to defined-benefit plans, where individuals don't bear the investment risk. In Germany, even under the new law, full defined-contribution schemes are not permitted, and pension funds are obligated to be members of the insolvency insurance association.

Quantitative investment restrictions could have a direct impact on the extent to which pension funds can play a role in corporate governance. In Italy, the holding of shares of closed-end funds is limited to 25 percent of the closed-end fund's assets. In Germany, pension funds cannot invest more than 35 percent of their assets in equities. Even under the new law, the government is authorized to issue detailed quantitative investment rules on pension funds. The European Commission has calculated that funds placing emphasis on quality management generated higher returns from the mid-1980s to the mid-1990s than those operating under quantitative rules.[41]

2. *What is the relationship between fiduciary responsibility and institutional responsibility?* Should European institutional investors have a duty to exercise their voting rights diligently as part of their fiduciary responsibility? Or should institutional shareholders exert greatest influence through the market? In each of the two cases, what should the government's role be in promoting institutional activism? After starting to exert their voting rights at shareholders' meetings and making some public actions, will European institutional investors start to gain a powerful bargaining power in negotiating directly with a company's management?

The U.K. government has decided to adopt the first alternative to increase the activism of occupational pension schemes, despite the ambiguous empirical evidence from the U.S., where public pension funds have the statutory duty to use shareholder powers to intervene in investee companies.

---

41. *Communication by the Commission*, Towards a single market for supplementary pensions, 1999, Annex, as quoted by Deutsche Bank Research, Pension Funds for Europe. See www.deam-europe.com/pension_reforms

Even without imposing the exercise of shareholder rights, European governments would have much room to maneuver:

• By introducing adequate regulations of conflicts of interest or several restrictive measures (e.g., limits to participation in managing companies) to reduce the influence of banking groups on money managers.

• By equalizing the treatment of all different occupational schemes (Italy).

• By simplifying the way of voting at annual meetings (Italy, Spain).

• By reforming the system of cumulative voting in order to ensure that the director designated with the vote of the institutional shareholders cannot be removed by the decision of the majority (Spain).

Although institutional activism has made significant progress in Europe, it seems that domestic investment funds still lack the power exercised by U.S. money managers, who vote "noisily" with their feet by directing harsh comments to managers, either privately or via the press.

Acknowledgments

We thank Professor Stewart C. Myers for his support of our research and for his coordination work. Special thanks also go to his assistant, Gretchen Slemmons, a "behind the scenes" leader.

This work would not be the same without the opinions and suggestions of all the inspiring people whom we have interviewed over the past year. Our sincere acknowledgments go to: Karl-Hermann Baumann, Siemens; Lori Belcastro, The Carlyle Group; Ilja Bobbert, Prime Technology Ventures; Professor Richard Brealey, London Business School; Albrecht Crux, Roland Berger; Rolf Dienst, Wellington Partners; Peter Englander, APAX Partners; Massimo Ferrari, Romagest (BancaRoma Group); Professor Julian Franks, London Business School; Arno Fuchs, Viscardi; Fabio Galli, Assogestioni; Anne Glover, Amadeus Capital; Professor Dietmar Harhoff, Odeon; Damien Horth, ABN Amro; Professor Simon Johnson, MIT Sloan School of Management; Professor Peter Joos, MIT Sloan School of Management; Dave Lemus, Morphosys; Professor Donald Lessard, MIT Sloan School of Management; Professor Richard Locke, MIT Sloan School of Management; Dirk Lupberger, Polytechnos Venture Partners; Marc Malan, Zouk Ventures; Professor Gordon Murray, London Business School; Sven-Christer

Nilsson, Startup Factory; Julia Otto, Cinven Ltd.; Andrew Phillips, Intermediate Capital Managers; Maria Pierdicchi and her team, Borsa Italiana Spa; Professor Malcolm Salter, Harvard Business School; Rene Savelsberg, Philips International; Raffaele Savi, Romagest (BancaRoma Group); Dario Scannapieco, Italian Treasury Ministry; Professor David Scharfstein, MIT Sloan School of Management; Professor Antoinette Schoar, MIT Sloan School of Management; Professor Lester Thurow, MIT Sloan School of Management; Roberto Ulissi, Italian Treasury Ministry; Professor Jiang Wang, MIT Sloan School of Management.

6.3   Financial Reform and Corporate Governance in China

Erika Leung, Lily Liu,
Lu Shen, Kevin Taback, and
Leo Wang

With the potential to develop into an economic superpower, China has undertaken the enormous task of developing market-based institutions. Confidence among market players is central to the market economy. Corporate governance provides an important framework to support this confidence. In fact, China's most prominent regulator in the drive to create efficient markets, the China Securities Regulatory Commission (CSRC), has declared 2002 the year of good corporate governance.

Corporate governance is a broad subject, intertwined with many areas of financial reform. The western concept of corporate governance has been codified by the OECD. The concept centers on the following principles: transparency, accountability, and fairness. The main mechanisms to look for include an independent board of directors, treatment of minority shareholders, and coordination of the interests of capital owners and business managers.

In its development of corporate governance, China will try to avoid financial crises and plundering of state assets. Retaining capital, fostering domestic investments, and raising badly needed cash to fund social obligations are recurring policy themes.

As China develops its markets and institutions, it enjoys the learning advantage of a late mover. It can take best practices from other economies and avoid major pitfalls. China's challenge is to develop its rules and institutions in a very compressed timeframe and create lasting markets.

Financial market development and reform in China started as a by-product of the state-owned enterprise (SOE) reform. However, as China's economy takes off, the role of the financial market becomes much more important to the growth of the economy. Some call corporate governance the "last pillar to be moved" in China's economy.

Financial market development and better corporate governance have become entwined.

This paper addresses some important issues in corporate governance and financial market reform in China. The first two sections provide an overview of China's securities market and discuss a range of problems arising from the securities market development. The significant hurdles China must overcome include:

- the legacy of a quota-based, politically driven listing process
- the role of the CSRC (China's SEC)
- the development of a liquid market with institutional investors
- the ability of companies to bypass domestic markets by seeking financing abroad

The third section examines issues arising from listing SOEs on China's stock exchanges and diluting state ownership. The questions we address here are: Does listing of SOEs really improve corporate governance? Are initial public offerings of SOEs sufficient, or should the state significantly dilute its ownership in SOEs to improve corporate governance? Finally, does better financial performance follow from listing?

In the last section, we examine the connection between nonperforming loans (NPLs), banking sector reform, and corporate governance. Specifically, how successfully will Chinese banks deal with NPLs? How fast can the Chinese government further deregulate the banking industry?

China's Financial Sector: Development Overview

A well-developed financial market is one of the crucial elements of corporate governance reform. In this section, we provide an overview of the current Chinese financial market by focusing on the securities and banking sectors.

Rationale for Forming the Securities Market

The securities market can be viewed as a first step toward creating domestic capital markets. The securities market can also be a tool through which the government can shift some of its SOE responsibilities to economic forces. In 1990 and 1991, the government set up the Shenzhen and Shanghai securities exchanges, respectively, as an experiment in installing a capital market apparatus in China.

The securities market has enjoyed much growth over the past ten years. Since 1995, equity market capitalization has risen to RMB5 trillion, or 400 percent (CSRC, 2000). Over 1,000 companies have listed between the two stock exchanges, with coverage expanding from a mainly local base to an extended national base.

While the exchanges enjoyed relatively high levels of autonomy in the first few years of operation, the combination of the extended coverage and the Asian financial crisis led the central government to tighten its control. The China Securities Regulatory Commission (CSRC) was created and became a governing body that answered only to the State Council. Regulatory enforcement thus became more centralized and local governments played a much less active role in formulating regulations and policy about the further development of the capital market.

Makeup of the Ownership Structure

The initial listings of public companies were politically driven. Some SOEs were performing poorly, and the securities market became an easy venue for companies to generate funding from the public and create some independence from political influence. A system of quotas was established by the central regulators and administered in the provinces. Each province was given a number of SOEs that could be listed, and it was up to local leadership to determine which firms it would list. Certain performance requirements had to be met, but the process was full of political pitfalls, with little resemblance to market forces.

In theory, consideration of SOEs for listing should be in the order of their financial health, that is, the best SOEs get listed first. However, the reality was that provincial governments used scarce quotas for companies who needed money the most. Because the listing law specified that a company had to show three years of continued profits to qualify for listing—a law that was borrowed from Hong Kong—provincial governments often bundled companies that had profits with poorly managed companies that needed money. As a result, companies with no apparent synergies were bundled together. In some cases, the managements of companies that got bundled together did not know

Box 6.3.1
Example of Bundling

Changhong Enterprise in Sichuan province, a television producer who had little access to large-scale state financing, managed to be successful in leveraging foreign technology and optimizing human resources within the enterprise. Further, it developed the market by establishing a comprehensive distribution network and a complete after-sales service. In 1998, Changhong's annual turnover of $2 billion was impressive and supported the locality's tax revenues.

Although an example of successful SOE strategy, Changhong is also an example of a contemporary whose success brought it responsibilities as part of a centrally planned economy. Changhong was asked to take over other less profitable—or at times simply unprofitable—SOEs. Even before the listing, Changhong was approached by the regulatory authorities to assume responsibilities for several SOEs in Nantong and Changchun. Although there is some vertical integration benefit inherent in the acquisition, the primary rationale was to balance the books so that the integrated SOE would appear to be more profitable than it actually was.

each other until just before going public (Neoh, 2002). An example of bundling companies is given in box 6.3.1.

The ownership structure of listed companies is distinctively Chinese. Shares of the listed companies are classified into three categories: state shares, legal-person shares, and tradable shares.[1]

State shares are held by central and local governments or by state-designated institutions (including SOEs). These shares cannot be publicly traded without the explicit approval of the state. While the exact definition is not clear, the "state" includes the local financial bureaus, state asset management companies, or investment companies. Sometimes the parent of the listed company, itself an SOE, can be counted as "state." Usually, the state comprises the controlling shareholders in publicly traded companies.

Legal-person shares are held by domestic institutions, including industrial enterprises, securities companies, real estate development companies, foundations, research institutes, and any other economic entities with legal-person status. A "legal person" is defined as a nonindividual legal entity or institution, but in effect they are just a nominal dis-

---

1. The following discussion of share types draws on Lin (2000).

tinction from state entities. The only distinguishing difference for legal persons may be the hierarchical differentiation between central and local governments. Most important, the legal-person shares are not publicly tradable, and they are subject to the same restrictions as state shares. Last, the legal-person shares are categorized by their ownership structure into SOEs, SONPO (State-Owned Non-Profit Organizations), collective enterprises, private companies, joint-stock companies, and foreign-funded companies.

Tradable shares are offered to—and are freely tradable in—the securities market. These shares are mainly held by individuals, and they provide the real liquidity in the securities market (where state shares represent 37 percent, legal-person shares 28 percent, and tradable shares 35 percent). The individual shares are also known as *A-shares*, held solely by Chinese citizens in domestic currency. There are also *B-shares*, which are domestically listed, foreign-held shares available only to foreigners. While the government tried to maintain a strict partition between the two markets,[2] recent trends suggest that there will be further integration of the different classes of shares in the Chinese market.

China's Entry into the WTO

While many believed that China's entry into the World Trade Organization (WTO) signified the end of its reform agenda, it has, on the contrary, just begun. Laura Cha, vice chairman of the CSRC, comments: "For all levels of the Chinese government, the work has just begun," and in fact, entry to the WTO has "galvanized reform efforts."

Under the current agreement, foreign securities firms can establish joint ventures—with foreign ownership less than one-third—to engage in underwriting A-shares, and in underwriting and trading B- and H-shares,[3] as well as government and corporate debt without a Chinese intermediary within three years of accession to the WTO. Furthermore, foreign insurance companies will also be allowed to operate in China, creating the foundation for institutional investors.

Commercial banking reform will also be accelerated under WTO. Currently, foreign banks lack the distribution network of domestic

---

2. This is mostly due to the fear that the state could possibly lose control over foreign exchange.

3. *H-shares* are shares of Chinese enterprises that are listed on the Hong Kong Stock Exchange.

banks, and domestic banks lack sophisticated products and operational systems. Enabling further domestic and foreign competition, and offering more products to domestic customers, will pose great opportunities and threats for the domestic banking industry.

Banking Industry Overview

Because bank loans are still the most dominant source of financing for domestic companies, the banking industry plays a key role in shaping economic development in China. With the various deregulations in the banking industry, more shareholding and private banks have entered into the picture, offering more products and services. After the founding of the People's Republic of China in 1949, three commercial banks merged into the central bank, which dominated all of China's banking services. Driven by the need to reform the SOEs, the banking sector started undergoing reforms in 1978. The most important reorganizations have been to separate policy banks and commercial banks from the central bank. By 1999, there were four state commercial banks, five national commercial banks, 12 regional commercial banks, and two housing savings banks. In addition, there were 274 foreign bank representative offices, 163 foreign bank branches, six foreign banks, and seven joint-venture banks, engaging mainly in trade-related finance and non-RMB business. Figure 6.3.1 depicts the current players in Mainland China's banking industry and outlines its historical development.

Inefficiencies in the state-run banking system led to the creation of a significant nonperforming loan (NPL) problem for the country. The size of the NPL problem is in the range of half a trillion RMB (US$518 billion), or more than 40 percent of total loans outstanding—almost half of China's GDP. To deal with the NPL problem, China established Asset Management Companies (AMCs) in an effort to deal with selling assets of debtor companies, recovering amounts owed, or writing off uncollectible debts.

Emerging Problems in Developing Mainland China's Securities Market

The development of the securities market in China has not been smooth. While the establishment and the continual metamorphosis of the securities market have caused some academics to applaud, we

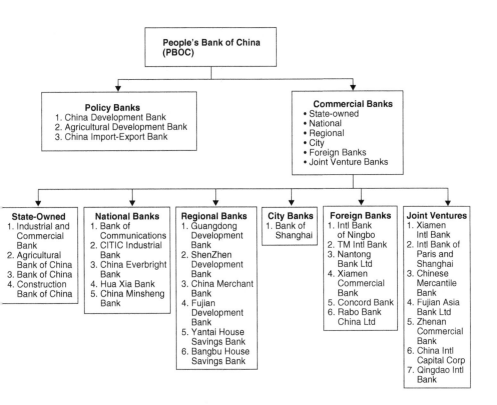

Timeline and history of banking reforms:

By 1984: The Agricultural Bank (ABC), the Construction Bank of China (CCB, the Bank of China (BOC) and the Industrial and Commercial Bank of China (ICBC) were separated from the central bank. Each bank dominated one sector of the economy: the peasants, the industrial enterprises, and the trade- or foreign-investment companies.

1984: As part of Monetary Reform, the four "specialized" banks (ABC, CCB, BOC and ICBC) became commercial banks aimed at profit making.

1986: The Bank of Communications was reestablished.

1992: Separation of commercial banking and investment banking.

1994: Three new policy banks were to be established: China Development Bank, Import and Export Bank of China, and Agricultural Development Bank.

1995: Release of Commercial Bank Law and Central Law Bank. The four state-owned banks began to function as commercial banks, subject to new rules and regulations holding them responsible for their profits and losses. The People's Bank of China status as a central bank was also legally confirmed.

Post 1995: Development of share-ownership commercial banks, in which various levels of government, Chinese institutions, and (in rare cases) individuals, hold shares.

1998: Lending quotas abolished.

1999: State Council approved the establishment of the four bank Asset Management Companies, which each acquired significant assets from one of the four state-owned commercial banks (Orient AMC to BOC, Great Wall AMC to ABC, Huarong AMC to ICBC, and Xinda AMC to CCB).

Figure 6.3.1
Banking structure in China.

believe that the inherent problems that are identified in the securities market reflect more systemic deficiencies within the Chinese financial infrastructure. In this section, we will delve into some of the more pertinent problems that we feel are key to a successful financial market transition.

Listing Process

As suggested in the previous section, the selection process for listing companies has historically been highly political. The Chinese stock market gained a reputation as a place to get free money for enterprises. The central government gave priorities to certain SOEs, and while minimum standards provided for the screening process, the actual procedure of getting listed fell to the level of favoritism, misinformation, and bribery.

First, the quota system and provincial recommendation format encouraged bribery on the local government level. The listings were based on recommendations from the local government, and since local officials were the gatekeepers to the stock market, they became obvious targets for corruption. Once the officials were successfully lured into a deal, the overwhelming incentive was to make the company in question as attractive as possible. As a result, rampant corruption, false documentation, and convoluted selection processes led to the overall disappointing performance of the listed companies.

Second, the state regulated the types of share issues and their liquidity. The state owns nearly two-thirds of the shares issued. These shares consist of two types, state-owned shares and legal-person shares. Both are nonliquid and not publicly tradable. As a result, state ownership significantly reduces the liquidity and financial disciplinary role of the stock market. Only shares belonging to individual investors are freely tradable, leaving two-thirds of the equity market illiquid and not exposed to financial discipline.

Recently, the CSRC initiated significant changes in the listing selection process. The changes reduced the role which local government plays, but the effectiveness of the new procedures still remains to be seen. Box 6.3.2 provides typical examples of corruption in the listing and investing process.

Box 6.3.2
Examples of Corruption

Listing-Related Corruption

Since a public listing is a limited commodity and the listing itself implied 'free money' from individual investors, enterprises go through all venues to try to guarantee their positioning for the next listing. The types of corruption extend from falsification of company financial information to the blind support of high government officials on all levels—from municipalities to city, provincial, and state levels. A typical example of this nature is the case of Kangsai Group, formerly known as the Huangshi Garment Factory in Hubei province, where the extent of the bribery system proved to be staggering.

From 1993 to 1996, prior to the company's listing, Kangsai's management offered discounted internal shares to more than 100 officials who were deemed useful during the listing process. The shares were offered to the officials at RMB1.00 per share, about one-sixth of the pre-listing value. When the group gained listing rights, the value went as high as RMB30.00 per share, a comparable return to the Internet start-ups during 1998. Among those who accepted these bribes were the vice minister of SETC (State Economics and Trade Commission) and the minister of MTI (Ministry of Textile). These two ministers are instrumental in making the listing of Kangsai a success, but it is also a sobering demonstration of the lack of integrity that is exemplary of an incomplete capital market.

Investing-Related Corruption

In 1992, the Shenzhen stock exchange experienced the first public protest of unequal opportunity given to individual investors. Since the stock exchange was still a new experiment, investors who were interested in getting in on the IPO investment had to first acquire an IPO application form, of which 10% would be awarded the right to subscribe. Following the announcement of the news, more than one million people waited in line to get their opportunity. Unfortunately, the distribution of the application was over before it hardly began, leaving the investors behind with the realization that these applications have already been allocated to the friends and family who got in through the back door.

Limited Role of the Governing Body—China Securities Regulatory Commission (CSRC)

In 1997, with the Asian financial crisis as the backdrop, CSRC was appointed as the sole overseer of the two exchanges in Shanghai and Shenzhen. This was a drastic departure from previous practices, because the local and municipal governments were in effect removed from the decision-making path. Further, with the passage of the Securities Law, the CSRC seemed to possess the dual power of overseeing and managing the securities market and of standardizing existing laws and regulations within a unified legal framework. In terms of the listing process, the CSRC reformed numerous aspects of the system. For example, the administrative approval system was revamped to abolish the right of local government to recommend stock listings. Instead, a set of listing criteria was set up and a central committee was created to review and evaluate the legitimacy of the potential listing companies. As compared to the CSRC's record of rejections under the local recommendation scheme, the record following the passage of the Securities Law was much more impressive—40 percent of applications have been rejected. Furthermore, the CSRC is currently promoting the use of internationally accredited law and accounting firms for the due-diligence process for potential listing firms. This, coupled with the demands of the WTO entry, seems to be promising for the establishment of a credible monitoring and enforcement system in the securities market.

In delivering new regulations, the CSRC has made an effort to improve compliance by reducing the discretion that companies have in interpreting laws. Templates have been provided for dealing with profit warnings, connected party transactions, ownership changes, and other important events. The Shanghai Stock Exchange now requires that companies issue warnings by January 30 if their profits will drop by more than 50 percent from the previous year or if they will report losses in the year.

According to statistics, the CSRC unveiled 51 laws and regulations from early 2001, when Laura Cha (the vice chair of the CSRC) first took office, to the end of the year. So far, the CSRC has established a basic framework of regulatory rules. During that period of time, more than 80 listed companies and 10 brokerages were publicly criticized, penalized according to administrative rules, and even put under judicial investigation (Hu et al., 2002). The CSRC has also delisted three companies and revoked the securities licenses of five local accounting firms that had been involved in the improper preparation of listed-company financial reports.

However, academics are at times skeptical of the long-term effectiveness of the CSRC. In terms of enforcement, new cases of delisting and other crackdowns seem to have subsided. While the establishment of a coherent regulatory framework and the continued disincentivization of corruption in the listing process is commendable, the real power that the CSRC holds—in enforcing the regulations and acting as a governing body independent of the central government—is in serious question.

Independent Directors

Although listed companies do have independent directors, these directors often do not fully understand their responsibilities. In the United States and other developed countries, directors are brought in when they have extensive knowledge of the industry, of financial markets, or of the legal system—all of which are relevant to the listed company. These directors are either active advisors or they act as independent checks and balances for the overall health of the company.

Box 6.3.3

"There are strict stipulations internationally on the qualifications of independent directors. Some emphasize accounting experience and some emphasize knowledge in law. But whatever aspect is emphasized, there is one common point: that is, the independent directors should have a certain professional background. For example, the U.S. National Association of Securities Dealers requires that an independent director should be able to understand the company's financial statement and the issuer should make sure that the auditing committee has at least one member with the professional background of financial accounting, who should be well versed in corporate accounting and disclosure of financial information."
(Hu et al., 2002)

Although the recent Enron case proves that even in the United States directors do not always fulfill their duties, China is still far behind in the basic understanding of the role that independent directors play.

China is also behind on the manpower required for the future needs of the listed companies. In August 2001, the CSRC issued detailed guidelines regarding independent directors, mandating that companies have three independent board members by 2003 and including strict board meeting attendance requirements. A sample of all 314 directors listed at 204 listed companies showed that nearly half were university academics (*The Chinese Entrepreneurs Magazine*; Zhang, 2002b). With 1,000 listed companies, this means there will be a need for at least 3,000 independent board members next year. The short supply of qualified directors will continue to be a challenge for companies needing to meet the CSRC's requirements.

Liquidity in the Marketplace

The tradability of stocks is one of the frequently discussed areas of the Chinese securities market. As mentioned in the previous section, tradable shares only account for about one-third of all shares, and the inferred liquidity of the Chinese capital market is only about 40 percent of the total market capitalization. Although the turnover ratio is 550 percent for tradable shares (Neoh, 2002), the highly volatile market suggests that the high turnover ratio is a product of the speculative nature of the market, rather than of a well-developed liquid market. Moreover, because of the lack of depth in the market, the stock market is also prone to manipulations.

Sophistication of Investors

Chinese investors are for the most part unsophisticated. They operate on a hearsay basis and are usually in the market for short-term gains. In China, large-cap stocks account for a very small fraction of total market turnover (Neoh, 2002). In more developed and less speculative markets, large-cap stocks usually account for a larger percentage of turnover, and investors maintain a longer investment horizon.

Retail Investors

Retail investors, individually, have no means or intention to exercise any influence over the companies in which they hold shares (Zhang, 2002b). Historically, having strong returns in the market makes people

Table 6.3.1
Successfully removing the "ST" stigma and staying listed

Code	Original name	New name	How they succeeded
0004.SZ	ST Shenzhen Anda	Beida High-tech	Debt restructuring, selling assets
0038.SZ	ST Shenzhen Dalong	Shenzen Dalong	As above
0502.SZ	ST Qiong Energy	Qiong Energy	As above
0550.SZ	ST Jiangling	Jianling Motors	As above
0555.SZ	ST Qian Kaidi	Taiguang Telecom	As above
600137.SS	ST Packaging	Chang River Packaging	As above
600696.SS	ST Haoshen	Fujian Haoshen	As above

Source: UBS Warburg, *China Securities News*

less interested in fundamentals and governance than in speculative stock returns. This is not surprising, since many of the investors that have the time to gamble in the stock market are retirees.

Another example of investors' lack of concern for company fundamentals and corporate governance is the case of ST-labeled companies. When listed companies have accounting losses for three years in a row, exchange regulations require "ST" to be placed in front of the company name. Zhang (2002b) points out that retail investors flock to ST shares despite their poor financial results, because investors know that a form of bailout will be in the works. Parent companies have been skilled at creating success stories through financial engineering and restructuring to prevent further losses. Of the seven examples listed in table 6.3.1, all were renamed and reengineered through debt restructuring and selling assets. The mechanism Zhang cites is that parent companies and local governments will buy assets at artificially high prices to generate profits for the listed companies.

Institutional Investors

Data compiled at the end of 2000 show that the capitalization of the U.S. stock market stood at U.S.$17.2 trillion, of which individual investors accounted for $6.6 trillion, or 38 percent, and institutional investors $10.6 trillion, or 62 percent. Clearly, institutional investors (including mutual funds, pension funds, and insurance companies) dominate the U.S. stock market and are critical for a well-functioning market. But things are different in China.

By the end of 2001, proprietary trading and investment in the funds by securities companies accounted for less than 10 percent of the capitalization of the negotiable shares in China's stock market, indicating that institutional investors are still a weak group in China. The presence of institutional investors has a stabilizing effect on the securities market because institutional investors make long-term investments in specific stocks, with less portfolio turnover. Moreover, institutional investors with a large stake in a particular company could exercise powerful influence over corporate governance in those companies. Although there is evidence that institutional investors in emerging markets tend to adopt a shorter-term investment perspective,[4] a stronger presence of institutional investors will benefit the Chinese securities market (Zhang, 2002b).

Raising Capital Overseas—The Hong Kong Securities Market

Beyond the mainland domestic market, Chinese enterprises can raise capital through the Hong Kong securities market. As of May 2001, among the 55 mainland enterprises that had sought overseas listings, 54 of them listed in Hong Kong, raising an accumulated capital of HK$124 billion (US$16 billion).[5] Kwong Ki-Chi, chief executive of Hong Kong Exchange and Clearing Limited, has stated that with China's entry into the World Trade Organization, "many mainland enterprises will need to raise funds to strengthen themselves in preparation for competition with foreign firms," thus increasing "the demand for mainland companies to raise funds in the SAR (Hong Kong) market."

With a very active market and the strong presence of institutional investors, the Hong Kong securities market provides an attractive avenue for Chinese companies to raise capital beyond the domestic market.[6] However, listing in Hong Kong is subject to strict listing and

---

4. According to a report produced by Credit Lyonnais, the average length of time money is invested by international players like Merrill Lynch and Smith Barney in emerging markets is only one-sixteenth of the time spent investing in developed markets.
5. Tdcstrade.com, Hong Kong Trade and Development Council, 2001.
6. Hong Kong was most active in Asia in 2000 and fourth most active in the world in terms of new capital raised. A recent Stock Exchange survey indicated that trading by overseas investors, mostly institutions from the U.S and the U.K, accounted for about one-third of the total turnover in 1999. Moreover, the implementation of the Mandatory Provident Fund (MPF) scheme in December 2000 also provides the Hong Kong securities market with a large-scale domestic institutional investor. It is estimated that the MPF scheme will inject an extra HK$30–40 billion a year of retirement funds for the next 30 to 40 years until the system matures.

disclosure rules, and only a handful of Chinese companies could realistically list on the Hong Kong Stock Exchange (HKSE). The recent failure of the Bank of China's attempt to list its Hong Kong branch on the Hong Kong and New York Stock Exchanges is a case in point. Nonetheless, the hope of gaining access to international capital and deeper pockets could accelerate the current reform efforts.

Will Shanghai Take Over Hong Kong as China's Financial Center?

With China rapidly developing its securities market and tightening its regulations, many people feel that it is inevitable that the domestic market—especially Shanghai, with its close proximity to Beijing—will one day take over Hong Kong as China's premier financial market. According to a recent (2002) report in the *Economist*, if Shanghai continues to grow at the rate of the past decade, its GDP "will match Hong Kong's in 15 years." In addition, Shanghai enjoys a range of advantages over Hong Kong, including close political ties to Beijing, access to relatively cheap and well-educated mainland labor, and substantial government spending on infrastructure. However, as the article also points out, Shanghai's close ties to Beijing are also its main disadvantage. Entangled with mainland China's murky political system, Shanghai's property market and financial system are "ill-regulated and chaotic," and its legal system is "arbitrary." Shanghai's skyline might rival that of any financial center in the world. But to become an international financial center, China has to build confidence and credibility, not more skyscrapers.

Box 6.3.4

> HKSE chief executive Kwong Ki-chi said he was not unduly concerned by the possibility of mainland companies listing on the domestic markets in Shanghai or Shenzhen instead of Hong Kong: "For the companies which want to raise funds in Hong Kong dollars or for those which want to have a wider access to international investors, Hong Kong will be their first choice," he said.
> (Lowtax.net 2002)

The Issues to Watch

China's ability to overcome its legacy of listed companies (companies brought to market through a political process) will be critical to the proper development of its markets. The CSRC will continue to play a pivotal role in developing market mechanisms, and its power will be sufficiently tested by all those affected. Without strong demand for liquidity and stability, efforts to reform securities markets will have little support. And finally, should China's market developments stall further, the best domestic companies will have alternative sources of financing.

SOE Listing and State Share Sales

Reforming China's state-owned enterprise (SOE) sector is at the core of China's economic reform. Since the reform started in the late 1970s, significant progress has been made in such areas as accounting standards, reporting, and reorganizations. Indeed, the need to reform the SOEs has been the most important driver of reform in the financial market. After twenty years, it is recognized that SOE reform has fallen short of the standards set by efficiently operating businesses in developed economies. The core of the problem lies in the difficult tasks of reforming the SOE ownership structure and improving corporate governance. In this section, we focus on the corporatization of SOEs and their subsequent listing—two major steps in ownership reform. Figure 6.3.2 illustrates the relationship between corporatization, listing, and privatization of SOEs.

Corporatization of SOEs to Clarify Property Rights and Improve Performance

Corporatization (*gongsihua*) of SOEs started in 1992 as a way of clarifying property rights of SOEs and improving their performance. After serious attempts to improve SOE performance through increased autonomy failed, it was recognized that the crux of poor SOE performance was the ambiguity of property rights inherent in state ownership. Ownership by "the whole people is almost equivalent to free goods, since nobody owns it" (Nakagane, 2000). The corporatization program sought to solve the problem by converting SOEs into Western-style corporate entities with more clearly defined ownership structures,

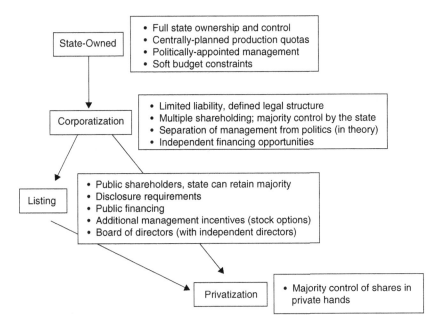

Figure 6.3.2
Corporatization and privatization in China.

such as joint stock companies (JSCs) and limited liability companies (LLCs).

There were political as well as economic considerations behind the corporatization program. Politically, corporatization was a way to reduce state intervention and improve corporate governance of SOEs *without full privatization*. By reallocating formal control rights from a single controlling entity to a small number of state institutions and SOEs, the state hoped the resulting multiplicity of shareholding would sever the link between an SOE and its controlling authority. The company would be subject to the checks and balances of a small number of owners. Thus, it would, we hope, become immune to excessive political interventions and only operate on economic objectives.

Economically, corporatization was to increase SOEs' access to funds beyond traditional bank loans and state subsidies, such as the vast amount of household savings. It was also to separate state ownership from the management of SOEs, and to hold company directors responsible for the assets of the company and prevent further asset theft.

Listing of SOEs to Mitigate the Agency Problem and Increase Transparency

Concurrently with the corporatization process, SOEs were given increased autonomy in management and operations. Corporatization separated the management of SOEs (agent) from its ultimate control (principal), creating an agency problem. In this context, increasing management autonomy without aligning incentives exacerbated the agency problem. Company management often acted in its own interests, stripping off company assets for personal gains. As a result, corporate performance further deteriorated, necessitating other remedies. This motivated the listing of SOEs on domestic stock exchanges, with sale of shares to private investors. It was hoped that the increased transparency and incorporation of private ownership interests through listing would provide the checks and balances on management to improve performance.

The questions we want to address here are: Does listing of SOEs really improve corporate governance? Is initial public offering of SOEs sufficient, or should the state significantly dilute its ownership in SOEs to improve corporate governance? Finally, does better financial performance follow from listing?

In principle, the listing of SOEs should ultimately create better management incentives with more objective performance feedback structures in the form of stock performance. Introducing apolitical shareholders with board representation that seeks to maximize firm values should improve monitoring and should mitigate informational asymmetries. It also imposes a more standardized set of disclosures that increase transparency. Furthermore, raising equity capital helps reduce debt loads and frees resources for investment. Finally, empowering employees through ownership also helps align interests with management and shareholders.

In practice, the story is a mixed one. As noted earlier, corporatization was a way of avoiding full privatization. With listing, an attempt is made to provide independence and structure to the corporatized SOE, but ultimate control (through ownership) is not fully transferred from the state. Only a small share of the equity in an SOE is listed in an IPO and sold to private investors. In fact, the state retains two-thirds ownership (through state and legal-person shares) in most listed companies, ensuring no substantive change in the nature of ownership and control by the state. The presence of outside shareholders and additional public disclosure requirements due to listing do, however, ensure more transparency and arguably better governance.

Nevertheless, it is important to note that transparency is only as good as the credibility of management, board members, and auditors. Investors will have a hard time acting on information just because it is disclosed—it has to be believable and predictable. Furthermore, liquidity and efficient markets are critical for such disclosure to have any value. China's market has not developed sufficiently—and regulatory compliance is not complete enough—to provide a clear link between performance, stock prices, and oversight of listed companies.

Effects of Listing—Discouraging Empirical Evidence

Empirical evidence on the effects of listing SOEs is discouraging. Wang, Xu, and Zhu have performed a compelling statistical analysis of listed SOEs from 1990 to 2000 (Wang, Xu, and Zhu, 2001). They found that the financial performance of SOEs deteriorated after listing. Measured in terms of return on sales and return on assets, post-IPO performance of listed SOEs trends worse than results in the periods leading up to IPO. Table 6.3.2 shows the average return on assets (ROA) drops steadily, from 19.6 percent in the year immediately prior to IPO to 2.7 percent in the sixth year after IPO. The average return on sales (ROS) also decreases, from 16.6 percent one year before listing to 0.2 percent in the sixth year after listing. In addition, capital expenditures as a percent of total assets declined rapidly after listing. However, Wang et al. did find that performance is positively correlated with a more balanced ownership structure among top shareholders, suggesting that less concentration of power in a single shareholder's hands leads to better performance. In the sample studied, all the firms were listed under the quota system that has since been phased out.

Table 6.3.2
Selected mean performance statistics of listed SOEs

	Year −1	Year 0 (IPO)	Year 1	Year 2	Year 6
ROA	19.6%	15.4%	9.7%	7.4%	2.7%
ROS	16.6	16.2	13.7	7.8	0.2
Capex/Assets	74.3	57.7	43.1	28.2	3.8
Annual sales growth	28.7	47.8	22.2	10.5	16.5

Source: Wang, Xu, and Zhu (2001), World Bank

Zhang also notes that post-IPO performance of many firms is disturbing. Of the 90 companies that went public in 1999, only 25 met forecasts disclosed in their prospectuses. Of the 25 that met forecasts, 11 did it through financial engineering (asset sales and restructuring). The most egregious examples include Changjiu missing its forecast by 75 percent, Hualin Tyre being 66 percent short, and China Agricultural Resources issuing profit warnings within six months of its IPO (Zhang, 2002b).

Wang et al. present traditional explanations of this evidence that center on "window dressing" or inflating pre-IPO performance to ensure successful IPOs. In addition, they argue that lack of ownership by management and dispersion of shareholders do not create the necessary incentives for performance (Wang, Xu and Zhu, 2001).

Zhang suggests additional sources for poor performance stemming from a lack of corporate governance. These problems are in the area of connected-party transactions and loans from listed companies to their state-owned parents. The relationships between listed subsidiaries and parent companies are fraught with governance problems and pose a major hurdle to better performance. Zhang cites the case of Luoyang Chundu going bankrupt because its parent owed it RMB330 million since Luoyang Chundu's IPO in 1998, which was 80 percent of its IPO proceeds (China Securities News; Zhang, 2002b).

The CSRC issued a set of guidelines in June 2000 called "Announcements Regarding Listed Companies' Loan Guarantees for Others," which prohibits related-party loans and loan guarantees. Yet a year later, New Fortune reported 159 new loans disclosed in 2001, which amounted to RMB 23.1 billion. (See table 6.3.3).

Even when loans do get repaid, a study from Southwest Securities shows that more than three-fourths of parent debts are settled in-kind, with the equipment and property given being of subjective value. Only 17 percent of the debts in this study were settled with cash (Zhang, 2002b).

In addition, ongoing transactions between parents and listed SOEs are a significant problem. New Fortune reported in December 2000 that 93.2 percent of A-Share companies have disclosed ongoing significant connected-party transactions with their parents (Zhang, 2002b).

Owing to these relationships and corporate structures, Zhang argues that many listed companies could never become fully independent of their parents. He cites examples of Kelon, which went public without any of the three brands of their refrigerators and air-conditioners. The

Table 6.3.3
Examples of Chinese companies making guarantees

Company	Guaranteed amount (Rmb m)	Guaranteed amounts/Equity
Founder Technology (600601.SS)	465	82%
Lujiazhui (600663.SS)	1,962	46%
Xinye Property (600603.SS)	878	231%
China High Tech (600730.SS)	494	150%
China West Medicine (600842.SS)	593	270%
China Kejian (0035.SZ)	820	also received counter guarantees
China Tech Venture (0058.SS)	415	249%
Shanghai Ninth Department Store	567	84%
Hero Corp (600844.SS)	472	82%
Shenzen Petrochem (0013.SZ)	1,673	307%
Tongji Tech (600846.SS)	2,240	67%

Source: *New Fortune*, December 2001, UBS Warburg

brands, Kelon, Rongsheng, and Huabao, are controlled by the unlisted parent. In the case of Yanzhou Coal, the mines went public without railway links to the public railway system.

Why Listing Did Not Significantly Improve Corporate Governance

While the Wang data set is robust given the firms that have listed to date, it is not necessarily a good representation of the average SOE that will be listed in the future. Historically, the Chinese quota system for determining listed SOEs was politically driven and administered geographically. First, the quota system for listing SOEs did not prevent poorly performing SOEs from being listed. Indeed, local governments often "bundled" poorly performing SOEs with better-performing SOEs before taking them to the market in the practice of "packaging" discussed earlier.

Second, abuse of listed firms is probably commonplace. If each province only receives one opportunity to access the public markets through a listed firm, the umbrella of political influence becomes even more imposing. Use of funds is not going toward productive investments in the listed firm but instead serves as payback to the community. Contrary to the goals of improving independence and corporate governance, listed SOEs that come through a political quota system can be strapped with obligations to the community, actually becoming less independent and less financially viable.

At a more fundamental level, SOE listing did not significantly improve corporate governance because the state did not—and still does not—want to give up its control of SOEs and embrace full privatization. As discussed earlier, the state merely views listing as a pragmatic way for cash-strapped SOEs to raise funds without full privatization. As long as the state maintains substantial ownership interest in SOEs, it will keep bailing these firms out of financial crises one way or the other ("soft budget constraint" à la Kornai). As a result, the disciplinary role of the financial market will be severely undermined, and SOEs will not really be penalized for poor corporate governance.

Finally, in a thin capital market with few investment opportunities, vast amounts of household savings seeking investment opportunities made—and still make—it easy for any listed firm to raise equity even without sound corporate governance (Lin, 2000).

Looking ahead, more opportunities to raise the quality of listed firms will be available as the market—not politicians—determines which firms most deserve to be listed. In addition, the CSRC has implemented an innovative way to improve quality by putting more screening responsibility on investment banks through its own form of quotas. In our interviews, we learned that each investment bank is only permitted to have five filings under review by the CSRC at any given time. This provides a strong incentive that only the best companies, with the best chance of clearing approvals, will be submitted after more extensive due diligence.

The CSRC has cracked down on poor performers and has been trying to remove the implicit government guarantee of solvency through delisting. Laura Cha says a primary intent of this crackdown is aimed at reforming packaged companies. "The first purpose is to avoid packaging-oriented reorganization. Pocketing money through reorganization is intolerable, and we will watch more closely the reorganization of listed companies. Second, if over 70 percent of the reorganized company is new business, it should be regarded as a new company that will go through procedures as a newly listed company and receive the examination of the Public Offering and Listing Review Committee under the CSRC. Only when it lives up to the conditions of a listed company can it continue to maintain the status of a listed company after the reorganization" (Hu et al., 2002).

Wang's empirical evidence should serve as a wake-up call for investors and listing SOEs, but it is not an outright indictment against listing SOEs as a means to improve corporate governance. Studies of privatization in other emerging markets generally agree about the productivity and performance benefits of reduced state ownership. Additional studies of listing and corporatization as a step toward privatization in other former socialist economies may provide further support for a more optimistic view.

Next Step after Listing: Dilution of State Ownership

In addition to reducing state ownership of SOEs, listing of SOEs is also a way of monetizing firm values to support pension and social safety-net obligations. However, initial equity offerings only amount to a small fraction of state ownership, and the state continues to control most listed SOEs. The next big challenge is how to sell additional shares and dilute the state to a minority shareholder to improve governance. The value of private ownership and independence of former SOEs is well documented in separate privatization studies by Megginson, Frydman, and Pohl (Nakagane, 2000). However, the mechanism in China is different from other successful privatization efforts.

In 1997, in President Jiang Zeming's speech at the National People's Congress, he announced a policy called "releasing the small and retaining the large enterprises" (*zhuada fangxiao*). This marked the start of a process of significantly diluting state ownership in small- and medium-sized SOEs, especially through listing. As a matter of policy, the state will continue to retain controlling ownership of the very large SOEs out of strategic considerations, even if these companies are taken public.

According to Elaine Wu, an analyst with China Southern Securities, "the state-share sell-down is the most sensitive topic in the markets. Whenever there is some news on it, investors immediately become nervous and sell stocks" (China Online, 2002).

The key conflict in state-share sales is between market prices for existing minority shareholders and for the beneficiaries of stock sales, namely social security funds. Without sufficient liquidity in the market, or investor appetite for the quantity of shares available for sale, stock prices would collapse with state shares flooding the market. Clear market reaction has been seen on this issue. In June of 2001, the announcement by the CSRC that the state would sell shares equal to

10 percent of public offerings was met with a 30 percent decline in the Shanghai index, which lost RMB600 billion (US$72.5 billion) in value over four months. The state social security fund was an investor in Sinopec and lost RMB160 million (US$19.3 million) in value over the same period. In early 2002, when confirmed rumors emerged that the CSRC would shelve any plans for the sale of shares, the market responded with a 10 percent rise.

As discussed in the previous section, China needs greater stability among its investors to absorb the quantity of shares that need to be sold by the state. With a market presently made up of many gambling retirees, it is not surprising that the market reacted so strongly to the issue of state share sales. Obviously, lack of liquidity and the speculative nature of China's market are other important issues at work, but the sale of state shares is an extremely sensitive topic.

There is also a lack of coordination among interested government parties on whether and how to continue to sell state shares. After halting the June 2001 plan in October, Zhu Ronji was already urging the CSRC to develop new measures to continue state share sales by December. At a conference in Beijing, Zhu said that China would not discontinue the sell-off of state shares because it is needed as a source of cash for the social-security fund (China Online, 2001).

It seems that everyone involved in the market has an opinion about how state shares should be sold off. In 2001, the CSRC solicited opinions on its website and received 4,137 suggestions (Hu et al., 2002). Recent comments from the CSRC on the subject outlined the CSRC's commitment to the following principles: state-share sales should create a favorable situation for all parties involved; they should be conducive to the long-term development and stability of the stock markets; they should realize full tradability of the stocks of newly listed companies; and the interests of all parties should be protected and investors' losses should be reasonably measured and compensated (China Online, 2002).

It is clear that any solution will take a modest approach, and most agree that the timeframe for execution will span one to three years. Some alternatives being considered include allowing investors to bid for state shares through open, competitive tenders, beginning with SOEs that were listed earliest. Compensating investors for losses caused by the flood of shares on the market might include the issuance of bonus shares or stock options. Lockup periods to prevent flipping were also suggested, as was the ability for companies to buy back their shares if their stock prices become too low (China Online, 2002).

In agreement with statements from Zhu Ronji, Anthony Neoh[7] thinks the central government's primary motivation for selling state shares is to raise cash to fund social obligations and government budgets. In that case, creating confidence and stability in the stock market is a driving force in the decision of exactly *how* to dispose of state shares and dilute ownership in SOEs. Failed experiments began in 1999, with the attempt to sell a portion of state-owned shares in 10 firms of various sizes and industries. The original plan was complicated and tentative, providing an unclear timeline and unclear quantities and trading restrictions for institutional investors.[8]

Neoh believes that a proposal to create a closed-end mutual fund of state shares in SOEs will deliver a number of benefits for investors and for the state. Creating a diversified index allows the state to monetize a large amount of shares in a wide variety of firms. Investors have the opportunity to limit their risk by investing in the broader market instead of investing in individual firms.

Other proposals include allocating shares directly to the social security fund, which then has the ability to sell shares as cash is needed to fund obligations. Chen Zhiwu, professor of finance at the Yale University School of Management, proposed this solution (China Online, 2001).

The Most Viable Proposals for State-Share Sales

The problem of selling state shares cannot be considered without considering the missing link: sufficient demand. Institutional investors, especially those with foreign money or western investment philosophies, are key to generating a stable market environment for state shares. Assuming this issue will be solved through the WTO and

---

7. Anthony Neoh is former Chairman of Hong Kong's Securities and Futures Commission, and special advisor to the CSRC.
8. The firms slated for share sales were Tangshan Jidong Cement Co., Ltd., the Yunnan Huayi Investment Co., Ltd., the Guizhou Tyre Co., Ltd., the Chongqing Taiji Industrial Co., Ltd., the China Jialing Industrial Co., Ltd., Huitian Heating, Fulong Heating, Tianjin Port, Chengdu People's Department Store, and Shanghai Lijiazui. Some of the terms were reported to be: existing shareholders were given first priority, institutional investors would be barred from trading over two years, and pricing of shares was to be between net asset value and 10 times earnings (China Online, 1999).

continued regulatory reforms, two of the proposals mentioned above seem to balance the needs of the state and the needs of investors.

First, the index fund plan sounds very credible and has the added benefit of offering a viable investment vehicle for institutional investors with low entry costs. It is not clear that this proposal will go far to improve governance, however. The problem of small shareholders having little influence and representation with management would persist in a closed-end fund arrangement. Significant shareholders in the fund may not be very significant holders at the enterprise level and thus have little power over management. The other question is about the long-term fate of the fund and the individual SOE shares. How long will shares be locked up in the fund, and will the fund eventually be dissolved with distributions to shareholders? Finally, will the closed-end fund be the best way to maximize value for state shareholders if net asset values of the fund are based on illiquid share prices of SOEs traded outside the fund?

Second, distribution of shares to social security funds is also a promising approach. After SOE shares are monetized, the funds should be permitted to reinvest in the broader market. The benefit is that cash reserved for long-term obligations can be plowed back into high-quality corporate bonds and certain equities to provide a significant institutional presence in the market. Implementation will be key with this proposal. If one or several funds are established and are given flexibility about when to sell shares, the approach may be no better than the CSRC's initial attempts at state-share sales.

Implementation Limits: Connection to Bank Reform

The institutional support structure required for strong governance and independence of SOEs cannot be ignored. Strong, independent institutions support the development of market mechanisms, and they impact managers' ability to finance and run a publicly listed SOE. If financial institutions continue to be controlled by the state, the layer of political influence is not far removed from a listed SOE. Foreign sources of financing without political baggage are only available to a small number of high-profile SOEs. Weiying Zhang recommends that both financial and nonfinancial state enterprises be privatized concurrently (Nakagane, 2000).

Since the equity market is so interconnected with the overall capital market, this discussion of SOE listing would not be complete without addressing reform in the debt and banking sectors. As competition for capital increases with SOE listings, so should competition increase in banking. The capital markets should serve as a source of oversight and incentives for SOEs to operate more competitively. In the next section, we will address banking reform and its connection to corporate governance.

Banking Reform and Corporate Governance

Much of the reform in the banking industry in China since 1978 has been driven by the need to recapitalize the SOEs. Past lending practices that were entirely based on political considerations, coupled with poor performance of the SOEs, have left Chinese banks with a large amount of bad loans. Against the backdrop of China's entry into the WTO and further penetration of the foreign banks, the state-owned banks and private banks are all struggling for independence and profitability.

In recent years, China has seen some dramatic growth in the real sector, and private enterprises contributed 30 percent of total GDP in 1999. However, only 1 percent of private enterprises' financing comes from bank lending and only 1 percent of listed companies on Shanghai and Shenzhen exchanges are private enterprises (Langlois, 2001).

Furthermore, given the disciplinary effect of banks' profitability and good corporate governance in the companies to which they lend, the banks should be a contributor to China's economic growth and not become an impediment to the growth.

It is therefore important to look at both drivers of the banking industry going forward: the legacy problems of the nonperforming loans (NPLs) and the future reforms of banking. Two key questions are:

1. How successfully will the Chinese banks deal with NPLs? NPLs have been the result of poor corporate governance both in the SOE debtors and within the banks themselves. The following discussion analyzes the recent efforts by the government to reduce NPLs.

2. How fast can the Chinese government further deregulate the banking industry? It is clear that further reform measures will be needed to ensure: a) healthy development of the private banking sector; b) true competition among the "big four" state-owned commercial banks and c) efficient allocation of capital in the economy. (See box 6.3.5.)

Box 6.3.5

Significant regulatory reform steps taken to reduce NPLs include:
• Abolition of the mandatory loan quota system. (As a result, state banks could lend according to commercial considerations.)
• Reclassifying bank loans into five categories in line with international practice (pass, special mention, substandard, doubtful and loss) in late 1998 to improve loan quality
• Establishment of four asset management companies (AMCs) in early 1999 to absorb the four state commercial banks' NPLs with AMC bonds swapped at full value
• Disclosing loan-defaulting companies in the interbank computer network and banning new lending to them
• Setting up a national credit bureau for banks' reference when extending loans. By FY99, the database already covered over 1 million borrowers in 301 cities

---

How Successful Will the Efforts to Reduce NPLs Be?

Since 1995, many of the banking reform measures have focused on solving the NPL issue. Several steps that have been taken are described in the sidebar above. However, at the end of 2000, even after transferring RMB 1.3 trillion of NPLs, the remaining NPLs still remained at 29 percent of total loans.[9] By any international standard, all of the Big Four banks are bankrupt. (See table 6.3.4.) Some have argued that as bad as the NPLs are, they are not an issue as long as the growth of new NPLs is curbed and the economy can slowly absorb the existing portfolio of bad loans. Others have argued that if the reforms are not successful, nonperforming loans will continue to grow and, ultimately, be the downfall of the Chinese economy.

Corporate governance is at the heart of solving the NPL issue. The four asset management companies (AMCs) set up to help reduce the NPLs will likely not solve the problem, because the corporate governance of the AMCs is not properly structured. The AMCs are in fact set up as another type of state-owned enterprise under the regulatory oversight of the People's Bank of China with input from the Ministry of Finance. Currently, their major activity is debt-equity swaps (i.e., AMCs acquire NPLs from the banks and then convert those assets at

---

9. RMB1.3 trillion of loans were transferred from the banks' balance sheet to the Asset Management Companies (UBS Warburg, 2001).

Table 6.3.4
Estimated size of NPLs, 2000

RMB (billions)	Outstanding NPLs transfer to loans	AMS	Remaining NPLs	NPLs as % of total
Industrial and Commercial Bank of China	$2,414	$410	$796	42.7%
Agricultural Bank of China	1,484	346	490	45.7%
Bank of China	1,378	296	394	41.2%
China Construction Bank	1,386	280	394	40.4%
Total	$6,662	$1,332	$2,074	45.5%

Source: UBS Warburg estimates
Note: For ICBC, ABC, and CCB, remaining NPLs assumed to be 33% of outstanding loans in 2000

par into direct equity holdings in the defaulting borrower, namely large SOEs). However, the SOEs chosen for this swap are selected by the State Economic and Trade Commission (SETC) and not the AMCs themselves. The AMCs also have no power to change the management of the banks or to perform any kind of restructuring of the banks. They also do not take any control of the board. Without power as shareholders and without political independence, the hope for successful loan recovery lies in the specific methods AMCs will apply. However, evidence shows that after the debt-equity conversion of the assets are transferred to AMCs, the governance structure of the banks remains unchanged, and thus the physical restructuring of the enterprises remains unchanged. After almost two years in operation, AMCs had only disposed RMB $90 billion in assets (7 percent of total transferred assets), and the recovery rates for the disposed portion did not even exceed 10 percent.

On the other hand, according to UBS Warburg, the growth of new NPLs in the last two years appears to be very low. The banks said that new NPLs should be below 5 percent of total loans, or even as low as 1–3 percent. According to the report, the improvement is mainly due to tightened credit risk control procedures. For example, the Bank of China has established credit evaluation committees within the bank to approve individual credit applications. If the banks can continue to slow the growth of new bad loans, then the existing NPL problem can be isolated and slowly absorbed by the banks. UBS Warburg suggested that for the past two years, however, the new low NPL figure is mainly due to more personal-mortgage lending and long-term infrastructure projects lending. According to China's accounting standard, these loans will not be considered nonperforming until maturity. Many experts also suspect that there is still a lot of policy lending masked by the commercial banks, which understates the ratio of NPLs to total loans. Because relationship-based lending continues to dominate, and commercial banks are taking on infrastructure lending, the NPL issue is not likely to be relieved soon. Therefore, it still remains to be seen whether the banks have really become more efficient at capital lending. (See box 6.3.6.)

Box 6.3.6

"China's big four banks need at least 10 years to deal with their problem loans and the cost of the necessary write-offs could equal US$518 billion," according to S&P. "Consequently, they are unlikely to meet the target set by the central bank—to cut their nonperforming loans to 15% of total loans within 5 years," said S&P director of financial services Terry Chan at a press briefing in Hong Kong on May 9, 2002. S&P's assessment of China's banks comes a day after economists at the Asian Development Bank's annual meeting in Shanghai called for urgent action on the bad loans problem.

Chinese central banker Dai Xianglong said that the NPLs of the Big Four could stand at 30 percent of their total loans, revising earlier, lower estimates. But S&P said on May 9, 2002, that the real figure is likely to be even higher.

The write-offs required are almost half of China's estimated gross domestic product of RMB1.1 trillion last year, or US$518 billion, said S&P. "The rate of NPL reduction desired by the authorities will almost certainly need some form of government intervention, possibly through injections of fresh capital and through further transfers of NPLs to asset management companies owned by the Ministry of Finance," S&P said.

Fresh equity could also take the form of a public listing of the banks, and S&P says it is more likely that the Big Four will tap the domestic market. "Thirty percent NPLs is too high a risk for the appetites of international investors. Technically, these banks are insolvent," said Mr. Chan.

The banks will have to balance the write-offs and provisioning against scaring potential investors off, so the rate of write-offs will be slow, said Mr. Chan. But he said that compared with Japan, China has bitten the bullet and is taking steps to reform the banking sector. "They need to do more, but at least they have acknowledged they have a problem."
—*The Business Times*, May 10, 2002

Continued corporate governance reform is also the key to curbing future NPLs because it will directly influence banks' risk management, asset allocation (loan portfolios), and strategy. Since 1998, most of the banks are holding branch managers responsible for poor performance and rising bad debts.

While government control gives rise to corporate governance problems across all corporations, it tends to be worse for banks. Banks are particularly opaque, and it is very difficult for outsiders to monitor and evaluate bank managers (Caprio and Levine, 2002). The tacit protection by the government further exacerbates the agency problem at the banks. Under the current Chinese banking system, in which the banks are still not allowed to compete effectively because the interest rates are not liberalized, the monopolistic nature further contributes to the opaqueness of the banks.

What is good corporate governance of the banks? Minsheng Bank has been publicized as a prime example of good corporate governance in China. Corporate governance, according to the OECD notion, is a set of relationships between the management and the board of directors, shareholders, and other interested parties. Separation of the functions with clearly defined accountability, responsibilities, and checks-and-balances among them is usually considered good corporate governance. Specifically for a bank, however, corporate governance will directly influence the bank's risk management, asset allocation (loan portfolios), and strategy.

Without the history of poor lending practices and unburdened by as many NPLs, the shareholding banks and the private banks are much more nimble and have been leaders in corporate governance. At the October 2001 Asia Pacific Summit held in Vancouver, Mr. Liu Ming Kang, chairman and president of Bank of China, specifically pointed to the following five aspects of corporate governance:

- Formulating development strategy
- Improving the decision-making process and internal control
- Adopting prudent accounting norms and increasing transparency
- Establishing a rigorous responsibility and accountability system
- Strengthening human resources management and building a distinctive corporate culture

For example, at the Bank of China, Liu has set up checks and balances so that no official, himself included, can make policy loans. Due diligence and risk management committees in the head office and branches now assess all loans. Liu has no seat on those committees. "If the committee says no, I could not say yes," says Liu. Conversely, if the committee approves a loan, he can veto it. At the same time, Liu is trying to ensure that each loan application gets approved or rejected within 10 working days, compared with the several months it sometimes took before Liu took over in 2000 (Mellor, 2002).

However, even given the amount of publicity on banks' corporate governance reforms, many experts believe that both central and local governments still have strong influences on lending practices at various bank branches. Although lending quotas have been abolished, new lending practices based on relationships with the SOEs are essentially the old practices under a different name. The government has also, at times, returned to old habits. For example, as economic growth slowed in 1998–99, the central government asked the commercial banks to contribute by taking up infrastructure loans to boost GDP (HSBC, 2001). An issue to watch, therefore, is whether the "healthy" banks in the industry have become independent enough to resist this kind of pressure in the future.

China's entry into the WTO will allow Chinese banks to seek foreign capital—through joint ventures, for example—and also penetration of foreign banks into the Chinese market. Will these changes drive the banking industry to greater health? Corporate governance and operational reforms can only function well when there is a foundation from which the firms can compete effectively. After much reform, the current Chinese banking industry still remains a heavily regulated market with the Big Four banks controlling approximately 70 percent of the total assets. Therefore, this naturally leads to the next key question: How fast can the government further deregulate? We will lay out some of the objectives for the government for the next few years.

How Fast Can the Chinese Government Further Deregulate?

A well-run financial market allows financial intermediaries to efficiently allocate capital across the economy. Under the existing structure, however, both the Big Four banks and the shareholding banks access the same resources, compete for the same clients with the same set of products, and essentially have the same shareholder. What further reforms are needed to bring true competition? There are five major areas in which the government should further deregulate:

1. *Regulatory rigidity:* Currently, the establishment of all financial services firms has to be preapproved by the central government. Firms with primary private sponsors are either not approved or approved with crippling business restrictions. Therefore, competition is only among the banks that are still government owned and controlled. Two other examples include: a) the requirement for banks to receive approvals for every line of business, and b) slow deregulations in allowing new sources of capital.

2. *Unliberalized interest rates:* The interest rates on loans and deposits offered by financial institutions are set centrally by the People's Bank of China (PBOC). Financial institutions have some leeway in setting lending rates: they can vary the centrally governed rates by 10 percent for lending to large institutions, and up to 30 percent for small- and medium-sized enterprises (SMEs). If banks are not allowed to price lending rates themselves, they will not be able to compete on the basis of interest rates. The three-year liberalization timetable announced by the PBOC governor in 2000 has basically been dropped. The reason given is that after the recent liberalization of foreign currency interest rates, there was a sharp jump in foreign-exchange deposit rates but little change in the foreign-exchange lending rate. This has resulted in a reduced interest spread. Currently, a high RMB interest spread is a major factor in domestic banks maintaining their financial strength. Therefore, the PBOC is worried that the push on interest rate liberalization will cause the interest spread of the RMB business to fall as well.

3. *Denial of market allocation of capital:* To date, the corporate bond market has been suppressed because the law requires that all corporate bonds be sold as public instruments and because the state imposes minimum requirements to issue: minimum net assets, maximum debt/assets ratio (40 percent), and one-year debt service capability. The result is that almost 100 percent of corporate risk in China is on bank balance sheets and is mispriced (Langlois, 2002).

4. *Excessive taxation:* Even though the banks make no money on lending, they still pay heavy taxes: 7–8 percent business tax, 33 percent income tax with extreme restrictions on provisions for nonperforming loans (<1 percent of loans) and restrictions on expenses (compensation) (Langlois, 2002). In 2001, however, the PBOC did announce a policy to cut banks' business tax from 8 percent of total operating income (after deducting interest income from financial institutions and government bonds) to 5 percent by 2003. In order to make the Chinese banks truly

competitive, we believe the business tax must eventually be scrapped. The corresponding tax loss to the government, estimated at around 2 percent of government revenue, should be bearable given the rising tax contribution from other sectors (HSBC, 2001).

5. *Continuing to open China to foreign banks:* Only in February 2002 did the government grant new licenses to provide foreign currency services in China for local customers. However, according to PBOC, as of the end of June 2001, foreign banks in mainland China had total assets of $41 billion, representing only 2 percent of total assets. Although foreign banks will have very limited distribution networks, their services are more competitive than Chinese banks. The rules published in February 2002 were considered by some to be a milestone in China's meeting the concessions necessary for entry into the WTO. Nonetheless, some foreign banks still felt that the rules fell short of the expectations because of the stringent capital requirements for foreign banks planning to enter China (*Peoples Daily*, 2002).

In the meantime, however, the banks are trying to become more competitive by becoming corporatized—more shareholding banks as well as the Bank of China are trying to get a public listing on China's stock exchange.[10] It is believed that going public can help support the capital expansion needed by the banks. Mergers, reorganizations, and business combinations will also improve banks' economies of scale, thereby increasing banks' capabilities for resisting risk and enhancing their competitiveness as a whole. However, will corporatization work? Listing banks is a step in the right direction, but without the necessary foundation (discussed above) and given the still underdeveloped securities market, the impact of listing on banks' profitability is still unclear.

Conclusion

We attempted to address some of the most important issues in corporate governance and financial market reform in China. The significant hurdles that China must overcome encompass four areas: the legacy of a quota-based listing process; the role of the CSRC (China's SEC); the development of a liquid market with institutional investors; and the

---

10. China currently has four listed banks: Minsheng Bank, Pudong Development Bank, Shenzhen Development Bank, and China Merchants Bank.

opportunity to bypass the domestic market and finance companies abroad.

Corporate governance in state-owned enterprises has the potential to be addressed through the process of listing SOEs and diluting state ownership. The results that remain to be seen are whether:

- listing of SOEs really improves corporate governance
- the initial public offering of SOEs is sufficient, or if the state should quickly dilute its ownership in order for better governance to take root
- better financial performance will eventually follow from listing.

We also examined the connection between nonperforming loans, banking sector reform, and corporate governance. Two factors are critical to success here: how successfully the Chinese banks deal with non-performing loans, and how fast the Chinese government will further deregulate the banking industry.

To compete effectively on a global scale and successfully transition to a market economy, China must have well-functioning securities markets and banks to establish the foundation for strong corporate governance.

Methods and Acknowledgments

The student research team would like to thank Professor Stewart Myers for his guidance and contributions to this work as our project advisor. Our research was conducted through a combination of primary and secondary research, including interviews on location in Hong Kong, Shanghai, and Beijing in early 2002. We would like to thank each of the following people for their contributions to our understanding of the background and challenges of financial reform and corporate governance in China: Laurence Franklin and T. J. Wong, Hong Kong University of Science and Technology; Leslie Young, Chinese University, Hong Kong; Earl Yen, Ascend Ventures, Hong Kong; Marjorie Yang, Esquel Group, Hong Kong; Laura Cha and Anthony Neoh, CSRC, Beijing; Lawrence Li, Hong Kong Securities and Futures Commission; Jaime Allen, Asian Corporate Governance Association, Hong Kong; Victor Fung, Chang Ka Mun, and Chin Wai Man, Li & Fung, Hong Kong; Joe Zhang, UBS Warburg, Hong Kong; Dr. Yuan Cheng and Zili Shao, Linklaters, Hong Kong; Fang Xinghai, Shanghai Stock Exchange; Lu Wei, Fudan University, Shanghai; Yibing Wu, McKinsey

& Co., Beijing; Wang Yi, China Development Bank, Beijing; Jin Shuping and Wei Shenghong, Minsheng Bank, Beijing; Chen Taotao, Tsinghua University, Beijing; Colin Xu, World Bank, Washington, D.C.; Stoyan Tenev, Shidan Derakhshani, Jun Zhang, and Mike Lubrano, International Finance Corporation, Washington DC; Mengfei Wu, CNOOC, Hong Kong; Edward Steinfeld, MIT, Cambridge; Dean Alan White, MIT Sloan, Cambridge. Of course, many comments were made in confidence, so we are unable to attribute every statement from these sources. Special thanks are extended to Laurence Franklin, Marjorie Yang, and Laura Cha, whose insights and referrals to other sources of information in Hong Kong and Beijing were most appreciated. Dean Allen White of MIT Sloan was also extremely helpful in establishing contacts for our team in China.

References

Caijing Magazine, January 23 through China Online.

Caprio, Gerard, Jr., and Ross Levine. 2002. "Corporate Governance of Banks: Concepts and International Observations," April 25, 2002.

China Online. 1999. Ten Chinese Firms Chosen to Sell Government Equity. November 30.

China Online. 2001. Zhu Rongji says sell-off of state shares must resume. December 19.

China Online. 2002. Worries over state-share sales trigger stock slump. January 28.

Cull, Robert, and Lixin Colin Xu. 2000. Bureaucrats, State Banks and the Efficiency of Credit Allocation: The Experience of Chinese State-Owned Enterprises. *Journal of Comparative Economics* 28: 1–31.

HSBC Securities (Asia) Limited, Banks / Financial Research. 2002. "Form Command to Demand in Financial Services—Entering the China Century," February 2001.

Hu Shuli, Wei Fuhua, and Niu Wenxin. 2002. An interview with Laura Cha, CSRC vice chair.

Langlois, John D., Jr. 2001. "China's Financial System and the Private Sector," presentation at American Enterprisse Institute, May 3, 2001.

Lardy, Nicholas. 1998. *China's Unfinished Economic Revolution* (Brookings).

Lin, Cyril. 2000. Public Vices in Public Places: Challenges in Corporate Governance Development in China. OECD Development Centre. Draft.

Mellor, Williams. 2002. "Cleaning Up Bank of China." Bloomberg Markets, April.

Nakagane, Katsuji. 2000. SOE Reform and Privatization in China: A Note on Several Theoretical and Empirical Issues. University of Tokyo.

Neoh, Anthony. 2000. China's domestic capital markets in the new millennium, Chinaonline.com

Neoh, Anthony. 2002. Corporate Governance in China. Talk at China Harvard Review conference, April 13.

People's Daily. 2002. "Detailed Bank Rules on Foreign Banks Take Effect," February 2, 2002.

Shleifer, Andre, and Robert W. Vishny. 1997. "A Survey of Corporate Governance," *Journal of Finance* 52, no. 2: 737–783.

Wang, Xiaozu, Lixin Colin Xu, and Tian Zhu. 2001. Is Public Listing a Way Out for State-Owned Enterprises? The Case of China.

Zhang, Chunlin, and Stoyan Tenev. 2002a. Corporate Governance and Enterprise Reform in China: Building the Institutions of Modern Markets. The World Bank. April.

Zhang, Joe. 2002b. China's Corporate Governance: A steep learning curve. UBS Warburg, January 17.

The Economist. 2002. "Special Report Hong Kong and Shanghai: Rivals More Than Ever." March 30.

Lowtax.net. 2002. Hong Kong Securities Market,
http://www.lowtax.net/lowtax/html/ hongkong/jhksec.html

Tdcstrade.com. 2001 "Profile of Hong Kong Major Service Industries: Securities." Hong Kong Trade Development Council, June 12.
http://www.tdctrade.com/main/si/ spsect.htm

6.4 Discussion

Professor Stewart Myers, Dr. Rolf Breuer, and Dr. Victor Fung all commented on the factors driving greater interest in corporate governance. Aside from the obvious issue of U.S. corporate scandals, changes in Asia and Europe are highlighting the importance of corporate governance.

In particular, the rising use of equity financing and outside shareholders in both Europe and China bring up the issues of greater transparency and shareholder rights.

Dr. Rolf Breuer, chairman of Deutsche Bank, described the European view of corporate governance. In describing the current situation, he noted the troublesome issue of unifying the 35 different corporate codes of conduct and regulatory frameworks in the European Union. This is a microcosm of the larger global problem of unified standards and the thorny issue of balancing global needs against local needs. Breuer warned that the European Union should avoid choosing the lowest common denominator when creating a common framework. It is important to use the commonality among the 35 frameworks but also to keep local laws where they serve local purposes.

Looking at the world stage, Breuer lamented the lack of convergence between U.S. international accounting standards bodies. For example, when Deutsche Bank listed on the NYSE, the bank was forced to switch to U.S. GAAP. The switch caused much consternation and confusion among the bank's European and world shareholders. And, although Breuer had no qualms about signing the U.S.-mandated CEO and CFO certifications, some heads of dual-listed European companies have objected to this recently mandated practice because they see it as a sovereignty issue: whether American watchdogs should oversee European companies or vice versa. To improve communication with shareholders and provide greater transparency, Breuer recommended using

scenarios when presenting issues to shareholders, analysts, and stakeholders. Too many corporate decisions are obfuscated by complex
legalistic documents. Complex legal documents adhere to the letter of
the law regarding reporting proposed actions to shareholders, but they
create a lack of transparency that brings a host of ill-considered practices such as excessive executive compensation or Enron's infamous
special-purpose entities. Instead, CEOs could explain proposed actions
using a set of scenarios (worst-case outcomes, expected outcomes, and
best-case outcomes). Such scenarios would help shareholders and
stakeholders gain a clearer understanding of the real impacts of proposed management decisions.

Dr. Breuer also commented on the U.S. practice of allowing the CEO
(head of management) to be chairman of the board (head of oversight).
In contrast, the dual-board system is common in Europe. In the dual-
board system, the heads of the two boards are purposefully distinct—
the executive board is in charge of running the business, and the
supervisory board performs a strategic oversight role and hires/fires
those executives.

When asked about the recent closure of Germany's Neuer Markt,
Breuer noted that this answer to America's NASDAQ failed because it
tried to copy the public-listing practices that were appropriate for
larger, more established companies. As Professor Myers had noted, different types of organizations require different types of governance and
regulatory frameworks. Aside from cultural and regional differences,
differences in the age, size, and history of a company affect how it
should be run.

Dr. Victor Fung, chairman of Li & Fung, focused on the Asian view
of corporate governance. The biggest story in Asia is the ongoing evolution of China from a communist-led command-and-control economy
to one that tries to meld the energy of free markets with the values of
socialism. The state-run enterprises have already shrunk from being
100 percent of the economy to being a mere 30 percent of the current
economy.

During his introduction, Professor Myers noted the crucial goal of
frictionless flow and efficient allocation of capital. In turn, Dr. Fung
described the obstacles to this process in China. The obstacles are
twofold: human resource issues at banks and the lack of sophistication
of investors. Like many Asian countries, China enjoys a phenomenally
high savings rate (some 40–50 percent). Most of this money flows into
low-yield bank savings accounts. In the past, banks played more of a

simple cashiering role, because the state made all the lending and investment decisions. In theory, the banks now have the responsibility for local lending decisions. Unfortunately, the banks have neither the personnel nor the expertise necessary to recycle all the capital socked away in savings accounts. Until the banks learn to lend—or consumers learn to invest in equities—China will suffer from inefficient allocation of capital.

Regarding his own company, Dr. Fung noted its efforts to promote ethical practices among Li & Fung's global network of trading partners. Although not mandated by any government edict, Li & Fung created a Compliance Officer position in the company. Li & Fung knows that its own reputation as a trading company is a function of the reputations of all the companies with which it does business. The Compliance Officer ensures that trading partners live up to high standards. Dr. Fung noted that although his company created this position simply because they believed in it, the practice has created a barrier to entry for Li & Fung competitors. Li & Fung can form tighter relationships with the better suppliers, leaving less ethical alternatives to its competitors.

Commenting on the Bank of China, Dr. Fung described how going public brings greater discipline to a company. Many believe that privately held companies have an advantage in being able to make better strategic decisions than do their publicly traded counterparts. Yet going public in Hong Kong forced the Bank of China to create better governance and reporting structures for the Hong Kong side of the bank. The bank learned much from the process and intends to transfer that learning back to the mainland and then take the remainder of the bank public.

Another issue being debated in Asia is whether companies should move to quarterly reporting. (Currently, companies report semi-annually.) Dr. Fung pointed out that the practice of quarterly reporting can actually reduce transparency. This view is in contrast to the argument that the longer reporting cycles of companies in places like Europe and Hong Kong mean a lack of transparency—that investors lack timely updates on affairs of the company. First, he pointed out that shorter reporting cycles tend to amplify the normal noise of business, having fewer months over which to average the ebb and flow of revenue and cost events. Thus, companies on shorter reporting cycles have more incentive to manage earnings, shifting costs and revenues using accounting sleight-of-hand to reach the magical "1 cent over

expected earnings" target. Second, shorter reporting cycles can actually delay the reporting of material events. If a material event occurs
two months into a six-month reporting cycle, the company is likely to
report it immediately. In contrast, a company on a three-month cycle
might delay the news for one month to coincide with the next routine
quarterly announcement.

The speakers also referred to the role of crises in bringing about corporate governance reforms. Dr. Fung said that the state of corporate
governance in Asia was not good before the financial crisis of 1997. The
crisis raised awareness, however, and Asian countries have made much
progress since them. Singapore and Hong Kong are the farthest along.
The United States, currently in the midst of crisis, is trying to create
reasonable reforms to prevent any future repeat of the recent corporate
scandals and to restore confidence in U.S. financial markets. Dr. Breuer
said that the events in the United States were eye-opening for Europe.
Europe is currently working hard to avoid being the next financial
crisis.

The speakers also discussed one of the differences between American stock exchanges and those in Asia and Europe, namely the size of
companies listed on the exchanges. For example, more than 50 percent
of the market cap of the Hong Kong Stock Exchange is made up of companies that are family-controlled, Dr. Fung said. Dr. Breuer, likewise,
commented on the large and vibrant role of small and midsize companies in Europe. This difference in corporate size requires a corresponding difference in corporate governance. Although some have
argued that family ownership is a poor form of governance, Fung dis-
agreed with this view. Family ownership creates extremely strong
incentives and alignment that other "professionally managed" companies must try to create using cruder mechanisms such as salary,
bonuses, and stock-options. Although family ownership can be abused,
Hong Kong regulations focus on those potential abuses (e.g., self
dealing and connected transactions). The point is that no single form
of governance is superior to all others. Each form of governance has
advantages and each needs regulations that address the potential
weaknesses or abuses inherent in that form of governance.

Finally, the speakers discussed the topic of strong independent
boards of directors and the challenges to creating these boards. Most
pressing is the shortage of qualified candidates. In China, the newness
of private enterprise implies a shortage of experienced business executives for boards, Dr. Fung said. In a country in which no one can claim

decades of for-profit management experience, finding board members is difficult. Fung also noted the low pay scales for board members and a tendency for the same people to appear on multiple boards.

Likewise, in the United States, the drumbeat for accountability will likely frighten potential board members. Increasing the responsibilities and liabilities of board members will shrink the pool of applicants. In her presentation, HP CEO Carly Fiorina cautioned that overregulation could make boards and management too risk-averse, which would threaten the innovation and experimentation that form the basis for value creation.

Even the definition of "independent" varies across countries. Dr. Breuer noted that U.S. regulators see European boards as lacking independence owing to the presence of employee representatives. At the same time, European regulators see U.S. boards as lacking independence owing to prevalence of stock ownership by members of U.S. boards. At issue is the role of the board in representing various constituencies during the boards' oversight of management. European boards have more alignment with employees; U.S. boards have greater alignment with shareholders. Board members can represent constituencies such as shareholders, employees, debt-holders (banks), the local community, governments (i.e., golden shares), and even the general public.

Aligning the board with any of these constituencies can make the board indirectly dependent on the company and management. With the fates of so many all connected in different ways to the fate of the company, no one is truly unbiased and independent. This is the prime driver for the need for ethics. In an interconnected world in which everyone is dependent on everyone else, ethics may be the only practical substitute for the ideal of independence.

7   Technology

7.1

The Next Technological Revolution: Predicting the Technical Future and Its Impact on Firms, Organizations, and Ourselves

Ellen Brockley, Amber Cai, Rebecca Henderson, Emanuele Picciola, and Jimmy Zhang

Technology changes the world. Steam power, the railroad, electricity, the automobile—these technologies have changed how we work and how we live in irreversible ways. Within the last ten years, advances in telecommunications and computing have revolutionized communications, provided virtually unlimited data, and opened up new possibilities for products and services in nearly every industry.

In this brief essay, we draw on current MIT research to look forward: to explore how technology is likely to develop in the next twenty years and to begin to speculate on how these developments will change the commercial world. We sketch out the three areas in which we are likely to see the most progress—in information technology and communications, in the life sciences, and in the science of the small, or "nanotechnology." Since each of these areas is far too large and far too complex to explore in any detail, we focus in depth on advances in medical technology, pervasive computing, and water cleansing technologies for developing nations in an attempt to give the reader a sense of the dramatic potential of current research. We also highlight developments in microelectro-mechanical devices to illustrate the ways in which current developments may interact with each other to create products and capabilities in ways that are almost impossible to foresee. Our goal is to give the reader a sense of the vibrancy, enormous potential, and sheer enthusiasm generated from the MIT research in these exciting fields. We hope to inform you, to pique your curiosity, and to provoke your thinking about the future.

We also hope to highlight some of the challenges that continuing advances in science and technology are likely to create for managers.

There is the immediate challenge of recognizing which of these advances is likely to be important for a particular firm, and of integrating them into complex organizations that are already under stress. More fundamentally, however, our results suggest that it will be increasingly impossible to manage "technology" or "science" as a thing apart from the complex human, social, and financial systems that make up a firm: that decisions about technology will have to be deeply integrated into the heart of the firm. This implies that the manager of the future will need to be much more technologically sophisticated than her predecessor: that technology will no longer be something that can be safely left to the technologists.

Our results also raise broader questions about issues of social justice and about the goals to which we harness technology. We describe below a number of developments that have great potential to improve the quality of life in the developing world—and a few that have the potential to improve the quality of life for the majority of the world's people who live in the so called "developing" world. We suspect that one of the great questions of the next ten years may be how we harness the imagination, drive, and creativity of the world's scientists to benefit all the world's population, rather than only a fraction.

General Trends

We are on the verge of the third industrial revolution—the convergence of Information Technology, Life Sciences, and Nanotechnology. *Information Technology* delivered the last technical revolution—the Internet. The volume and creativity of current research guarantee that the pace of innovation in networks, telecommunications, and computing will not slow. In fact, the rate of progress is probably accelerating. Advances in chemistry and biology in recent years have propelled *Life Sciences* to the forefront of scientific attention. New discoveries and improved understanding of cellular processes have spawned entirely new and exciting scientific fields such as proteomics, pharmacogenomics, and genotyping. Each contributes to the real possibility of dramatically improving our health and extending the human life span. *Nanotechnology*, the study of matter at the atomic scale, promises to revolutionize our view of materials and offers unprecedented options for new machines and intermediate products. As the newest of the three, nanotechnology has achieved the fastest start from a funding perspective and is poised to surpass biotechnology and semiconductors in both scale and scope.

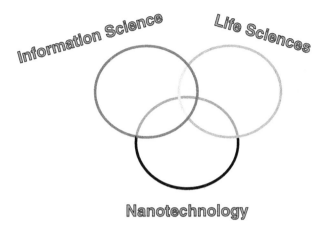

Figure 7.1.1

Information Technology

Look how far we've come! In the last 15 years, information technology and computer science have brought us into the Information Age with pocket telephones, e-mail, automobiles that talk to us, laptops—a panoply of technical innovations that we take for granted but which were unheard of 10 years ago. New developments promise to continue at an aggressive pace. We can look forward to persistent computing and ubiquitous networks that sense conditions in our environment, control variable factors, analyze huge stores of information, and even predict the future. In a later section we focus on the impact of pervasive computing, but we offer highlights of a few compelling technologies here.

Network Grids

Computer network technology has evolved from loosely connecting communication paths among computers (i.e., sharing data via the Internet), to extremely tight coupling of multiple computers that create virtual super computers capable of sharing computational resources as well as data. These integrated systems will perform as a single machine, combining processing capacity and performance capable of solving some of the big scientific questions such as protein folding.

Neural Networks

Neural networks are software designed to mimic human brain activity and learning models. Neural networks are currently applied to a wide range of predictive computing applications, from sales forecasts based on historical data to mapping developments in cognitive science and neural biology. Professor Amar Gupta of the MIT Sloan School uses neural networks in manufacturing operations analysis to minimize inventory requirements and optimize operational efficiency. Other applications include financial market forecasts, medical diagnostics (especially for tumor growth potential), and product market projections.

Quantum Computing

Although real applications are probably 20 years away, quantum computing is pushing the frontier of computational possibility. Scientists are beginning to harness the power of quantum mechanics to control and interpret atomic spin cycles that may solve currently unsolvable problems such as the prime factoring of large numbers used in encryption. Professor Isaac Chuang, MIT Media Lab, has created a quantum computer and is leading multiple research projects to build powerful quantum computing architectures that aim to improve processing capacity, efficiency, and speed of classical computing.

Life Sciences

We are in the midst of one of the most remarkable revolutions in the history of mankind. The revolution was sparked by scientific curiosity about life, but its consequences will be so far-reaching as to touch every aspect of society. It is an information revolution, unlocking databases of human heredity and evolutionary history. It is a medical revolution, holding the prospect that our children's children will never die of cancer. And it is an intellectual revolution that may reshape—for better or for worse—our notions of human potential.

I refer, of course, to the revolution in Genetics and Genomics.

Dr. Eric S. Lander
Director of the Whitehead Center of Genome Research
Professor of Biology at MIT
Millennium Evening at the White House, October 12, 1999

Dr. Lander's prophetic comments heralded the dawn of a new age of possibility. With the completion of the human genome map, we suddenly face the prospect of understanding—and possibly controlling—the mechanisms of life itself. Scientists, governments, and investors have responded with unprecedented fervor, launching a range of research designed to capitalize on these discoveries and propel our knowledge even further. Below are four examples of current life sciences research taking place at MIT.

• The Whitehead Institute, a nonprofit, independent research laboratory affiliated with MIT, was one of the leading contributors to the recent mapping of the human genome. Current work includes projects exploring molecular genetics, cancer genetics, neurobiology, infectious diseases, X-ray crystallography, biomedical engineering, and cell and developmental biology.

• DNA microarray techniques now test hundreds of thousands of compounds against a target field in a matter of weeks instead of the many months it used take to analyze only a few hundred. More and better information is now available in a fraction of the time, raising hopes for the discovery of many new drugs.

• Will we someday be able to determine the genomic sequence of an individual while they wait in a doctor's office? Paul Matsudaira, professor of biology and bioengineering and a member of the Whitehead Institute for Biomedical Research, is creating hand-held bioanalytic devices designed to identify human disease genes. Other forms include disposable, plastic "lab-on-a chip" platforms that can analyze a tiny amount of body fluid (e.g., blood or saliva) for biomarkers to determine the health of an individual or the status of a disease process.

• Many promising drug therapies fail clinical trials owing to high toxicity in a small number of patients. Because we can evaluate the genetic make-up of individuals, and therefore isolate risky candidates, many of these discarded compounds could be revived, potentially saving the lives of people who are genetically receptive to the treatments.

The Science of the Small

Much of the most interesting work at MIT today focuses on the "science of the small"—on machines, materials, and processes constructed at very small scales. Broadly, this work can be divided into two: into "micromachines"—structures that are tiny but still visible; and into "nanotechnology"—technology at the molecular level.

Micromachines

Microelectro-mechanical systems (MEMS) are tiny machines, often only a cubic centimeter in size, designed to interpret information about our physical world at a microscopic level and execute multiple tasks as sensors, computers, communications devices, and actuators. This is the concept behind development at the MIT Microsystems Technology Laboratories (MTL): Highly sensitive electronic sensors interpret physical stimuli such as light, sound, etc., and produce electronic signal input to the device. After analog processing, signals are translated to digital signals and then reconverted to analog. At various stages, they initiate appropriate communications protocols to external optical or electronic devices, to on-board microchips, or to internal actuator mechanisms that compel a physical response such as mechanically moving or controlling something, displaying information, or generating electric power.

Over the last 15 years, the MEMS industry has grown to annually generate revenues of USD 4 billion with projections that it will approach USD 10 billion by 2005 (source: Electronic Business, III-Vs, Electronic Buyer News, Solid State Technology). Advances in fabrication technology such as Professor Emanuel Sachs's "three-dimensional printing" have helped to generate a number of exciting developments. In addition to highly specialized equipment such as aeronautical components and medical diagnostics, MEMS devices are included in increasingly common consumer goods such as accelerometers that trigger automobile airbags, microfluidic inkjet printer heads, optical projection displays, and radio frequency devices in cell phone filters.

Many of the new developments in MEMS technology will be focused on biology, optics, and power generation:

• *Health monitor*—Implanted microchip devices could relay the status of blood composition, hormone levels, and various pressures—basically ubiquitous sensing that cannot be accomplished any other way. Information could be used to identify precursor conditions for disease or even provide early warning of a heart attack.

• *Power Generation*—Researchers are focusing on energy generation and efficiency with a goal to design a miniature power source that can produce at least 10 watts of power for a few hours. This alternative to batteries, which are not good at small scale, could remove a key obstacle keeping electric cars from the mass consumer market: the large size and very heavy weight of enough conventional batteries to power a car for an acceptable distance.

• *Fuel Cells*—The U.S. Army is investing in research to develop a small fuel cell, literally a micro engine with a generator. They envision a day when a piezoelectric transducer is stored in the heel of a soldier's boot, which is connected (wired) to the rest of the uniform. Each step generates a charge, providing power to communication equipment and other devices carried by the soldier.

• *Persistent Sensing*—MEMS sensors could also be used for civil engineering projects (e.g., bridges, buildings, and roads) to identify small changes in structural integrity, providing an early warning system to maintenance engineers.

Nanotechnology

Nanotechnology is the study of matter at the nanometer scale—one billionth of a meter—the size of a single water molecule. Researchers have drawn from all scientific disciplines, including biology, chemistry, physics, and engineering, to develop techniques that isolate molecular components for study under unusual and complex conditions. Scientists are now capable of creating new materials with advantageous features not found in natural compounds and have discovered new properties and behaviors of existing matter when addressed at the molecular level. With the aid of new scanning probe microscopes, they can even isolate individual atoms, picking them up and rearranging them at will.

Theorists paint astonishing pictures of the possibilities of this new technology that is poised to change the world by creating a U.S.$1 trillion annual market within ten years. Some of the claims are almost certainly simple hype; some are very real. Scientific development and market creativity will define the winners over the next five to ten years. Here are a few possibilities:

• Passive applications—materials that accomplish a task by virtue of their presence—are first to market and are available today in the form of impenetrable coatings for machine parts, protective clothing, and even the inside lining of tennis balls.

• Nanoelectronic circuits built from carbon nanotubes may some day break through the theoretical limits of silicon and allow production of a microprocessor with up to 5 billion transistors.

• Nanowire arrays built from nanoparticle crystallization may potentially store trillions of bytes of data per square inch of storage medium.

• Fabricated nanomaterials that exceed the strength of steel at a fraction of the weight and cost may revolutionize many consumer goods and manufacturing processes.

• Nanoparticles called quantum dots reflect different waves of light depending on their size. They are used as biological markers and potentially as food coloring.

• Non-invasive diagnostics may be able to detect a tumor only a few cells in size when marked with nanoscale contrast agents.

Interactions across the Three Fields

Despite their differences, we believe that it is likely to be in the areas of overlap between technologies in all of these three areas—in IT, in the Life Sciences, and in the "Science of the Small"—that the most dramatic advances are likely to take place. This is for two reasons. First, all three fields face very similar challenges, and solutions that benefit one are likely to benefit the others.

• *Development of Tools*—progress in every field is dependent on the availability of interpretive tools that will measure, control, and diagnose the results of research. Appropriate tools are likely to be valuable across areas.

• *Fabrication*—successful implementation of many of these technologies requires new processes and factories to manufacture high volumes of precise machines at low cost. Again, progress in one area is likely to benefit the others.

• *Multipurpose Use*—the viability of a technology will be determined by the variability and versatility of the applications it influences. Commercial success of a single development may depend on whether it can be integrated into multiple technologies or products.

• *Scale*—as technologies become more sophisticated, products often become increasingly smaller. Understanding the behavior of molecular particles and developing design techniques to harness them will be essential enablers of new technology.

Second, the most compelling and most important developments may well occur in the areas of overlap across the technologies. Below are just a few examples.

• Almost every facet of biotechnology generates massive amounts of data. A new field called bioinformatics, which crosses into the information technology realm, has evolved to address the particular requirements of storing and processing information generated from genome mapping, drug discovery, and patient diagnostics.

• If we are to leverage the information provided by genotyping, we must understand the effect of gene expression at the cellular level. Kim Hamad-Schifferli, a postdoctoral associate in the MIT Media Lab, combined her knowledge of nanotechnology and biology to develop nanoscale biomolecular tools that dehybridize DNA and ultimately regulate intracellular activity. This revolutionary invention allows researchers to "turn off" a particular gene—without impacting the entire system—to observe the impact on the cellular pathways.

• In the quest to achieve further miniaturization and increased capacity, semiconductor researchers have cultivated the realm of nanoelectronics and nanophotonics. Electrical engineers and computer scientists have come to rely not only on a new understanding of quantum physics for their work, but also to leverage the lessons biologists have learned from observing the pathways of various biomolecular devices.

• Biological computing—the pursuit of nanoscale circuits and wires built from biomolecules for computational purposes—lives right in the sweet spot. The burgeoning field of silicon biology draws from every hard science to develop biomolecular machines, field-effect biosensors, wireless biosensors, protein biochips, and nanoelectronic devices.

Diving Deeper

With this "broad brush" overview of our technological future in mind, in this section we now focus in on a few particularly promising research programs. We have two goals. The first is to begin to put some flesh on the bones of our very general description. The second is to give the reader a sense of the uncertainty inherent in forecasting technological progress today with any precision. These technologies are fascinating, but they are also extremely complex. Trying to understand what may happen opens one up to the problem of the fractal: the more one understands, the more complex the phenomenon becomes.

We focus on four groups of technologies: on pervasive computing, on advances in medicine, and on two technologies designed for the developing world—water purification and instant eyeglasses. While the latter two are much less "high tech" than the first, we include them deliberately since it seems to us one of the most important unresolved uncertainties of the next twenty years is that of the degree to which technological progress will benefit the poor and the disadvantaged.

Pervasive Computing

In 2015, the developed world will contain billions of micromachines capable of sensing, manipulating, and communicating information about the environment, people, and objects. Buildings, homes, and vehicles will become central computing platforms through embedded devices that interpret and modify conditions such as temperature, light, and sound, based on the predefined preferences of the individual using them. Convenient and powerful handheld devices will identify you and your preferences to the physical environment, provide the information you want, and allow you to communicate with your friends and colleagues. Wireless communications will facilitate all of these activities by connecting requests and creating sophisticated ad hoc networks as devices are moved throughout the network grid.

MIT's "Project Oxygen" is dedicated to realizing this idea through the development of integrated systems that are as available, accessible, and useful to us as the air we breathe. Organized within the MIT Laboratory for Computer Science, Project Oxygen brings together world-renowned expertise in software, networks, hardware, knowledge management, artificial intelligence, and security to create a new paradigm that weaves computing and communications into every aspect of our lives. The research focuses on four key technologies: on "environmental devices," or "E21s"; on handheld devices, or "H21s"; on networks, or "N21s"; and on work in knowledge and semantics.

Devices

The Oxygen researchers envision environmental devices called "E21s" will be embedded within the physical structures of "intelligent spaces." They will serve as the nerve center, directing communications requests, completing computational tasks, and managing network connectivity.

E21s will interpret presence and activity in open spaces and facilitate seamless communication among people and the central network through microphones, cameras, and computational interfaces. Human communication with E21s will be as simple as a voice command or a waving arm gesture.

Mobile handheld devices called "H21s" will provide the personal link for users to communicate with the E21 platform. They will also provide functions like telephone service, Internet access, streaming video, and voice recognition. The network and communication pathways used by the H21s will be dynamic and self-changing, because the devices will determine their function and choose the device or network interfaces that are most appropriate to meet the needs of a particular user in a particular time or place. For example, your verbal request to see budget spreadsheets you created last week would prompt your H21 to connect to the company intranet, conduct a search for the appropriate files, and display them in a logical order.

Networks

Communication among these devices will be controlled by networks called N21s that will configure themselves based on the changing requirements of the E21s, H21s, and people in the room. In addition to managing network traffic and authentication, N21s will create and control ad hoc networks called collaborative regions, comprised of a group of devices gathered for a particular purpose or timeframe. N21s will enforce security and access policies, and they will support multiple communications protocols that will adapt as applications and device standards evolve.

Knowledge and Semantics

E21s, H21s, and N21s will not reach their full potential without the move from an information source that requires human interpretation to one that embeds meaning within the data itself, so that machines can navigate and solve problems independently. The evolution of our current World Wide Web to this kind of "Semantic Web" is the vision of its inventor, Tim Berners-Lee, and represents a critical component of Oxygen.

The Semantic Web will provide a structural framework that will define data and guide automated processing by identifying the data type, defining potential uses, proposing logic, and imposing rules related to the information. Specifically, the Semantic Web will use RDF language that documents the relationships between objects. Objects have meaning, and the relationships between the objects (semantic links) have meaning as well. By documenting the meaning of data and the links between data, applications can merge or interconnect disparate data from other applications. In this environment, software agents will be able to understand relationships between objects and perform work on our behalf.

The Future of Pervasive Computing

If these technologies are successfully developed they will have dramatic implications. The following business conference scenario developed by the Project Oxygen team provides one possible example:

Hélène calls Ralph in New York from their company's home office in Paris. Ralph's E21, connected to his phone, recognizes Hélène's telephone number; it answers in her native French, reports that Ralph is away on vacation, and asks if her call is urgent. The E21's multilingual speech and automation systems, which Ralph has scripted to handle urgent calls from people such as Hélène, recognize the word *décisif* in Hélène's reply and transfer the call to Ralph's H21 in his hotel. When Ralph speaks with Hélène, he decides to bring George, now at home in London, into the conversation.

All three decide to meet next week in Paris. Conversing with their E21s, they ask their automated calendars to compare their schedules and check the availability of flights from New York and London to Paris. Next Tuesday at 11am looks good. All three say "OK," and their automation systems make the necessary reservations.

Ralph and George arrive at Paris headquarters. At the front desk, they pick up H21s, which recognize their faces and connect to their E21s in New York and London. Ralph asks his H21 where they can find Hélène. It tells them she's across the street, and it provides an indoor/outdoor navigation system to guide them to her. George asks his H21 for "last week's technical drawings," which he forgot to bring. The H21 finds and fetches the drawings just as they meet Hélène.

Advances in Medicine

The right medicine for the right patient at the right dose at the right time. Current research in genetics and in materials technology has the potential to dramatically improve the range and effectiveness of existing biomedical treatments. Here we touch briefly on three exciting developments: on the use of single nucleotide polymorphisms, or SNPs, to find new drugs; on new techniques for controlled drug discovery; and on recent advances in tissue engineering.

Personalized Medicine: Using Individual Phenotypes to Find New Drugs

The Human Genome Project produced a consensus DNA sequence map of the human genome that describes 99.9 percent of the genetic composition of individuals. The remaining 0.1 percent—one in every 1,000 letters—describes the characteristics that make an individual genetically unique and also determines predisposition to or protection from disease. These variations are called single nucleotide polymorphisms (SNP).

On the clinical side, information from SNPs can be used to map a patient's genetic makeup, sometimes referred to as genotyping. Knowing a patient's genotype will allow doctors to better diagnose diseases and prescribe medicines accordingly. On the drug development side, pharmaceutical companies can take advantage of SNP information to develop drugs that act with more potency and fewer side effects on patients with specific genetic profiles.

Many researchers see SNPs as the genomic keys that will open the doors to personalized medicine. SNPs may help explain why individuals respond differently to the same drug. As we learn more about the influence that human genetic composition has on the disease process, we will understand more about the metabolism of medicine. Once these pathways are further understood, targeted gene expression and protein synthesis may be controlled to achieve optimal individual reaction to a drug.

Herceptin, produced by Genentech, is a successful example of this type of personalized therapy. Herceptin (Trastuzumab) is the first targeted, humanized monoclonal antibody for treatment of women with HER2 (human epidermal growth factor receptor 2) positive metastatic breast cancer. Herceptin is designed to target and block the function of HER2 and is only effective on the subset (about 20 percent) of breast cancer patients who have a genetic profile of HER2 overexpression. A genetic test to determine whether the patient over-expresses HER2 is needed before Herceptin is prescribed.

Controlled Drug Delivery
To date, most malignant brain cancers were largely untreatable owing to two complications. First, although the brain tumor is localized, the vast majority of chemotherapy drug therapies are delivered systemically, and significant doses of chemotherapy must be frequently administered. This exposes the entire body to the action of the drug and results in potentially significant side effects and substantial patient discomfort. Second, the blood-brain barrier prevents a variety of blood-born chemicals from penetrating the brain and reaching brain cancer cells.

Dr. Robert S. Langer, Kenneth J. Germenshausen Professor of Chemical and Biological Engineering at MIT, has changed the way brain cancer is treated. His approach offers new hope to patients with this severe, life-threatening disease. Langer designed a biodegradable polymer that releases medicine at a controlled rate. About the size of a dime, the surface-degrading wafer is impregnated with cancer chemotherapeutic drugs. The wafers are implanted during the tumor removal surgery. The chemicals are released locally, directly to the tumor site, in high concentrations over a period of two to three weeks. Consequently, the drug is contained within the brain where it is needed and therefore does not cause the systemic toxicity typical of anticancer drugs that often result in liver, kidney, or spleen damage. In clinical trials, the wafer has been shown to significantly prolong patient survival while improving the quality of life. Approved in 1996 by FDA, the wafers became the first new treatment for brain cancer in 25 years. This is the first polymer-based treatment to deliver chemotherapy directly to a tumor site, and there is hope that this kind of approach may prove useful in the treatment of a variety of other conditions.

Langer has also pioneered research in remote-control systems for drug delivery. The rate at which the drug is released can be controlled using ultrasound, electric pulses, or external magnetic fields. Eventually, the drug release can be controlled and activated on demand by a biosensor to create a smart delivery system. An implantable "pharmacy-on-a-chip" was recently prototyped in the Langer Lab. (See figure 7.1.2.) The microchip is made of silicon and contains multiple (up to 1,000) drug reservoirs. Scientists in the Langer Lab hope that someday doctors will be able to monitor a patient's vital statistics and blood chemistry as well as administer appropriate medicine remotely. In addition to treating prostate cancer, ovarian cancer, endometriosis, and severe bone infections, the same type of slow and controlled-

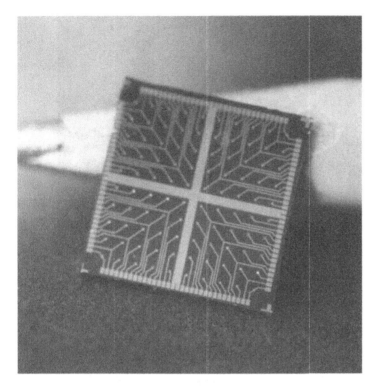

Figure 7.1.2
Pharmacy-on-a-chip. Photograph courtesy of Dr. Robert S. Langer.

delivery system is being applied to insulin, growth hormones, gene therapy agents, and vaccines.

Tissue Engineering
Dr. Langer is also a pioneer in tissue engineering, developing methods for synthesizing artificial cartilage, skin, liver, nerves, and blood vessels for human transplant. (See figures 7.1.3 and 7.1.4.) Langer's method is to build biodegradeable polymer matrices in an appropriate shape and infuse them with biomolecules, often cells from the patient's own body, to create replacement tissue. This approach provides tremendous flexibility in design and application and can be applied to a wide variety of structural requirements. Langer entered the tissue engineering field upon learning about a boy who was born without external ears. After preparing the matrix in the approximate dimensions, the ear was implanted on the ear of a rabbit for incubation and grown to the appropriate size for the child.

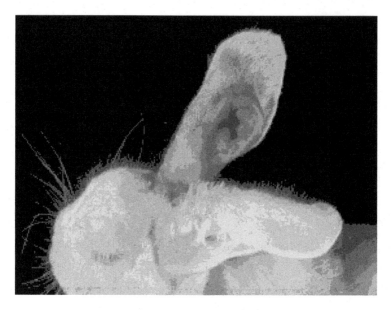

Figure 7.1.3
Ear growing in rabbit. Photograph courtesy of Dr. Robert S. Langer.

Cartilage Tissue Engineering

   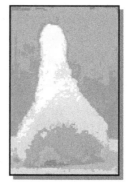

BEFORE   AFTER
cell seeding   2 weeks in culture

Figure 7.1.4
Cartilage tissue engineering. Photo courtesy of Dr. Robert S. Langer.

For blood vessel engineering, Langer and Shulamit Levenberg, a postdoctoral associate in the MIT chemical engineering department, took a similar approach. They have achieved artificial structures that exhibit all the characteristics and strengths of natural blood vessels. A polymer structure is coated with cell culture that mirrors the cellular structure of a natural blood vessel: smooth muscle cells on the outside, endothelial cells on the inside. Although endothelial cell cultures can be grown from a variety of sources, human stem cells provide the greatest efficacy. After the structure is cultivated to the desired dimensions, the vessel is pulsated with an electric pump that propels fluid at an ideal rate and pressure.

Langer, always searching for new applications of his technology, is working with Julie Andrews, the singer, to develop new repair techniques that will restore the delicate tissues of damaged vocal cords. In collaboration with physicians at the Massachusetts Eye and Ear Infirmary, researchers at the Harvard Medical School, and Mariah Hahn, an MIT graduate student in computer science and electrical engineering, Langer is considering three approaches to solving the problem: injection of an elastin or collagen to improve elasticity, introducing engineered material to replace portions of the vocal cord tissues, or "growing" a new vocal cord via introduced matrices.

Dr. Shuguang Zhang, associate director of the Center for Biomedical Engineering, is tackling similar problems using biological scaffolds rather than polymer matrices. The self-assembly properties of human proteins were discovered in 1993, and stimulated the research that led to the discovery of synthesized peptides that create a biological matrix scaffolding for cell attachment and cell-based transplants for regenerative medicine. The peptide gel is about 98 percent water with very high viscosity for good support. It allows cells to move freely and combine in 3D structures just as they would in nature. "Cartilage gel," the first application, may repair damaged cartilage, potentially providing relief to weekend athletes as well as osteoarthritis patients. John Kisiday, a graduate student in the biomedical engineering division, is hoping to create a gel that will transport living cartilage cells directly into the joint and provide a supportive environment while the implant takes hold. After it is no longer needed, the extraneous material will simply erode away.

Clean Water for a Billion People

Today, over 1.1 billion people do not have access to safe, clean drinking water. Two and a half billion people do not have access to sanitation services. Each year, 2.2 million people, most of them children, die of illness related to unclean water, poor hygiene, or unsatisfactory sanitation.[1] These are typically the poorest citizens of developing countries. With global population expected to increase by 20 percent to 7.1 billion by the year 2015, the problem will only get worse.

In addition to the high mortality rate, waterborne illnesses claim close to half the population in the developing world at any given time.[2] Diarrhea, ascaris, dracunculisis, hookworm schistosomiasis, and trachoma are responsible for severe malnutrition that leads to stunted physical growth, impaired cognitive development, and blindness. Poverty manifests as a continual negative spiral for underserved communities—poor people cannot easily pay for access to clean water that will improve their health because they are too sick to work and earn income.

Susan Murcott, lecturer in the Department of Civil and Environmental Engineering, founded the Nepal Water Project to provide onsite water analysis and household cleansing solutions to people that need it. Her graduate students conduct research and design experiments during the academic year and spend at least a month in the field, testing and applying their theories and solutions. Last year, Murcott's students won three separate awards: the MIT IDEAS Design Competition for colloidal silver ceramic filters for Nicaragua; the Lemelson international prize for a microbial/arsenic treatment system in Nepal; and the MIT $1K Business Idea Warm-Up Competition for very low-cost chlorine manufacturing for water treatment systems in Haiti.

In addition to providing the technology solutions that will clean household water, Murcott and her students are interested in making people become self-sufficient in their water cleansing efforts. For example, local potters are engaged in clay vessel and filter design and production. Similarly, community leaders are trained in appropriate hygiene behavior and learn about the dangerous health effects of

1. World Health Organization, UNICEF, Water Supply and Sanitation Collaborative Council, *Global Water Supply and Sanitation Assessment 2000 Report*, 2000, www.unicef.org
2. Ashok Gadgil, "Drinking Water in Developing Countries," Lawrence Berkeley National Laboratory, Environmental Energy Technologies Division, 1998.

contaminated water so they can provide education and local support throughout the year.

Murcott emphasizes that no single technical solution will work for all regions. Sustainable treatment programs must address the specific purification needs of local water and support the cultural norms of the community. However, all solutions share the following characteristics:

• Perform well technically—consistent particle removal to reduce turbidity and microbial (bacteria, virus, protazoa, helminth) removal at acceptable levels

• Low-cost—not more than USD 3–15 per household per year

• Socially acceptable—gender sensitive, acceptable taste, e.g., minimal chlorine residue

• Locally available and appropriate—parts and systems from acceptable materials that can be easily distributed, especially to rural areas

• Simple to use—transferable to illiterate users

• NO ELECTRICITY REQUIRED![3]

One of the difficulties of treating water in the field is identifying the composition and level of contaminants in the water. Typical diagnostic processes depend on incubating water with a substrate for at least 24 hours. Most incubators require plentiful electricity, which violates the most emphatic rule. To solve this problem, Murcott teamed with Amy Smith, who won the Lemelson-MIT Student Prize for Innovation and Invention for her laboratory incubator. Smith's design maintains temperature via phase-change material without the need for electricity or electronic parts.

Typically, household water cleaning systems that meet these qualifications are contained within simple, spigot vessels, usually produced locally from plastic or pottery. (See figure 7.1.5.) Filtration systems are comprised of at least two containers that hold various sand aggregates or fibrous material that trap impurities as the water transfers from one well to the other. Most sand filters are easily maintained by simply stirring the top 5 cm of sand, breaking up the biofilm layer that forms through use, and replacing the highly turbid water that results with relatively clean water. There is no incremental cost or labor associated with filter cleaning. (See figure 7.1.6.)

---

3. Susan Murcott, lecturer, MIT Department of Civil Engineering and Environmental Science and Director of the Nepal Water Project, interview November 2001.

Figure 7.1.5
Making water filtration units.

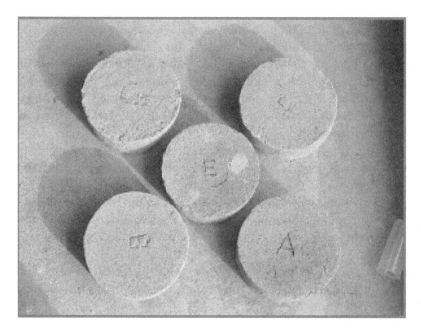

Figure 7.1.6
Water filtration units.

Figure 7.1.7
Arsenic removal system.

The arsenic removal system shown in figure 7.1.7 is comprised of three vessels. Contaminated water is poured into the top portion containing course sand and iron nails. The water flows to the second stage containing fine sand and charcoal. Finally, the clean water is collected in the bottom chamber. This relatively simple and elegant design meets the core criteria and effectively removes 98 percent of arsenic concentrations of 300 parts per billion, bringing the level to internationally accepted levels of 0 to 5 parts per billion.

Solar disinfection systems use solar ultraviolet and thermal radiation to purify water in clear plastic bottles that are filled and left in the sun for at least 48 hours. Estimating that each person requires 10 liters of water per day, a family of five will have 75 1-liter bottles in transit over 3 days. While a bit cumbersome, this method is simple, inexpensive, and requires no chemicals. Murcott's students are concentrating on the variations in diurnal temperatures in different climates as well as whether bottle materials can be enhanced through insulation or other materials to increase the temperature of water in the bottles.

Chlorine is an effective water cleanser. A few drops added to a bucket of contaminated water will clean it to acceptable drinking levels in a few minutes. Residual chlorine taste and availability of the chlorine itself are the greatest obstacles to this method. In Nepal, powdered chlorine bleach is available only as an import from India, making an inexpensive and consistent supply nearly impossible.

However, a portable machine that generates sodium hypochlorite from local salt and tap water may provide an acceptable solution and build a cottage industry for local communities. Because the machine requires an adequate supply of electricity, production facilities should be established in central locations, probably cities. Establishment of supplier and distributor networks is planned to ensure efficient delivery to local and remote dealers, NGOs, hospitals, and centralized water treatment plants, thus creating an economic boost while solving a social problem.

Low-Cost Eyeglasses

Saul Griffith, doctoral candidate in the MIT Media Lab and technology history buff, solved a nagging problem using technology that is over 140 years old. While on a volunteer mission to provide people with free glasses in Guyana, Central America, Griffith and his colleagues felt with increasing frustration that their efforts weren't really solving the problem. "We could determine the right prescription using portable diagnostic equipment and that was okay. But then we had to search through boxes of donated glasses to find something close to the solution."

Previous attempts to solve this problem had focused on creating water-filled lens that are pressurized to achieve the desired refraction, but these proved unsatisfactory because of the high manufacturing complexity and weight of each pair of glasses, as well as the fact that the multiple interfaces led to many internal reflections in certain lighting conditions. The range of correction was also limited and would not correct for astigmatic error. Griffith reversed the standard approach such that the complex flexible surface became the mold, not the final product. By modifying this technique, he was also able to produce arbitrary mold surfaces programmatically that included astigmatic and even progressive lenses. All of this was fitted into a portable device that produces a plastic lens of uncompromised quality to specification in about 10 minutes.

He partnered with two Harvard Business School students to found a company called Low-Cost Eyeglasses and won the HBS Social Enterprise Business Plan Contest in March 2001. The business model aims not only to improve the vision of billions of people but also to create entrepreneurial opportunities for people who live in developing economies.

Forecasting the Impact of Advancing Technology

These brief descriptions leave unanswered the question of exactly how and when these kinds of technologies will impact the commercial world. Many of these technologies—perhaps half—will never reach the market at all. They will prove to be technically infeasible, or there will, in the end, be no real need for them. Unfortunately, we have no way of knowing, ex ante, which half will prove to be the ones that do make it to the market. Predicting their likely impact is even harder. Recall ADL's famous prediction that the entire world market for the computer was likely to be less than ten units—or the skepticism with which the telegraph was initially greeted. Really important, world changing technologies have a history of being used in ways that no one—least of all their inventors—really expected. Who would have predicted that the teenage market would be critical to the development of wireless communications?

Nevertheless, we speculate below on the four ways in which we believe that these technologies will change the world: on their implications for the firms and industries for whom these technologies are likely to be "disruptive," for the privacy and security of individuals, for the global structure of production and distribution, and, finally, for the changing strategic role of technology inside the firm.

The Disruption of Firms and Industries
The technologies that we have discussed are likely to have their most obvious impact on those individual firms whose business models and product lines they threaten to replace. While the collapse of the Internet bubble has made it less fashionable to worry about "disruption," significant technological shifts have a history of creating very significant problems for established firms. IBM and Digital Equipment did not make money from the PC revolution: Intel and Microsoft did. Even in the much maligned case of the Internet, it is clear that many industries—notably travel and financial services—will never be the same again. The kinds of advances in IT, in the life sciences, and in

nanotechnology that we have discussed above are likely to have similarly dramatic competitive consequences.

In IT, it is already clear that a move to embedded, mobile computing based around an open architecture presents the business models of many of the current industry leaders with tremendous challenges. The collapse in telecommunications stocks and Microsoft's announcement of its ".NET" architecture are symptoms of this uncertainty.

In the life sciences, a move to personalized medicine and the development of therapies that are targeted to an individual's genotype would run directly counter to the pharmaceutical industry's current focus on the development of "blockbuster" drugs. Will the major pharmaceutical firms be able to cover their research and development costs if there are many more drugs, each selling to a much smaller population? Will the considerable skills they have developed in marketing and sales be rendered obsolete by the new technologies? Will diagnostic laboratories be disintermediated when lab-on-a-chip technology provides immediate feedback on a patient's condition?

The new materials and the move to nanotechnology open similar questions. Du Pont, for example, has announced a major commitment to "biologically based materials" as a long-term replacement for their petrochemically based business, but such a switch will make many of their existing competencies obsolete, and presents the firm with very significant organizational challenges.

The flip side of these concerns, of course, is that the new technologies will open up enormous opportunities for newly founded, entrepreneurial firms. Truly ubiquitous computing coupled with the widespread deployment of integrated micro sensors will probably lead to an order of magnitude increase in the amount of available information. The ability to instantly obtain this information will launch new service lines and may even create new industries in manufacturing, distribution, data mining, and analytics and a wide range of security and privacy applications.

The Impact on Individuals

These technologies are also likely to have a very significant impact on us all as individuals. The initial rumblings about the importance of individual privacy that have surfaced around the Internet and around the increasing consolidation of commercial data banks are likely to become a shout. The technology will soon be available to link nearly every data base on earth; to have that information instantly available at any point; to track every transaction, and even every movement of every "connected" individual. Such power has an obvious potential for abuse. How much do you wish others to know about you? How vulnerable is your life if much of it is instantly visible to possibly unauthorized eyes?

Advances in medical technology will raise similar concerns. There has already been much discussion about the pros and cons of genetic screening: do you want your employer to know that you have a genetic susceptibility to depression? If a company knows an employee is predisposed to a fatal illness, can it compel that person to undergo preventative therapy? But it will very soon be possible to implant a sensor that will transmit detailed data about your moment to moment physiological condition to . . . your employer? Your estranged wife? The technologies of the next twenty years are not "out there." They will not happen "somewhere else." Their small size and their ubiquity will make them truly pervasive, and this ubiquity will bring with it either a vigorous and sustained conversation about the appropriate use of information or an extension of control and the associated opportunity for abuse that will have transforming implications for our society.

From a more optimistic perspective, these new technologies have the potential to significantly increase our quality of life. Better therapies will bring obvious benefits, but it may be that the biggest benefit we can expect is that local, embedded, micro sensors will give us a better idea of where our time is going and of how we are reacting, physically, to what we are doing. Perhaps the next wave in technological development will help us become a significantly less stressed, more aware society.

The Global Structure of Production
Third, there is the possibility that these technologies will change the very structure of firms and organizations. We have already seen that recent advances in telecommunications have made it possible for ten-person firms to become truly global in a way that would have been unthinkable twenty years ago. It may be that the new technologies will only accelerate this trend. As products and machines become very small, production and distribution may become very local. This may preclude the need for large-scale and expensive factories and could

encourage companies to establish a larger number of smaller facilities. Will organizations become more decentralized and therefore smaller? They might.

However, implementation of the Semantic Web and corresponding device development will allow companies to control ever increasingly large volumes of information, support huge employee bases, and potentially capture even greater market share. Will emerging economies of scale in data management remove the limits to growth and encourage formation of monolithic companies? Will we see a world in which the consolidation of economic power into a few very large firms continues? We might.

There is also a real possibility that these new technologies may open up qualitatively different development paths for some of the developing economies. Does the move toward small-scale, low-energy products open up the potential for broader application? Will developing countries exploit future research, development, and production opportunities to leapfrog over the established competition? We know that cellular phone technology in South America and wireless infrastructure in China exceeds the U.S. standard. In many ways, developing countries are well positioned to participate in the next wave of technological innovation and production. The move toward small scale, and low-energy products may open up the potential for broader applications, further expanding the potential market. New fabrication facilities to manufacture new devices and tiny machines will be built in areas with low-cost land and labor forces. Research, development, and production opportunities abound. A significant percentage of nanotechnology researchers, for example, are from rapidly developing economies. If they return en masse to their countries, expertise in advanced technology will migrate with them. Can the new technologies have a significant impact on the quality of life for the billions of the world's inhabitants who are so much less fortunate than we are?

A Changing Strategic Role for Technology?
Lastly, we predict that the days when technology could be safely left in the hands of R&D are over, if they were ever here. The work that is in the labs now has truly startling potential. If there are real interactions between the three streams of work, between advances in computing, biology, and the "science of the small"—and the beginnings of such interactions are already visible—then they will have advances that

no one can predict. The innovative networks that we see now between the public and private sectors and between large and smaller firms are likely to become increasingly important and increasingly pervasive. Making decisions as to which technologies to invest in internally, which externally, and which to simply "watch" will become increasingly costly and increasingly important.

The returns to managing technology strategically, to being fully aware of what is likely to happen, and to having thought through how the organization will respond to the future while simultaneously maintaining the ability to run "conventional" businesses continuously in an appropriate way will be enormous.

Some organizations are already experimenting with the appointment of a "Chief Innovation Officer" and with integrating technology much more closely into the strategy of the firm. These are clearly important steps and we expect that they will become commonplace. However, we suspect that they may not be enough. Twenty years from now sophisticated technological literacy will be as central to the CEO's job as financial literacy is now, and technology will have transformed the world in ways in which we have not even begun to imagine.

Conclusion: Implications for Sloan and for Management Education

What implications for the future of management education can be drawn from this very brief and necessarily highly selective account of the ways in which science and technology might evolve and of the implications that such evolution will have for people and organizations?

Our work suggests that it will be increasingly critical for managers to develop at least a basic technological and scientific literacy: to have a sense for what science and technology can do and for the problems and opportunities that they create. But we suspect that our results also suggest something both more subtle and more complex than this. They suggest that successful managers will come increasingly to manage science and technology as an integrated part of an increasingly complex and interconnected world: to understand how social and human systems both shape and are shaped by technology, and to attempt—in what will surely be one of the great challenges of this century—to ensure that advances in science and technology benefit not only their own organizations but the larger world of which we are all a part. It is our hope that the MIT Sloan School will play a leading role in preparing managers for this challenging but critically important role.

Sources

http://oxygen.lcs.mit.edu

http://web.mit.edu/lms/www/research.shtml

http://web.mit.edu/tdp/www

http://web.mit.edu/cheme/langerlab/langer.html

MIT News, 28 March 2002

MIT Tech Talk, 17 July 2002

http://therics.com/

Scientific American, Special Issue, September 2001

Technology Review, May 2002

7.2 Discussion

Several MIT scientists and engineers underscored the importance of linking management and technology in the lab, at the earliest stages of the development process.

Provost Robert Brown pointed out that collaboration across academic departments has been a hallmark of MIT since its early days. At most universities, academic departments are like castles in Scotland— each self-contained and defensible, but not well positioned for collaboration among the fiefdoms they protect. At MIT, faculty move outside their academic "structures" to do interdisciplinary research. This tradition dates back at least as far as the interdisciplinary labs that helped develop radar systems and other critical technologies during World War II. The Media Lab is a current, highly visible example of this tradition. So is the Nanotechnology Lab. "Research goes on here that wouldn't have existed in a traditional academic environment," Brown said.

Brown also described the organizational impact of complex technology on MIT. Just as the world is becoming more interconnected, organizations like MIT are becoming more interconnected. Complex new technologies draw on and have implications for many disciplines. This interconnectedness is at odds with the tendency toward specialization. MIT uses a "research center" approach to create structures that encourage collaboration across what were the feudal castles of traditional academic disciplines.

But this issue of local fiefdoms versus global connection is far more than just an academic phenomenon. **Professor Rebecca Henderson** noted that all organizations have the issue of local silos that conflict with the need to create connected, mutually-optimized global solutions. And when Kofi Annan spoke of the need for more understanding and inclusiveness, he was talking about breaking down the barriers that separate the far-flung cultures of the human race. Finally, the fundamental fact that the constituencies are broadening speaks to the reality that leaders of every local culture, corporation, or academic department must connect with a broadening array of others.

One issue becoming more pressing and prevalent is about how to take the fruits of technology and make them relevant to people who are not as fortunate as we are. Henderson said: "In the next ten years, there will be an increasing effort to link our enormous resources to help those who don't have enough food to eat or clean water to drink." Inventions such as MIT Professor Susan Murcott's water cleansing solutions demonstrate how technology can help solve such world problems.

Technology also has an important role to play in the fight against world hunger and disease. For example, **Professor Susan Lindquist** described work to add vitamin A to rice. Thousands of preschool children in developing countries go blind from vitamin A deficiency, a problem that could be averted if common staple crops were nutritionally more complete. Although genetically modified foods have their own ethical issues, the potential to improve nutrition or reduce hunger (by improving yields) should not be ignored.

The idea of adding vitamin A to rice prompted the question whether a scientific advancement, like the addition of Vitamin A to rice, can be distributed to the world when it was created by a for-profit company. Lindquist addressed this point, and the related notion of whether companies should be able to get patents for genetic discoveries. Lindquist said that until recently she was against patents. But then she talked with drug companies and learned that they were not developing a new discovery because the discovery was in the public domain. Because it was in the public domain, it presented no competitive advantage for a drug company to develop it. Lindquist said that new incentive programs were needed to get the best minds working on these pressing problems. "There must be other ways than just a small number of individuals making millions while the others are left in the dust," Professor Lindquist said. Creating consortiums of companies was one suggestion. Another was to develop a profit motive that would work in the third world.

Professor Lindquist also described the sheer joy and intellectual exuberance of figuring out how life works. Hundreds of millions of years of biological evolution have created some amazing materials. Nature allows for flexibility, and a diversity of new structures can be invented which will profoundly affect our lives, Professor Lindquist said. "There is tremendous power in the material world. Consider the protein that forms spider silk. A spider web looks gossamer, but its tensile strength exceeds that of steel. A roll as thick as a pencil can stop a 747 airplane." Learning to harness this power of proteins will change the world.

Similarly, the human genome project is not only teaching us about ourselves, but it is reinforcing some basic philosophic principles, Lindquist said. "It shows the brotherhood of man. We realize that we are extraordinarily similar." The differences between us amount to a few words changed in a book the length of Herman Melville's *Moby-Dick*.

She noted that differences between people are a natural resource for new talents, but they also give us different susceptibilities to disease. By exploring these differences, we can determine the precise nature of the disease and develop therapeutic strategies that will target it. Curing diseases—and eventually preventing diseases—follows.

Professor Linda Griffith's description of research on Hepatitis C illustrates another benefit of taking account of ethical issues. Sometimes it leads scientists to alternatives they might otherwise not discover or pursue. Hepatitis C is a dangerous virus that drives the need for most liver transplants and afflicts 200 million people around the world. Combating Hepatitis C is a research question, but even studying the disease presents ethical issues. This disease is hard to study in a test tube because liver cells in a test tube do not act like liver cells in a live person or animal. This brings the need to study the disease in living animals. But issues of human rights and environmental protection are expanding the list of constituencies to include animals. Many people are opposed to the use of animals, such as monkeys, rabbits, and mice, for biomedical experiments. Yet pharmaceutical companies and biomedical researchers need accurate models for human diseases. They need ways to test the efficacy and safety of new treatments prior to giving them to people.

New biomedical breakthroughs, however, are now providing scientists, drug developers, and doctors with test tube tools to combat disease without the controversial use of animals. Griffith described how new fabrication techniques and an advanced understanding of the structure of the liver let scientists create a functioning synthetic liver-like environment where liver cells behave normally. The result is a better model for studying liver diseases, like Hepatitis C, without infecting animals. Thus, technology can sometimes create a third path that alleviates the need to make a tough trade-off between the rights of two constituencies.

Professor Rodney Brooks's Project Oxygen is pushing the forefront of computing. At the same time, computing professor Brooks is working with management professor Rebecca Henderson to identify viable business models for the new technology concepts being developed.

In discussing Project Oxygen, Brooks emphasized the shift to people-centered computing. Under Project Oxygen, the computer has the intelligence and the software to focus on the person using it rather than the current paradigm that forces the person to focus on the computer. The intent is that people can spend less time on the technology and more time achieving their goals.

Yet as we give technology the power to serve us better, we also give technology more information about us. Core components of Project Oxygen track the locations of people so that these people have any needed files or software wherever they go. Such advances are a real boon to virtual workers and highly dynamic work and home environments. But data on where a person is and whether he or she is working or doing something else could be used in unethical or undesirable ways. So too can the "personal robots" under development that can do a variety of household chores and monitor people as well as physical environments. Technology provides the power, but it does not provide the wisdom to wield that power.

The panel members agreed that the key to dealing with these issues and getting the maximum benefit out of new technologies is to get managers involved early in the development process. Management must have a deeper understanding of the technology and the potential of the technology for returning value to the corporation and to society as a whole. New technologies often raise ethical issues. These issues should not be left to science alone. Rather, discussions with business and with society as a whole need to take place, to position the technology within the context of the larger world.

Postscript: Moving Forward

We believe the vision for the future of management practice and education laid out in the previous chapters is compelling. The challenge now lies in continuing the dialogue begun here, in developing this vision, and in translating it into concrete actions. We invite you to join us in this process.

Starting in fall 2003, we plan to organize a range of forums and workshops each term for MIT Sloan students and faculty to engage the issues and themes addressed in this book directly with practitioners who are dealing with these issues in industry and society. We invite you to join in these discussions and add your comments and experiences to the learning process. For more information on how to participate in these sessions on-line, in person, or by having Sloan students study how these issues are being addressed in your organization, send us an e-mail to the address we have set up for this purpose, management@mit.edu, and you will receive information on upcoming forums, workshops, and other opportunities for participating in these discussions as it becomes available.

In the meantime, if you have comments on the issues raised in the book or would like to share your experiences in dealing with them, please send them to us at the e-mail address above. We will summarize the comments received and post them back to you and bring them to the attention of our students when we discuss them on campus.

We look forward to continuing the stimulating dialogue begun here.

Contributors

Kofi Annan	United Nations
Alex d'Arbeloff	MIT Corporation
Vince Barabba	General Motors Corporation
Rolf Breuer	Deutsche Bank
Ellen Brockley	MIT Sloan School of Management
Rodney Brooks	MIT Artificial Intelligence Laboratory
Robert Brown	MIT Office of the Provost
Amber Cai	MIT Sloan School of Management
Giovanni Carriere	MIT Sloan School of Management
Philip Condit	Boeing Corporation
Andrew Cowen	MIT Sloan School of Management
Joel Cutcher-Gershenfeld	MIT Engineering Systems Division
Carly Fiorina	Hewlett Packard Corporation
Victor Fung	Li and Fung Ltd.
David Gagnon	MIT Sloan School of Management
James Goodnight	SAS Corporation
Linda Griffith	MIT School of Engineering
Rebecca Henderson	MIT Sloan School of Management
Jeff Katz	Orbitz Inc.
Melanie Kittrell	Merck and Company
Thomas A. Kochan	MIT Sloan School of Management

Susan Lee	MIT Sloan School of Management
Erika Leung	MIT Sloan School of Management
Susan Lindquist	MIT School of Science
Lily Liu	MIT Sloan School of Management
Richard M. Locke	MIT Sloan School of Management
José Antonio Marco	MIT Sloan School of Management
Donald Monson	MIT Sloan School of Management
Stewart C. Myers	MIT Sloan School of Management
Meg O'Leary	Price Waterhouse Coopers Inc.
Wanda Orlikowski	MIT Sloan School of Management
Emanuele Picciola	MIT Sloan School of Management
Federica Pievani	MIT Sloan School of Management
Fernando Ramirez	MIT Sloan School of Management
Tienko Rasker	MIT Sloan School of Management
Siva Ravikumar	MIT Sloan School of Management
Jessica Santiago	MIT Sloan School of Management
Richard L. Schmalensee	MIT Sloan School of Management
Peter Senge	MIT Sloan School of Management
Lu Shen	MIT Sloan School of Management
Kevin Taback	MIT Sloan School of Management
Glen Urban	MIT Sloan School of Management
Telmo Valido	MIT Sloan School of Management
Charles M. Vest	MIT Office of the President
Rick Wagoner	General Motors Corporation
Leo Wang	MIT Sloan School of Management
Jimmy Zhang	MIT Sloan School of Management

Index